NORTHER[N]

1914 – 1918

Allied line at the end of 1917 ▬▬▬▬
Hindenburg Line ▬ ▬ ▬ ▬

Scale of Miles

10 5 0   10   20   30   40

Antwerp

ALBERT CANAL

ssels

R. Dyle

enne

Liège

L G I U M

Namur *R. Meuse*

Sambre

A R D E N N E S

Mezières

Sedan

Luxembourg

R. Meuse

ne

Verdun

MAN OF VALOUR
The Life of Field-Marshal
The Viscount Gort,
VC, GCB, DSO, MVO, MC

"Today is Trinity Sunday. Centuries ago words were written to be a call and a spur to the faithful servants of Truth and Justice: 'Arm yourselves, and be ye men of valour, and be in readiness for the conflict: for it is better for us to perish in battle than to look upon the outrage to our nation and our altar. As the Will of God is in Heaven, even so let it be'."

From an address broadcast by Winston Churchill on 19th May 1940.

J. R. COLVILLE

MAN OF VALOUR

The Life of Field-Marshal
The Viscount Gort,
VC, GCB, DSO, MVO, MC

COLLINS
ST JAMES'S PLACE, LONDON
1972

FIRST PUBLISHED, 1972
COPYRIGHT © J. R. COLVILLE 1972

ISBN 0 00 211290 6

PRINTED IN GREAT BRITAIN
COLLINS CLEAR-TYPE PRESS: LONDON AND GLASGOW

To the memory of
JACQUELINE DE L'ISLE

Contents

Illustrations

Acknowledgements

I thank The Queen for permission to publish extracts from correspondence between King George VI and Queen Mary. The Duke of Windsor was good enough to supply me with an account of his contacts with Lord Gort and the French High Command during the winter of 1939-1940.

Field-Marshal Sir Gerald Templer, Admiral the Hon. Sir Guy Russell, Sir John Shaw, Admiral Sir Geoffrey Hawkins and Mr. Ford Geddes have greatly contributed by providing me with written accounts of important episodes in Lord Gort's career. Viscount De L'Isle, the Earl of Munster, Admiral Sir F. Dalrymple-Hamilton, Helen, Lady Hardinge of Penshurst, Sir George Fitzgerald and Mrs. Gerald Yorke have given me permission to quote from letters in their possession, and Mrs. Stephen Lloyd allowed me to use extracts from letters written by her father, Mr. Neville Chamberlain, to his sisters; Mrs. O. A. Archdale made available part of her husband's diary; Viscount Hood and Mr. V. G. Lawford sent me extracts from theirs; and Lt-Col. Miles Reid lent me the notes he wrote during the retreat to Dunkirk. Mr. Brian Bond, with the consent of Colonel Pownall Gray, gave me access to the relevant parts of General Sir Henry Pownall's diaries. Mr. David Grigg and the other heirs of Sir P. J. Grigg have allowed me to quote from his personal papers. Lady Liddell Hart kindly let me see and use those of Sir Basil Liddell Hart's files relating to his long association with Gort.

Gen. Sir Andrew Thorne, Viscount Chandos, Maj-Gen. F. G. Beaumont Nesbitt and Colonel R. Lambert eased my task and conscience by scrutinising with critical Grenadier eyes the chapters about World War I. Gen. Sir Ronald Adam, Maj-Gen. Viscount Bridgeman, Maj-Gen. P. Whitefoord, Lt-Col. Reid and my former Director of Studies at Cambridge, Professor Sir James Butler, have been equally helpful with regard to the years 1938-40; and Lord Munster, Admiral Russell, Sir John Shaw and Mr. Ford Geddes have vetted the chapters relating to Gort's proconsular appointments.

Maj-Gen. J. C. Haydon gave me useful information about the War Office under Hore Belisha and Gort; and no trouble was too great for Lt-Col. Rory Macleod, particularly in respect of the part played by Field-Marshal Lord Ironside in this story.

Many others who knew or served with Gort have given me their

ACKNOWLEDGEMENTS

assessment of his personality and achievements. I am indebted to his brother, the 7th Viscount, to Field-Marshal Earl Alexander of Tunis, the Earl of Avon, Brigadier C. R. Britten, the Duke of Buccleuch, Maj-Gen. Sir F. de Guingand, the Dowager Lady Ironside, Lt-Gen. Sir I. Jacob, Maj-Gen. Sir J. Kennedy, Gen. Sir H. C. Loyd, the Right Hon. Harold Macmillan, Field-Marshal Viscount Montgomery of Alamein, Lady Morrison-Bell, Lt-Col. W. S. Pilcher, Lt-Gen. Sir W. Platt, Gen. Sir F. Simpson, Maj-Gen. Sir E. L. Spears, Sir Gordon Vereker, Lt-Col. U. Verney and Col. G. Westmacott.

I owe Lord De L'Isle thanks for his help in many different ways; and I am especially grateful to Dr. Richard Vereker who himself contemplated writing Gort's life and with great good nature placed at my disposal the carefully chosen supply of material he had assembled for the purpose.

I would like to thank General Spears for the quotation from *Prelude to Victory* in Chapter VII and Mr. Christopher Sykes for permission to quote from his book *Cross Roads to Israel* in Chapter XX.

Mr. Peter Bradley researched most competently, especially among the files at the Public Record Office; and Mrs. N. L. Taylor has shown limitless patience in typing my untidy manuscript.

No acknowledgement whatever is due to my devoted wife and children, who have countless virtues but whose constant interruptions added enormously to the burdens of authorship.

J. R. COLVILLE

The Making of a Soldier

CHAPTER I

INTRODUCTION TO
LIFE AND WAR

I N the seventeenth and eighteenth centuries Ireland provided a
rich hunting ground for opportunists. Fame and prosperity came
to those who married judiciously, for girls survived more successfully than their brothers and heiresses abounded. This was also
true in the neighbouring kingdom of England and Scotland,
where many an estate and noble name passed through a sister or
a son-in-law; but in Ireland dispossession on religious or political
grounds increased at once the insecurity of ancient tenures and
the opportunities available to the shrewd.

At the end of this period, after long ancestral experience of plots
and civil wars, and generations of discriminating bridegrooms
who too often begat spendthrift sons, the heir to some heavily
encumbered property in Counties Galway, Limerick and Cork
was Colonel Charles Vereker, Member of Parliament for Limerick
and Commander of the city's Militia.*

In 1798, when the flag of Irish rebellion was raised, a supporting
French force under General Humbert landed in Killala Bay on
the coast of Mayo. At Castlebar the seasoned French troops put
the British defenders to flight and Humbert moved into County
Sligo on his way to Ulster, where he believed the Cromwellian
traditions of the Orangemen would produce sympathies towards
Republican France more abundant than those of the peasantry of
Munster or Leinster. He was unable to put this improbable
theory to the test because, in spite of a command from the British
general to retire into Fermanagh, Colonel Vereker decided to
disobey orders and stood barring Humbert's way at a place
called Coloony. The colonel placed his artillery, consisting of two
curricle guns, on a hill to his left, since he foresaw that the larger
enemy forces would try to outflank him. Then he attacked the
French with 250 members of the Limerick City Regiment,
twenty of the Essex Fencibles, thirty yeoman infantry and a troop

* A brief history of the Prendergast and Vereker families is given in the
Appendix.

of the 24th Light Dragoons. The action lasted an hour and a half and the Militia withstood a full charge of the French cavalry. At last the hill on the left flank was taken by the French and the colonel was obliged to fall back, leaving twenty dead and thirty wounded Frenchmen on the field as well as a fair number of rebel corpses. His own losses were light. The remarkable thing was that the French, convinced that no adversary could behave with such bravado unless there were a large army advancing to his relief, abandoned their march on Ulster and turned southwards straight into the arms of superior British forces to whom they were obliged to surrender. On giving up his sword General Humbert is reported as saying: "I met many generals in Ireland, but the only soldier among them was Colonel Vereker." The skirmish was hailed by the public as a major triumph and it was proved, to the rebels' discomfort, that the Irish Catholic Militia were loyal to the British Crown when faced by an invader. It was the last engagement with foreign troops in the British Isles. The colonel received the thanks of both Houses of Parliament and adopted "Coloony" as the family motto.

In 1817 the hero of Coloony succeeded an uncle as the 2nd Viscount Gort and became the owner of an embarrassed estate. Most of the land he was able to retain was mortgaged to a speculator who foreclosed some years later, at the time of the Irish Famine. However, before his uncle died, Vereker had commissioned Nash to build a castle on the shores of Lough Cutra from which he could gaze across the lake to the rugged mountains that divide Munster from Connaught. Far away in the Isle of Wight Nash built East Cowes Castle as his own residence. It bore a striking resemblance to the castle at Lough Cutra.

The next three Lords Gort were worthy but undistinguished. They maintained the family genius for discovering heiresses. In particular, the 3rd Viscount married as his second wife Mrs. Tudor, widow of the Member for Barnstaple and owner not only of Nash's East Cowes Castle but also of four acres of the Tottenham Court Road. This valuable property, which she obligingly left to her stepson, more than compensated for the vanished Irish estates. When the 5th Viscount married the daughter of Mr. Robert Surtees, creator of "Jorrocks", whose ancestors had lived for over three hundred years in County Durham, the family were able to divide their time between East Cowes Castle, Hamsterley Hall in Durham and No. 1 Portman Square. Little that was Irish remained except the peerage.

Three generations. The 4th, 5th and 6th Viscounts Gort

Lieutenants of the Grenadier Guards, Gort (right) and Eban Pike

The heir to this comfortable fortune, John Standish Surtees Prendergast Vereker, elder son of the 5th Viscount Gort by his wife, formerly Miss Eleanor Surtees, was born in London on 10th July, 1886. Eighteen months later another son, Robert, was born. There the family ended. The two boys spent a dull and uneventful childhood. The River Medina separated East Cowes Castle from the fashionable glamour of Cowes Roads and the Royal Yacht Squadron, and since Lord and Lady Gort did not move in royal circles the close propinquity of Osborne and of Norris Castle, where the Empress Frederick sometimes spent her summers, had little bearing on their lives. Lady Gort, though an admirable manager of her business affairs, showed no affection for her children. She treated them as chattels. Their father, too, was a distant, aloof man who became seriously ill before they were in their teens.

After five years in a preparatory school at Malvern Link, Jack, as the elder of the two boys was called, was sent to the Head-master's House at Harrow, a school as popular in the nineteenth century with the Whig, Scottish and Irish nobility as was Eton with the English and the Tories. The headmaster of Harrow was Dr. Wood, who was much less admirable than his predecessors, Dr. Welldon and Dr. Montagu Butler; but Jack spent five con-tented years in his house, conformist, well-liked and displaying slightly above average ability in his work. He was preceded and succeeded in the Headmaster's House by two boys who, some forty years on, had a part to play in his destiny. Winston Churchill was his predecessor; Field-Marshal Alexander his successor.

When Jack was sixteen his father, long incapacitated by illness, died and he succeeded to the peerage. He had already decided to join the army and the Grenadiers appeared to be a suitable regiment. Therefore, like Churchill before him, he joined the Harrow Army Class and he passed with flying colours into Sand-hurst where he arrived in January, 1904, for the customary eighteen months' course. His contemporaries included future generals such as William Platt, Andrew Thorne and Hastings Ismay as well as his eventual colleague on the Chiefs of Staff Committee, Cyril Newall. He was considered a decent, clean, likeable and, above all, exceptionally keen cadet. He was made a sergeant and christened "Fatboy", a nickname which remained for life on account of his squarely built figure, even though his insistence on strenuous physical exercise, in middle age no less than in youth, effectively denied him one ounce of surplus fat.

On leaving Sandhurst in July, 1905, he was gazetted an ensign in the Grenadier Guards. His brother officers were of two distinct varieties. There were those who had joined because, after all, a young man must have something to do and it was quite unthinkable that a gentleman should go into business or become involved in anything so undignified as earning money. Money, of course, was essential; but either one had it or else one married an heiress, perhaps even an American, and thus procured it. Life in the Officers' Mess of the Grenadier Guards did little to interrupt the really important things such as hunting or going to balls, and it provided a universally accepted social *cachet*.

There were, however, Grenadier officers of a different kind, men who were determined to be professional soldiers and who knew they were likely to have better and more diverse opportunities in the Brigade of Guards than elsewhere in the army. Pre-eminent among these was Gort. He had the gift of powerful concentration and he turned it to useful purpose in studying all imaginable aspects of the military art. While the attention of others was directed to wine and women, his main, indeed almost sole, interest was in reading or discussing tactics, strategy and the history of war. He was taught that attention to detail was essential to military success and this was a maxim readily acceptable to his tidy mind. He knew, too, that a good soldier must be fit and so, though a naturally bad horseman, he acquired a stable of serviceable hunters and hunted when he was quite sure this did not interfere with regimental duties. There was, he maintained, no better way for a soldier to acquire "an eye for country". In 1910 he rode his "Hooligan III" to victory in the Manners Cup, a steeplechase reserved for officers of the Grenadier Guards, and he came third on "Blazer" in 1912. On exercises he was seen to carry the fullest possible pack and he insisted on doing everything at the double. He revelled in leading a spartan life; he sought austerity for its own sake; and he displayed a martial enthusiasm that amazed and disconcerted his fellow subalterns in the peaceful reign of King Edward VII. He was indeed far from popular during his early years in the regiment. Honest, good-humoured and imperturbable though he might be, there were occasions when his brother officers thought his devotion to duty went altogether too far, and on one such occasion they threw him into the Basingstoke Canal at Pirbright as a punishment for taking life too seriously.

Guard duties in London were not in themselves the training for an ambitious professional soldier; but they sometimes required unexpected talents. On the death of King Edward VII Gort, by now a lieutenant, was in command of the Grenadier N.C.O.s detailed to bear the coffin and attend the catafalque. For several days before being called on to place the King's body in the coffin, he was engaged in supervising ten undertaker's men, dressed in deepest black, whose task was to show the sergeants how to carry a dummy coffin up and down stairs. The instructors in this art looked, he wrote, "as if they have been dug up themselves for the occasion, have faces a yard long, find it impossible to smile and would make a fortune on a music hall stage. I shall be quite a good amateur undertaker myself soon." For this macabre service Gort was summoned to Marlborough House to receive his first decoration: Member of the Victorian Order, Fifth Class. The next five, a Military Cross, three D.S.O.s and the Victoria Cross, were to be acquired in still more trying circumstances.

Shortly after the coronation and its attendant celebrations, for all of which the Grenadiers lined the streets of London, a railway strike was declared. It must have been something of a relief to be called on to man Norwood signal box, to escort a convoy of hay to Hackney marshes and to move a load of bullion to Newcastle, even though to a subsequent generation it seems strange that the guardsmen were ordered to perform these tasks wearing full marching order and bearskins.

In 1908 Gort's mother had married again and, since he cared little for his stepfather, his mother receded still further from any corner of his affections. She insisted on continuing to call herself Eleanor, Viscountess Gort; she resided at East Cowes Castle; and neither Gort nor his brother saw more of her than duty positively required. He had no sister nor other close feminine relation and such interest as he might naturally have felt for the other sex was subdued by a lack of self-confidence in addressing himself to them combined with an overpowering desire not to waste time which could be more profitably spent on attention to military studies. However, all men require some measure of affection and as his mother provided no home for him, he was driven to make one for himself. He was rich, he was a peer and he obviously had a fine military career ahead. There was no shortage of mothers anxious to find such an eligible young man for their daughters.

Female relations were easier company for the diffident than totally strange young ladies standing shyly in a ballroom under surveillance from the chaperones' bench. Besides, a man who preferred to spend the evenings in barracks reading about Wellington's Peninsular Campaigns was scarcely tempted to take part in the sport of outwitting the chaperones. Gort happened to have a second cousin of outstanding beauty called Corinna Vereker, commonly known as Kotchy. She had been brought up, largely in France, in a more cultured branch of the family; she revelled in gaiety; she was a brilliant linguist; she was consistently untruthful and she was incorrigibly fickle. At the age of twenty it was considered time to settle down and what better catch could she make than the head of her own family?

In the autumn of 1910 Gort had taken a brother officer, Lieutenant W. S. Pilcher, to Canada in pursuit of moose. They set off with a solitary Red Indian into distant uninhabited lands and succeeded, to Pilcher's dismay and Gort's satisfaction, in roughing it to a degree of almost unbearable discomfort.

However, the trip ended unhappily. Gort, whom Pilcher considered one of the finest men in the world but one of the worst shots, fired at what he thought to be a moose and killed the Indian guide. He recompensed the justifiably aggrieved squaw and, leaving Pilcher behind, hurried to New York, whence he sailed for home in the first available ship. He had not so much as mentioned matrimony to Pilcher during their weeks together in the wilderness and perhaps the distress which the accident caused him precipitated his decision to propose. Be that as it may, soon after his return to London he announced his engagement to the beautiful Kotchy. On 23rd February, 1911, they were married at the Guards Chapel, Wellington Barracks. Lieutenant Eben Pike, Grenadier Guards, who remained a lifelong friend, was the best man and the bridegroom, in a generous mood, gave Kotchy a diamond tiara, a diamond Grenade brooch, a diamond and emerald ring and a diamond cluster ring. The bride was suitably attired "in a white satin gown trimmed with silver and pearls in a design of true-lovers' knots and shamrocks".

Once the honeymoon, the coronation and the railway strike were over, Gort and his friend Andrew Thorne, no less keen a soldier than himself and known to the Brigade of Guards as "Bulgy" with even less good reason than Gort was called "Fatboy", turned their minds to the next essential step in their career, entrance to the Staff College. They were still young for selection, but they were ambitious and finding a German tutor called Zimmerman, they applied themselves assiduously to their task. This scarcely suited Kotchy, who longed for the bright lights and who found that her husband, though willing to buy her horses and take a hunting-box in the Bicester country, kept a tighter hold on the purse-strings than she would have chosen and was totally averse to taking her out in the evenings. Nevertheless, she remained faithful to him in the early years of their marriage and she bore him three children. The eldest, Charles Standish, always called Sandy, was born in 1912; another boy, Joscelyn, followed a year later; and Jacqueline, born in 1914, became one of the two women who throughout the critical years of her father's varied and often unhappy life retained a constant and unshakable hold on his affections.

On 3rd September, 1913, Gort, who had settled down with his wife and the baby at 77 Cadogan Gardens, was appointed A.D.C. to Major-General Sir Francis Lloyd, the General Officer Commanding London District. British generals have often felt it added lustre to their names to have noblemen or the sons of noblemen on their personal staff. Indeed, in the South African War, when decorations were bestowed all too frequently on staff officers wholly protected from shot and shell, the D.S.O. was irreverently labelled "Dukes' Sons Only". Sir Francis certainly believed that a peer, even an Irish one, was a valuable embellishment to London District. Gort, however, did not allow the general's or anybody else's social considerations to divert him from the military studies on which his attention was concentrated. At the beginning of August, 1914, admission to the Staff College was still his urgent target, and Kotchy was too busy having babies to be troublesome, when the first great whirlwind of the twentieth century was reaped and officers of the Brigade of Guards were called upon to put into practice in the field rather than the classroom the lessons which, some more studiously than others, they had been learning at Aldershot, Tidworth and Pirbright. The Staff College would have to wait.

Although the event which finally led to the outbreak of European war, the murder in Sarajevo of the heir to the Austro-Hungarian throne, took place on 28th June, 1914, it was only in the last few days of July that the full gravity of the situation was apparent. Until then the imminence of civil war in Ireland was the principal British anxiety. As soon as it became clear that hostilities were probable Gort, who had no intention of remaining at the Horse Guards, responsible for Sir Francis Lloyd's comfort and personal affairs while his brother officers embarked for France, contrived to have himself transferred as senior A.D.C. to

Major-General Charles Monro, commanding the 2nd Division of the prospective Expeditionary Force.

There were some, in particular Lord Kitchener, the newly appointed Secretary of State for War, who foretold a long, hard-fought war. Most people believed that even if the British force of six well-trained infantry divisions and one cavalry division, commanded by the Inspector General and former Chief of the Imperial General Staff, Sir John French, could only make a marginal contribution to victory, the magnificent French army, with its offensive spirit, its determination to retrieve Alsace-Lorraine and its thirst to avenge the disgrace of Sedan forty-four years previously, would win the war on land before Christmas while Britain swept the German navy from the seas. It was thus with excitement, often amounting to elation, that young men hurried to join the colours, afraid that the war would be over before they had a chance to participate. Those already in the army could at least expect a glimpse of action before a brief and glorious campaign ended in victory.

On the afternoon of 3rd August Gort left Cadogan Gardens in his Mercedes motor-car, called for General Monro and drove him to Aldershot. The next day, as the Germans, in defiance of their solemn treaty obligations and of a British ultimatum, began their pyromaniac march through Belgium, mobilisation of the army was decreed and war was declared. On 5th August Gort was promoted captain and while urgent preparations were being made for the Expeditionary Force to leave, he was inoculated against what he described as "interic" and retired to bed with a temperature of 103°. He recovered in time to assist the advance party of the 2nd Division and its three brigades in their departure for France and early on 15th August he set off by train for Southampton with General Monro and Divisional Headquarters. Every bridge and culvert on the London and South Western Railway was guarded by eager territorials against spies and saboteurs.

They found themselves sharing the S.S. *Minneapolis* with the 2nd Dragoon Guards ("The Bays") and the horse-deck was so crowded that although Gort was able to find room for his favourite charger, Blazer, there was no place for the second horse he had hopefully brought with him. Cowes Roads, where less than a fortnight previously the great yachts had been assembled for Regatta Week, was now the anchorage for a fleet of transports and thence one by one they steamed away under sealed orders.

They landed at Havre and entrained for the front three days later. The train took almost twelve hours to reach Amiens, the entire route being guarded by French soldiers and the loud cheers of the populace accompanying it along the line. At Arras General Monro, to his acute embarrassment, was ceremonially presented with a bouquet, and at 3.30 a.m. on the 19th his Divisional Headquarters unloaded themselves and their possessions at Wassigny. The fact that theirs was the twenty-fifth train to discharge its load in twenty-four hours did something to explain the length of the journey and was, at the same time, a tribute to the administrative arrangements made for the reception of the B.E.F.

The advance towards Belgium began and by 22nd August the 2nd Division was twenty miles south of Mons, where the battle was expected to take place. Gort was sent off in the general's Sunbeam car with orders for the three brigades, but on his return journey he was so held up by the troops advancing northwards towards Mons that he found his general had gone without him. The car was a useless appendage behind the dense columns of marching infantry and so mounting Blazer he rode through the night in pursuit of Divisional Headquarters, finally catching up with them before dawn. By noon the next day the division was deployed a few miles south of Mons, whose inhabitants, "regular industrial hollow-chested white-faced men and women", as Gort described them with evident distaste, came "slouching round" General Monro and his staff. Neither soldiers nor civilians had any idea of the avalanche which was approaching and which was already sweeping before it the French armies on the right of the B.E.F.

At 2.30 p.m. German shells began to fall. Shortly afterwards a squadron of the 15th Hussars and a contingent of soldier-cyclists came full tilt down the road from Mons, reporting that twenty horses had been killed by shell-fire and forty bicycles irremediably smashed. Officers and men of the 2nd Division began to gird themselves for a night attack, but to their disappointment it was cancelled and then, bewilderingly, at 2.0 a.m. on 24th August orders were received to withdraw. The retreat from Mons had begun.

Back they went across the French frontier, along the straight, dusty roads, recoiling on their own transport wagons which often blocked their way, leaving rearguards in each successive village to hold off the advancing Germans, perplexed by the absence of contact with the French troops, whom they believed to be on their flank. "On our west," Gort wrote, "we have the forest de Mormal which to the French nation is a great military obstacle." Twenty-five years later the French nation suffered from the same illusion.

An August heat-wave grew daily more intense and Gort noted that the men were beginning to show signs of fatigue although they remained strikingly cheerful and lacking in resentment. Thanks to Blazer and the Sunbeam, he himself suffered less physical exhaustion on the march than most of the officers and men of the division, and it was with a mixture of disgust and envy that Lieutenant Pilcher, footslogging wearily westwards, saw him drive past with his general in the car. But at night, when the streets of the small towns and villages were jammed with cavalry, transport wagons and the impedimenta of an army in unexpected retreat, it fell to the staff to unravel the tangles as best they could and there was little time for repose. On 25th August the division's 4th (Guards) Brigade were holding Landrecies against overwhelming odds. Gort wrote in his diary: "Everybody felt that we had been surprised by the Germans (motor-car army) who had pushed through the forest and that we were practically surrounded." That night they all but suffered a catastrophe: "As we withdrew it was noticed that the 5th Bde was not to be found: Col. Perceval went off in a car to find them and finally discovered them trekking in the opposite direction, General Haking having misread his orders." On the 27th the Germans, advancing on St. Quentin, were already abreast of them to the westward. The division entered Guise and Gort, who had been used to snatching a few hours' sleep each night on the seat of the Sunbeam, unexpectedly found himself billeted "in the house of two dear old English spinsters from Brixton".

On the 28th the troops and transport of two infantry divisions and an entire cavalry brigade were struggling down the same narrow road leading to La Fère and the infantry's sufferings were acute. March discipline had to be relaxed and many packs were thrown away, but good humour still prevailed and there was, Gort was proud to observe, a total absence of anything like insubordination. Blazer chose an inconvenient moment to cast a shoe, but a farrier of the South Irish Horse replaced it expeditiously. The heat became still more oppressive and by the 29th they had marched 143 miles in nine days. On the 30th they reached Soissons and the River Aisne. German cavalry were already across the river to their left and by 2.15 a.m. on 1st

September ("Sedan Day", Gort noted with two exclamation marks) they were off again through the Forêt de Compiègne towards Villers-Cotterets. Here the 4th (Guards) Brigade was attacked in force by enemy infantry, but the Germans suffered severely from the "five rounds rapid" which had been brought to its highest efficiency by the Brigade of Guards in their peace-time training. Deceived by the volume and accuracy of this rifle-fire the Germans overestimated the numbers opposing them. The descendants of the archers who fought at Crècy and at Agincourt had perfected a modern deterrent of comparable efficiency. .

Several of Gort's friends and contemporaries fell that day. He himself, collecting a band of men from the King's and the Berkshire Regiments, led them into the fray. He was struck in the groin by a shrapnel bullet but "it bounced off, leaving a nasty bruise". The next morning, in conditions of still greater heat, the British took up a position on the River Marne, covering the town of Meaux. The bridges were destroyed, the barges sunk and the boats ferried over to the south bank.

There was still a little farther to go. They spent a night at Tresnes "in a house which contained some lovely Louis XV gold furniture. Especially exquisite chairs. The dear old General was very restless and unnerved and wouldn't go to bed until 2.0 a.m. although he was dead beat." On 5th September, the last day of the retreat from Mons, the headquarters of the 2nd Division reached Fontenay, only twenty miles from Paris, whence the French government had already retired to Bordeaux. Meanwhile great events of which General Monro and his senior A.D.C. were ignorant had swayed the decisions of the German High Command and altered the course of history. East Prussia, homeland of the Junkers, was thought to be threatened by a Russian pincer movement. In consequence the High Command, sensitive to the nightmare of Cossacks galloping over the lands from which so many Prussian officers came, detached two corps from the right wing of the armies which were closing on Paris. At the same time the French, in the desperation of defeat, rallied their beaten armies and with only slight help from the British won that most Crowning of Mercies, the Battle of the Marne.

Thus on 6th September Gort was able to write: "Commenced to advance. We apparently took the Germans by surprise after our long retreat." On the 7th they entered Rebais, but Colonel Perceval, arriving by car a little too soon, was unceremoniously chased out of the town with a squadron of Uhlans galloping in hot pursuit. The inhabitants told many stories of the plunder and excesses from which they had suffered during their brief ordeal of occupation, and one of the more moderate came from an old lady who claimed she had been "*violée, mais pas brutalement*". The next day a German machine gun post held up the division as they attempted to cross the River Morin and it was eventually Gort, seeing a German soldier move in a hedge in the valley below, who brought fire to bear on the spot where resistance was concentrated and destroyed the enemy detachment. Twenty corpses and the machine gun were retrieved from the hedge. By 12th September, after several days of torrential rain, they were back to the River Aisne, where a battle lasting nearly a fortnight was waged. Gradually, as the armies dug themselves in, the front became stabilised. The long, tedious and miserable era of trench warfare was inaugurated on the Western Front.

CHAPTER 2

COMMAND IN THE FIELD

I N the middle of October, 1914, the 2nd Division was despatched to Ypres, where Gort first saw a countryside with which he was to acquire a long familiarity. From Poperinghe they attacked north-east of the Ypres–Menin road towards Passchendaele. The battle reached its culminating point in the early days of November. No great territorial gains were made, but the allied salient at Ypres, of bitter memory, was held at the cost of many young lives and became part of the line of trenches stretching across Flanders and France.

General Monro's headquarters were at Hooge Château, which he shared for a time with Sir Douglas Haig's I Corps. It was here, on the morning of 31st October, that Monro and his staff held a conference with Major-General Lomax, commanding the 1st Division. During the meeting two high explosive shells struck the building, wounding Lomax and killing five of the assembled staff officers. Neither Monro nor Gort was touched, but at this early stage of the war none complained that the generals and their staffs were too far behind the front line. Nor were the troops in danger of being spoiled by over-indulgence. Among the stranger entries in the divisional diary, and in Gort's handwriting, is this:

"12.XII.1914. Sandbags were issued to the troops of the 2nd Division. One bag issued to each infantry soldier for tactical purposes. This bag is to be carried on the soldier and in very cold weather permission is given for them to be used as footmuffs."

On 26th December Haig was given command of the new 1st Army. Monro, who was judged to have led his division with distinction, succeeded Haig in command of I Corps and he took Gort with him. Promotion to General Staff Officer, Grade 3, followed in February and there were five days' home leave. At Bicester Station, Lady Gort and Sandy, now nearly three, awaited him. "Sandy," he recorded, "was full of himself and had grown a lot. Joe can walk and Babs looked too sweet."

It was a brief interlude. In March, 1915, there was an expensive and unrewarding attack at Neuve Chapelle, and then on 1st April Gort was appointed brigade major of the 4th (Guards) Brigade under the command of Brigadier-General the Earl of Cavan. In May he was for a short time in the forefront of the battle at Festubert, but hardly had the brigade returned to billets when he received the heart-rending news that his second child, Joscelyn, "my poor little Joe," had died. The agony of those at home, who knew nothing and imagined everything about the dangers facing husbands, sons and brothers in France, was matched by the misery of men at the front unable to return to an afflicted wife or family. A soldier had to suppress his personal sorrows.

The summer was a hot one and Gort gave close attention to the health of the men in the brigade and to the state of the trenches in which they lived and fought. He found much to criticise when the 5th Brigade took over a sector of the line from the French. "The Brigadier and I thought they were without exception the worst trenches we had ever seen." Again, on 7th June, he wrote: "Scorchingly hot. 19th London Bttn. left trenches in a very dirty and insanitary condition. 20th London Battn. left the right sector in apple pie order. A credit to any unit. The trenches were made by the French and though in a degree good, they are made on a bad principle. The front parapet is undercut – always a temptation to men to stay in the dugouts while shelling is on and very difficult to get them out in time to resist an attack. A fire trench should have no dugouts, but there should be any number . . . in the support line."

In August a new Guards' Division was formed, with Lord Cavan in command. Throughout the autumn and winter Gort remained with it. Whether they were fighting at Loos or undergoing periodic weeks of intensive training behind the lines, he was invariably to the fore, a staff officer with some responsibility for planning and administration, but without the slightest inclination to examine the situation from a safe or sedentary position. Indeed, he had already achieved five Mentions in Despatches, as well as a Military Cross, before he first reported for regimental duty.

On 30th June, 1916, the eve of the Battle of the Somme, he was summoned to the general headquarters of the British army at Montreuil and appointed a G.S.O.2 on the staff of General Sir Douglas Haig, who had succeeded Sir John French as commander-in-chief. In the long months of alternating fear and boredom, and perhaps particularly during the Battle of the

Somme when there were over fifty thousand British casualties on the first day and two hundred thousand in the first week, it was galling for a soldier of undoubted courage to be imprisoned as a planner on the staff, even though Gort's duties also included active liaison with units in the line of battle. In days when the average life of a subaltern was counted in weeks, there were many who preferred the probability of death with their company or platoon to safety with what they regarded as dishonour. Gort suffered torment as he saw his contemporaries die and, highly sensitive about his reputation, he could not fail to be distressed by what might be thought of his comparatively sheltered appointment. Yet, serving as he did on the staff of a number of senior officers, he learned more about strategy and profited more by witnessing the success and failure of other men's initiatives than could have been his lot had he commanded a company in the trenches.

The battles of the Somme and of Verdun in 1916 were on a scale unprecedented in history. If the French and the British suffered hundreds of thousands of casualties, the Germans for their part were left reeling. In December, political intrigues in France resulted in the replacement of the French commander-in-chief, General Joffre, by one of the Verdun heroes, Nivelle. Nothing could have been more disastrous, for he at once extended and postponed the plans for an offensive in the coming spring which Joffre and Haig had devised in complete accord. He was supported by Lloyd George, who sought to place the British army under Nivelle's operational command.

There was gloom at Haig's G.H.Q. In the early months of 1917 the staff were busy with plans for a limited British offensive at Arras as a means of diverting German reserves from the area south-east of Soissons which had been chosen for a great and final breakthrough by the French armies. During March and April, amidst decisions and counter-decisions by the supreme British and French authorities, three momentous events occurred. America declared war on Germany; the Russian revolution erupted in St. Petersburg, its influence percolating rapidly to the French trades union movement; and the U-boat campaign against the British Isles achieved such startling success that threats of starvation and perhaps invasion had to be taken seriously, particularly if the Channel ports should be lost. Memories of these events, and the fears or expectations they aroused, were still vivid to the British and French Governments and their commanders in the field twenty-three years later, in the spring of 1940.

In March the Germans forestalled the allies and drew their armies many miles back to the carefully prepared Hindenburg Line. This should have induced a commander-in-chief more flexible than Nivelle to revise his plan drastically, but he refused to admit any change in what he had prepared with confidence and had already advertised widely. The Channel ports, which Haig saw to be endangered by the shortening of the front, and the consequent release of many German divisions, did not concern Nivelle: his mind was set on a brilliant and final solution in the south.

The British offensive at Arras opened on 9th April with startling success on the first day. After an artillery barrage by over two thousand guns, the 1st and 3rd British Armies seized all their objectives, advancing in alternating snow and sleet, and the Canadians triumphantly captured Vimy Ridge. Through lack of initiative this early success was not exploited to the full and it was commonly believed that the fault, at any rate in part, lay in the fact that general headquarters at Montreuil was too far to the rear of the fighting. There is no doubt that Gort, seeing victory turned into stalemate and no orders given for pursuit of the disintegrating German forces, read into the story a moral which influenced his decision to move his own command-post so close to the front line in 1940.

By 16th April the British had performed their allotted task of drawing substantial German reserves northwards. Nivelle therefore launched his attack on the Aisne. It was intended to be the battle to end the war and it was a complete failure. The French fought with gallantry, but the Chemin des Dames has become notorious in French history as a graveyard of thousands who could not break through the barbed-wire defences and were slaughtered by well-protected machine-guns. It was the end of Nivelle and the end of hope for victory in 1917.

For Gort, after the weary winter months of planning at Montreuil, release both from emotional suffocation and paper responsibility came on 17th April, 1917. He was appointed Commanding Officer of the 4th Battalion, Grenadier Guards, in the 3rd Brigade of the Guards' Division.

His first active command began quietly enough. At the time of his arrival the men were engaged in manual labour, helping the Royal Engineers to push forward a broad-gauge railway line towards Peronne at the junction of the British and French armies.

It was territory vacated by the Germans in their withdrawal to the Hindenburg Line and seldom has a scorched earth policy been more ruthlessly and efficiently practised: there was not a cottage left standing, not a well or waterworks that was usable, not a public utility of any kind that had survived deliberate destruction. It was vital to repair the roads as well as the railways and the hard-fighting warriors of the Guards' Division cheerfully converted themselves into navvies. An order was issued to remind commanding officers of the old established custom in the Guards that officers should take off their tunics and work with the men.

Early in May these laborious tasks were completed and the division went into training for three weeks, an experience which under their new commanding officer the 4th Battalion, Grenadier Guards, found anything but relaxing. The entire corps then moved northwards to the area near Ypres occupied by Sir Hubert Gough's 5th Army.

On 3rd June Gort was awarded the D.S.O. in the Birthday Honours List. It was in recognition of his services on the staff and he was far from proud of the fact. When the adjutant, Captain Lambert, congratulated him at breakfast his good wishes were acidly received and Lambert felt obliged to warn others against referring to the matter. However, things were now different and it did not take him long to gain the respect of his officers and men. Tin-hat aslant, a meerschaum pipe in his mouth, he strode about no-man's-land entirely regardless of shot and shell. There was no task he ordered his men to assume which he would not readily undertake himself; there was no point of danger in the battalion front where he was not to be found. He seemed to revel in personal discomfort while priding himself on maintaining the personal smartness and cleanliness which should go without saying for a Grenadier. Danger he disregarded entirely because, as the troops quickly discovered, fear did not seem to be included among his emotions. He overlooked no point of detail; no offensive possibility escaped his attention. Officers joining the battalion would be taken straight to a point where some German "minenwerfer" was concentrating its fire and would have the tactical position shown to them in practice rather than theory. Some of them tended to think that this immediate baptism might have been delayed until they had at least found their way about the trenches; but their commanding officer expected from others the standards he set for himself. Two young officers who had obtained leave to visit Boulogne were chided on their return for not having exercised their powers of observation in calculating the number of trains that could turn round in the station and the shipping capacity of the harbour. Gort, who was disinclined to relax when off duty, assumed that this would have been a natural and useful employment of leisure hours.

The failure of Nivelle's offensive and mutinies which infected half the fighting units in the French army during June added weight to the burden which fell on the British later in the year. Not so much as a ripple of disaffection stirred Haig's troops. However, the French armies, shattered by the slaughter at Verdun a year before and their morale once again reduced by the bloody anticlimax of the Battle of the Aisne, subjected to organised agitation by anarchists and syndicalists on their home front, embittered by the unfairness of their leave arrangements and politically conscious of the egalitarian developments in Russia to a degree that the British "Tommies" most certainly were not, came near to total collapse.

General Philippe Pétain was selected to deal with the situation. It is to his enduring fame, which his actions in the Second World War can never erase, that he saved France and the allied cause by his handling of the crisis which followed Nivelle's inglorious departure. His firm leadership and his personal visits to the mutinous units restored confidence in a surprisingly short time. The French recovered their health, but there had to be a period of recuperation and during that period it was the British, fighting once again in the pockmarked fields of Flanders, who were called upon to bear the brunt. The surviving flower of the British regulars and most of Kitchener's New Army had fallen at Loos and on the Somme: at Passchendaele a renewed blood-bath, still more horrible and only a little less extensive, now awaited the conscript army which had taken their place.

On 10th June battalion commanders of the Guards Division were summoned to discuss plans for an attack across the Yser Canal some three miles north of Ypres in order to capture enemy positions on the Pilckem ridge. There was to be a general advance by the 5th Army over the Passchendaele ridge and on to the vital railway centre of Roulers. During the temporary lull which followed the earlier battles there was plenty of time, in a stiflingly hot June, to prepare for this full-scale offensive and it was recognised that specialised training was necessary since the canal was a formidable obstacle. It contained very little water, but the mud on its bottom was deep and clinging.

Gort and his elder son, Sandy, at East Cowes Castle

In *Carlotta* off the Needles

The 3rd Guards Brigade was selected for the task and Gort made a number of visits to the forward trenches from which his battalion would attack across the canal towards Pilckem. Before the brigade moved into immediate reserve, the 4th Battalion had time to celebrate the second anniversary of its formation. There was a football match, a tug-of-war, a gay dinner in the Sergeants' Mess which the corps commander, Lord Cavan, attended and a free issue of beer to all the men. Fortified by the evening's entertainment, the battalion moved into the front line on 19th July with the 2nd Guards Brigade alongside the 3rd.

Early on the dank, grey morning of 31st July the leading battalions of the two brigades, fortified by the issue of rum and tea usual before a battle, crossed the canal. The task of Gort's battalion, almost six hundred strong, was to follow with the second wave of attackers and to capture the third line of objectives, thereafter allowing the 1st Guards Brigade to pass through them to Pilckem Ridge itself. At 4.30 a.m. their turn came. They moved to the attack under cover of an artillery barrage, but while deploying for the assault they were raked by heavy machine-gun fire, and finding it impossible to recognise landmarks in the half-light they were obliged to advance by compass bearings. Led by Gort, they put down a smoke barrage and succeeded first in blinding and then outflanking the German position. Most of the defenders surrendered. Without pausing, the Grenadiers advanced towards their goal, storming and capturing two enemy-held farmhouses as they went. They arrived at their objective exactly on time, but not before Gort had been wounded in the arm. Although he was clearly in pain, it was not his nature to retire hurt until the position he had won was consolidated. The 1st Battalion of the Grenadiers was added to his command so that by 2.0 p.m. the defences were complete and the area efficiently wired against counter-attack. Only then did he retire to have his wound dressed and as soon as this had been done he insisted on returning to lead his battalion in a later phase of the offensive. It was brilliantly successful: the ridge was captured, the enemy were driven back two and a half miles on a front nearly a mile long, over six hundred Germans were captured and Gort, who had meanwhile been sent to hospital for a short spell, was awarded a bar to his D.S.O. And then it began to rain.

A great deal has been written of the callous and senseless profligacy with which the generals of the First World War, issuing their orders far behind the lines, threw hundreds of thousands of young men into artillery barrages and against prepared machine-gun posts. No doubt there is justice in much of this criticism. Nevertheless, a later generation of authors and script-writers, judging by the standards of another time and totally divorced from the political and military thought which prevailed in distant years, give little consideration to the ceaseless pressure to achieve rapid success and an end to the war that was brought to bear on the generals by anxious governments and an agonised public at home.

The British decision to attack in the late summer of 1917 was mainly due to Nivelle's failure and the mutinies which followed. The enemy must be engaged before he could recover his strength for one last desperate throw against the temporarily weakened French armies. Partly, too, it was taken on account of reports that German morale, civilian and military, was on the verge of cracking: one more strenuous blow and the crack would become a cleavage. Finally, nobody could forget the menace of the U-boat bases on the Belgian coast which could be outflanked by means of a successful attack north-eastwards, including the capture of the junction at Roulers. The British army had, after all, carried everything before it at Arras in spite of atrocious weather conditions. Why should it not do the same at Ypres, and this time consolidate its early success, in the clement month of August?

After two months of glorious summer weather, it was in the afternoon of 31st July, as the Guards Division consolidated their territorial gains, that a Scotch mist descended and visibility deteriorated disconcertingly for infantry and artillery alike. In the early evening the heavens opened and they so remained for three days and three nights. On 3rd August Major Rory Macleod, commanding a battery to the right of the Guards Division, wrote home: "I am still alive though at present I am more likely to die from drowning than hostile fire." What he wrote was the literal truth. The ceaseless deluge turned the naturally boggy fields of Flanders into a sea of mud so deep that men were drowned in shell-holes and whole gun-teams disappeared from sight in the brown, quaking morass which was churned and re-churned by hundreds of thousands of bursting shells. There were breaks in the weather, occasionally there were fine spells and drying winds, but always the heavy rains returned and in the barren, battle-scarred land there was no shelter, night or day, for the attacking armies as slowly, yard by yard, they edged their way towards the still distant goal of Passchendaele.

The Guards Division, with occasional spells of rest in billets behind the Yser Canal, suffered as much exposure and bombing but rather less fighting than the units on their right, until on 5th October they took over the battle front in preparation for a renewed attack. The weather was fine, but such was the state of the ground that Gort's No. 3 company, instructed to lay some "mat crossings" over the swampy surface, worked for six hours on the night of the 6th, up to their waists in marshy water, and only succeeded in performing a part of their task. However, if the rains of August had been unprecedented, perhaps October would make amends. The Australians of the 2nd Army had attacked on 4th October with such vigour that the Crown Prince of Bavaria, commanding the opposing German army, had proposed evacuating Flanders altogether. The Guards went in on the 9th and, as usual, all went well with the initial attack. Three days later October decided not to be outdone by August: torrential rains, to which the Germans added a severe barrage of poison gas shells, brought the advance to a standstill. There was a physical limit to the depth of mud through which men could wade. For five days they endeavoured to struggle forward, but they had been relieved before finally, with a Herculean effort, the Canadians took the village of Passchendaele on 6th November. Eighty-six German divisions had been engaged in this, the third Battle of Ypres. They had been outfought for the first time and forty thousand of their men lay shot or drowned in the mud surrounding Passchendaele. Thousands more were wounded or taken prisoner. The British could claim the victory: they had reached their goal with the loss of only thirty-five thousand dead; and at this cost they had achieved in over three months what they had hoped to do in three days. One important objective was gained: the French armies were uninterrupted in their convalescence; and if the sun had shone that summer on heat-baked fields success might well have come rapidly. Seldom have climatic conditions played a more decisive part in the history of war.

This third Battle of Ypres was scarcely over before the British 3rd Army made an attempt to break the Hindenburg Line at Cambrai. It was ideal tank country and there were enough tanks – nearly three hundred and fifty of them – to test the merit of this British invention as leaders of an offensive in their own right. At the Somme the sight of such monsters had struck terror, but they were too few to be effective; at Passchendaele they wallowed, like stranded prehistoric animals, in the mud; but on 20th November at Cambrai the Tank Corps, with infantry and cavalry in support, and the fortunate co-operation of a thick mist, broke right through the German lines. Once again, as at Arras, early success was not exploited. By fatal hesitation, the cavalry lost the one great opportunity that was given them in France during the whole war. The tank crews were tired out, but the gap was open wide and for a few brief hours the men on horseback could have taken over the advance from the men in machines. With half his armies exhausted and brought to a standstill, Haig had decreed a limited operation only. There were but six infantry divisions in support and although reinforcements, including the Guards Division, were rushed towards the scene of the battle, they arrived too late to hold the great gains which had been made. The Germans, recovering from their surprise, counter-attacked powerfully on both flanks and the British were driven back, not indeed to the starting post but to the Hindenburg Line. In one sector alone the Germans were held. It was on the southern flank where the Guards Division, including Gort and his battalion, went into action on 25th November as snow began to fall.

Not far from the important strong-point of Flesquières was a wood, some hundred acres in extent, still unscarred by war, a refreshing contrast to the gaunt and battered tree stumps which stood like scarecrows on most of the western front. It was called Bourlon Wood and nearby there was a small country house or lodge formerly used by quite different kinds of shooting parties. The 40th Division was finding Bourlon Wood all but untenable against the strength of the German assault and so the 3rd Guards Brigade was placed at their disposal. The 4th Battalion of the Grenadiers moved up through a vicious artillery barrage so calmly that General Ponsonby, commanding the 40th Division, subsequently issued a special order of the day to the effect that the battalion had come to his support as steadily as if it had been on parade. This was partly because its commanding officer, believing constant drill to be the best antidote to fear, had drilled his battalion rigorously when they were out of the line. "No doubt you want something to help you over your fears," he subsequently declared, "and if you get control of the nerves, as you do in drill, it helps to drive the man forward in war." On this, as on other occasions, Gort's men proved in action the effectiveness of this old-fashioned conviction. For once the elements, too, co-operated: a violent hailstorm to some extent hampered the accuracy of the enemy fire.

By the night of the 26th the prospects for attack seemed reasonable. Gort retired to the Shooting Lodge, now filled with the wounded and the dying, to confer with Lieutenant-Colonel Harold Alexander, commanding the Irish Guardsmen who were to attack through his own battalion at dawn. He summoned the company commanders. One of them, Captain Charles Britten, describes how while shells were falling on and around the lodge Gort gave them his orders for the assault as if they were all taking part in a peace-time exercise at Aldershot. He then asked Britten to show him his company positions and they started on their way through the thick undergrowth of the wood, led by the company runner. Rifle fire from the German lines was so heavy that, although entirely unconcerned by the bullets, Gort concluded they must be walking into the enemy lines. He disapproved, he said, of short cuts; and turning round he walked slowly back to their starting point insisting that the visit be made by a more circuitous route.

That night in the front line there was a bed in a former German dugout where Gort could have reclined in safety and comparative comfort, suspended well above the liquid slush. Instead he spent four hours of darkness inspecting every inch of the battalion line and only shortly before dawn, his task as commanding officer completed to his own satisfaction, did he lie down for a brief rest. He gave orders to be awoken five minutes before zero hour. The Germans attacked simultaneously. Both sides had been awaiting the same zero hour, and for both sides the attack was a failure. It was evident that the enemy were in much the greater force and for the British there were but scanty reserves available. So Gort, for whom courage was not synonymous with recklessness, discussed the situation with his close friend Lieutenant-Colonel Andrew Thorne, now commanding the 3rd Battalion, Grenadier Guards, who agreed that a renewed attack would destroy the 4th Battalion without any compensating advantage in the battle. The Grenadiers therefore stood fast, unsuccessful but by no means ashamed, until they were relieved later in the day and could encamp in the rear of the battle zone while fresh units sought to stem the still unbroken force of the German counter-attack. The trees of Bourlon Wood were now skeletons and the dead, in khaki and field grey, lay thick in the undergrowth.

There was not long to rest. On 30th November the Germans broke through near the village of Gonnelieu and the British line was in danger of being outflanked. The Guards Division were summoned to the rescue and the 3rd Guards Brigade were given the task of evicting the enemy from the village itself if an earlier attack by other British troops should fail. The 4th Grenadiers were to lead. It was not till 1.0 a.m. on 1st December that this order was received and the potential zero hour was prescribed for 6.30 a.m. Thus the plan of attack, the conferences with neighbouring formations and the briefing of company commanders had to be completed in a race against the clock. Moreover, in the pitch dark there was no opportunity for the personal reconnaissance of the ground to which Gort always attached special importance. Shortly before zero hour news came that the previous British attackers had recoiled: the Guards were to take their place.

At first light, without any artillery support whatever, Gort's battalion moved forward across almost a mile of ground where there was no cover, up a gentle slope leading to the village. The sun had not risen, but it was light enough for the German machine-gunners to see their targets and they opened fire remorselessly, relieved that for once the accompaniment of a creeping artillery barrage was absent and they could concentrate undisturbed on the advancing Grenadiers. Gort knew, and the men knew, that they were being sacrificed to save a desperate situation and that they must succeed where other gallant soldiers had failed and died. On they went, never wavering, in open order, regardless of their comrades dropping to right and left. Gort himself, carrying a walking stick, moved among them checking every aspect of the situation, urging them on and galvanising them by his disregard of his personal safety.

For a time he seemed to have a charmed life: the bullets of the machine-gunners passed harmlessly by this stocky figure, clearly visible as the commanding officer, whose presence was inspiring his men to feats of heroism. But it could only be for a time. More than two hours after the attack he collected his three surviving officers and the remnants of the attacking companies in a trench they had captured just outside the village and he set about organising a defensive position. This done, he moved forward alone to examine the situation on the left of his battalion line where the neighbouring unit was reported to be in retreat. At last the bullets struck and he fell wounded, in the side and in the left arm, more severely than at Pilckem three months previously.

Although elements of the battalion had actually entered the village, the 3rd Guards Brigade could not hold Gonnelieu; but the rest of the division recaptured the neighbouring railhead of

Gouzeaucourt and brought the German counter-offensive to a halt. In the brigade alone thirty-four officers and 928 other ranks fell that morning. It was an expensive epilogue to the Tank Corps' first successful outing. Gort was sent to hospital in England. He was one of the few soldiers in the British army to regard such an event as a calamity.

CHAPTER 3

VICTORIA CROSS

WHILE Gort was recovering from his wounds, the Allies and the Germans rested in their inhospitable trenches. The defenders of the Ypres salient stood cold and wet on the ridge at Passchendaele. No lasting dent had been made in the enemy defences. In Germany General Ludendorff had become the power in the land. It was clear to him that an irresistible offensive against the British and French armies was an immediate necessity. The Americans had begun to land in Europe. They were inexperienced and they had not a single field-gun or aircraft of their own. Indeed, in striking contrast to the Second World War, it was the British and to a lesser extent the French munitions factories which armed the American forces until the war was over. But they were fresh troops, strong, brave and enthusiastic, untouched by privation and ignorant of the horrors of the Western Front. It was essential for the Germans to win before the American threat became a serious reality and before the Royal Navy's blockade produced results unbearable to the civil populations of Germany and Austria-Hungary. Europe shivered, starved and waited.

Preparations for a mighty German attack were far advanced when, on 8th March, 1918, Gort returned to the front, appointed to command his regiment's 1st Battalion. It formed part of the 3rd Guards Brigade which was included in the 3rd Army defending the line from Arras to the Flesquières salient. To the south lay Gough's 5th Army, containing more newly conscripted troops and fewer experienced junior officers than any of the other four British armies in the field. Between them these two armies covered a front of seventy miles, the major part entrusted to the weaker and less battle-experienced 5th.

The Ludendorff offensive was launched on 21st March and it became apparent that the Germans had decided to use new tactics. Selected storm troopers, men of the highest fighting quality, threw themselves at the allied trenches after a bombardment with mustard gas and a short artillery barrage of an intensity unequalled in any previous assault. Nearly six thousand guns opened up on a forty mile front. Assisted by a thick fog, which bewildered the already shell-shattered defenders, the Germans leaped on the 5th Army, which bent and then broke before the storm. With equal ferocity they attacked the 3rd Army; but here, although the 51st Highland Division, at the southern end, was cut to pieces, and others were seriously mauled, they were confronted by a tougher adversary manning better prepared defences.

The Guards were in close reserve when the attack began. No less than sixty-four German divisions had been hurled at the chosen sectors of the British front where there were but thirty available to oppose them. On 23rd March the 3rd Guards Brigade took over the front line at Henin, a village a few miles south of Arras. Even as they relieved the exhausted defenders they were confronted by hordes of advancing infantry whom they repulsed with rifle and machine-gun fire. Gort had only been in command of his new battalion for a fortnight, but they had responded immediately to his leadership and when the Germans began a mass attack, advancing across the front of the 1st Battalion, it was the steady, accurate fire of the Grenadiers which destroyed the enemy vanguard. But the Germans came on without respite, new formations advancing as their predecessors fell or withdrew, until the divisions holding the line to the right were overwhelmed or driven back. At 6.0 p.m. on the 25th, as dusk fell, the Guards were ordered to retire too, so as to maintain the line intact. Gort stayed behind with two of his platoons in order to ensure that no British troops were left east of the Arras–Bapaume road and to maintain contact on his left flank with the Royal Scots Fusiliers, commanded by the Boer hero, Lieutenant-Colonel Deneys Reitz, who after a notably gallant resistance had also been ordered to withdraw.

Back they all went to the next line of defence, deluged with thousands of shells from the German artillery but beating off the pursuing infantry on the morning of the 27th. To the south all was chaos as the remnants of the 5th Army struggled westwards towards Amiens and the Somme. Yet it was not at the 5th Army front that Ludendorff had aimed his main stroke. Even greater masses of men and material were initially concentrated against the British divisions to its north. On the morning of 30th March the Guards Division was subjected to a violent assault with the main brunt falling on Gort's men, who were entrenched before a village called Boyelles. There were three hours of intensive bombardment by artillery; the dreaded "minenwerfer" lobbed their missiles accurately into the trenches; machine-guns swept the parapets; and at 11.0 a.m. fourteen German aircraft flew in single file along the line of the trenches unloading their bombs and firing machine-guns as they passed.

Drenched by this storm of shell, mine and bomb; covered with earth by the explosions; many of their number killed or mutilated; the trenches in some places totally obliterated; the Grenadiers stood their ground. It seemed to the Germans, confidently awaiting their moment, that none could survive to confront them. A sunken road ran from Boyelles at right angles to the British line and up this road, as soon as the aircraft had passed, dense masses of enemy infantry advanced, some of them breaking into the open for an outflanking movement. To their surprise and dismay, Gort's men, or such as were left of them, rose to the defence and, shooting with a coolness and accuracy that would have been commendable on a rifle range, mowed down the Germans as they emerged from the cover of their sunken road. Only in one place, where the road crossed the British line, did fifty of the enemy actually reach the trenches and these were counter-attacked with grenades until they withdrew leaving eighteen dead in the trenches and others in the path of their retirement. The attack had been a costly failure to the Germans; but the 3rd Guards Brigade had lost twelve officers and 332 men during those morning hours.

The worst was over, at least for the Guards. To the south Ludendorff pressed his infantry forward and in April, after the British Government and Haig had voluntarily submitted their armies to the overall command of General Foch, a renewed offensive was launched against the British 1st Army in the Ypres salient. All the painful gains of Passchendaele were lost and the Germans once again threatened the Channel ports. Then, in May, it was the turn of the French, supported by five battle-weary British divisions, at the Chemin des Dames and on the Marne. The Germans stormed through to within forty miles of Paris, and for a time during that anxious spring the allies were in straits almost as sore as in August, 1914. The Germans had come within an ace of winning the war on the Western Front; but Ludendorff had failed in his objective of splitting the French from the British armies and defeating each singly.

Meanwhile, south of Arras, comparative peace reigned. The Guards went in and out of the line and Gort, the depleted ranks of his battalion filled by new recruits, had time to train his men to the standard he expected of them, a high and exacting standard in which, because of his gift for leadership and the esteem in which they held him, they took a positive pride. One summer's day, Gort's battalion relieved the 2nd Battalion, Scots Guards, in a sector of the line near the village of Blairville. It consisted of a track, cut deep into the side of a hill, which had been converted into a trench. Over the parapet the German front line, known to the British as the Highland Trench, was plainly visible eighty yards away on the flat top of the hill. On the British side of the track the hill sloped gently downwards to a small stream. As the Scots Guards left, two of their officers said to Captain Beaumont Nesbitt, the brigade major, that now Gort had arrived this agreeable scene and sector would certainly lose its peaceful character.

They were right. Gort was never content to leave well alone. The object of being there was, after all, to fight the enemy. Moreover, the German trench was uncomfortably close. He had been told that it required careful watching and that no less than three unsuccessful night assaults had been made on it by a British brigade previously in the line, the last having been repulsed with heavy casualties. Gort did therefore watch the German line carefully and he reached a conclusion.

He gave orders for a night reconnaissance to be made by Captain Harry Crookshank, an officer as much admired for his gallantry and devotion to duty in battle as he was subsequently respected for his firmness and astringency as Leader of the House of Commons. At the dawn "stand-to" Gort interrogated Crookshank. What information had he brought back? Had he patrolled right up to the German wire? Had he got into the trench and how was it held? The unhappy Crookshank was forced to admit he had succeeded in none of these things, whereupon Gort said: "I suppose your commanding officer must do himself what you have failed to do." He summoned his orderly – it was no sinecure to be Gort's orderly – climbed out of the trench and walked straight to the enemy line. Not a shot was fired and some time later he was seen returning, the orderly carrying a German military overcoat on his arm. As Gort had surmised, the enemy trench was only occupied at night and was vacated in the daytime One of the Germans had presumably left his overcoat behind in readiness for the next night's chilly vigil. Meanwhile Gort and his orderly had taken the trench single-handed and when the Germans returned they were pained to find it occupied by the British Grenadiers. They made no serious effort to dispute the fact.

August came and the German effort was at long last exhausted. In their hearts they knew they were beaten: they did not have the resources to try again on a scale comparable to the Ludendorff offensive; the Americans were now actively engaged; hunger in Berlin and Vienna was beginning to amount to starvation; and the front line troops were increasingly aware of the misery and discontent afflicting their families at home. Yet nobody on the allied side believed the war was nearly over and planning for the campaigns of 1919 was well under way. Nor did the German army give any indication whatever of disintegration in the field. It is impossible not to admire them, in spite of the passive, indeed approving, support they had given to their Government in breaking the treaty to respect Belgian neutrality, and in spite of the atrocities they committed in Belgium and France. Their most bitter opponents could not fail to salute the fierce courage with which, when almost two and a half million of them were already dead and hope of victory had gone, they fought gallantly on for a vainglorious Emperor and a guilty Fatherland. Never have there been more indomitable soldiers.

It was men of this quality that the Allies must still expect to face when, on 8th August, 1918, Foch gave the orders for the Battle of Amiens to begin. Moreover, for the first time since 1914 the war became one of movement and officers and men who had known nothing but trench warfare found themselves expected to manœuvre against the enemy in open country. It was then that Gort, whose whole adult life had been devoted to studying war in all its aspects, had the opportunity to show a resourcefulness and ability to improvise which was often lacking in the most experienced trench-warriors.

On 21st August the 3rd Army, with fifteen divisions, began an advance towards the Arras–Albert railway over country from which they had been driven, fighting all the way, in the previous March. Gort was given temporary command of the 1st Guards Brigade while his second-in-command, Major the Hon. W. R. Bailey, took over his battalion. In this interlude, advancing three miles and capturing every objective, it was said by Brigadier-General Follett, commanding the 3rd Brigade, to have given "the finest exhibition that has ever been made in this war". He ascribed this to Gort's training combined with the leadership provided by Bailey, a second-in-command who had been constantly in action since 1914 and was fully worthy to stand in the shoes of his commanding officer. When Gort returned to the battalion on the evening of 24th August, Bailey had been wounded and the losses had been such that the total strength was down to seven officers and just over two hundred men, scarcely more than a third of the complement. Gort's first act was to go round the line and impress on the surviving officers that whatever the normal routine might be, the men must be spared as much fatigue as possible since worse and even more strenuous trials were to come.

At dawn next day there was an autumnal mist and when it lifted groups of Germans, in bodies of fifty and more, could be seen in the open a few hundred yards away. Gort was no believer in killing for its own sake and he hoped they might be contemplating surrender. He therefore held the battalion's fire. However, the intention of these groups appeared increasingly doubtful and after five minutes' grace Gort, who could take no unwarranted risk with so small a force, gave the order to fire. With three tanks in support, he then led his men forward until they were pinned down by machine-gun fire and two of the tanks were put out of action. The remnant, and a remnant indeed it was, withdrew to rest, reform and reorganise. Gort was faced with the necessity of training and enthusing new recruits whose slight consolation for their short expectation of life lay in the knowledge that their commanding officer would expose them less readily than himself to the fire of the enemy.

In early September they were engaged in light skirmishing and there were a few days, out of immediate contact with the enemy, during which Gort subjected his men to intensive training in the methods of attack appropriate to warfare in the open. The trenches and defence were things of the past: the time had come for swift and offensive measures against a wounded but still most dangerous prey during the steady eastward push towards one of the strong defences of the Hindenburg Line, the Canal du Nord. By 11th September they were close to the outer zone of the main German position. It was necessary to reconnoitre the front defences. Gort was not prepared to risk the lives of junior officers and inexperienced patrols. Therefore, alone with Captain Simpson, his senior company commander, he spent the night in advance of his men and secured information sufficient to enable him to lead his battalion on before dawn to take what a whole infantry brigade had failed to capture and to withstand a counter-attack. The next day was supposed to be one of rest, but when he heard that the troops on his right were advancing, Gort moved his own men forward in order to keep pace with them. Each night he would go ahead alone or with Captain Simpson to reconnoitre; before each dawn he would lead his battalion to the objective he had chosen under cover of night. By 15th September the battalion stood on the banks of the Canal du Nord itself and, as was said in the citation to the second bar to the D.S.O., which recognised his conduct in the advance, it was "impossible to speak too highly of this officer's initiative".

For the next step forward even greater initiative was required and was given. On 27th September the leading troops of the 3rd Army were across the canal. The remainder were ordered to attack on a wide front and sweep the Germans from their strongly defended trenches behind it. The 3rd Guards Brigade were to capture a German-held beet factory at Flesquières and then to take possession of Prémy Ridge, strongly defended, swept by machine-gun fire but dominating the surrounding country. Accompanied by the adjutant and some orderlies (including Guardsman Ransome, his soldier servant) Gort strode along at the head of the battalion. They crossed the canal. The brigade on the right had progressed well, but on the left it was a different story and it seemed that the entire advance would be held up by the resistance of the enemy at the strong-point of Graincourt. Communications had broken down, but Gort saw no reason to hesitate and he decided, with or without support on his flanks, to make for the targets he had been allotted. The Grenadiers found themselves in undulating country and he so conducted the advance, using dead ground and every fragment of natural cover, that scarcely a man fell to the observant and persistent enemy machine-gunners.

As the hours went by Brigadier-General Follett was mortally wounded. Instructions were sent that Gort should take over command of the 3rd Brigade. Whether or not he received the order, he went ahead with the task in hand. As soon as the leading companies reached Flesquières, he led them round the northern edge of the village, threading his way between the houses and successfully masking his men from the machine-gun fire on the flank. Three tanks he had been promised in support were slow to arrive and so he detached two leading platoons and led them forward to a wood from which they could wheel right and attack the Germans holding trenches behind the beet factory. He was wounded over the left eye by a fragment from a shell-burst. Guardsman Ransome bound up his head and paying no further attention to this mischance Gort directed the platoons to the attack. It was completely successful and resulted in the capture of two hundred Germans.

The troops which should have been supporting him on both flanks were nowhere to be seen and he had to decide whether to advance without them. A battalion of the Welsh Guards arrived and so he made up his mind that the Grenadiers should capture Prémy Ridge, with the Welsh Guards protecting their flanks. A tank appeared. Gort strode across the open, regardless of a hail of bullets, to tell the tank crew how he wished them to co-operate. At the same time an enemy aeroplane signalled to the German artillery the position of the two Guards battalions, but before the shells began to fall Gort, the wound on his forehead stanched by the bandage, had devised and communicated the tactics to be employed in capturing Prémy.

As they advanced along the ridge he moved, walking-stick in hand, backwards and forwards among the soldiers, encouraging them onwards and instilling into them that resolute determination which only a natural leader can inspire. A shell burst near him and one of its fragments severed an artery in his left arm. Ransome applied a tourniquet and Gort forced himself onwards until he collapsed from loss of blood. Now lying on a stretcher he persisted in directing the advance and when his men reached the first line of the enemy defences, known as Beet Trench, he struggled up and was there with the foremost companies to lead the assault. The trench was taken and so was the next line, together with many prisoners and two whole batteries of field-guns. But Gort had collapsed again and the medical officer insisted that he be taken from the field. The success signal went up: all objectives had been gained. Captain Simpson, who had accompanied him on his lonely nightly reconnaissances on the way to the Canal du Nord, assumed command and wisely decided that the time had come to consolidate the battalion's gains; but the men, inspired by the example of their commanding officer, showed obvious disappointment when the order was given to halt.

Even then it was not finished. As Gort walked away, assisted by the faithful Ransome, German batteries opened up at the two figures clearly visible on the ridge. A shell burst close to them, and this time it was Ransome who fell, one arm blown off and a deep gash in his leg. Gort stumbled on, faint from loss of blood and dizzy with pain, until he met a medical officer of the Irish Guards with whom he struggled back to his wounded servant. They bandaged him up and, still under heavy fire, they began the return journey. It was too late, and the wounds were too severe. As Ransome died, his last words were: "Get out of this, sir, as quick as you can." Gort afterwards wrote of him: "He was a young upstanding Guardsman of the very best type. He was one of the finest men that ever lived. More than that, he was a comrade of mine."

As a result of Gort's initiative in capturing Prémy Ridge, the advance of the 3rd Army could continue, Graincourt was taken and the whole German line was forced back. He received the Victoria Cross and seldom has its award been more generally acclaimed.

The army's recognition of his removal to hospital was bleak indeed. Dated 28th September, 1918, it read:

"Supplement to the London Gazette,
Foot Guards (Regular Forces)
Captain & Brevet Major J.S.S.P. Vereker, Viscount Gort, relinquishes the acting rank of Lieutenant-Colonel."

For him the war was over. Six weeks later, on a grey November morning, it was over for everybody.

CHAPTER 4

SOLDIERING ON

IT is one of history's more dependable lessons that when a great deliverance takes place, the bells will scarcely have stopped ringing before disillusionment grips the people and anticlimax prevails. The months following the 1918 Armistice were no exception. Spanish influenza, more virulent than any epidemic in living memory, lowered still further the vitality of an under-nourished nation. Demobilisation was neither so efficiently nor so equitably arranged as after the Second World War. As often as not, soldiers returning home found no jobs available. The Land Fit for Heroes was strangely less attractive than it had appeared in recent day-dreams. As if to prove that man is incorrigibly combatant, industrial strife replaced the fighting in the trenches and the bitterness felt for the outward foe was turned inwards against employers, local authorities or the Government. It is easy to exaggerate. There was nothing approaching a threat of revolution in Britain; prices, unlike those in the rest of Europe, were reasonably stable; and the essential fabric of society was intact. All the same, expectations of Utopia quickly receded and the long winter of misery was succeeded by a political, social and economic season that was scarcely recognisable as spring.

Gort was certainly more fortunate than the majority of his comrades. Belgrave Square, where he now acquired a house, needed repainting. In other respects his possessions were largely unaffected by the war. He had been wounded three times and a severed artery, with great loss of blood, is a debilitating experience; but his natural strength and zealously maintained fitness combined to speed his recovery and, unlike so many, he had suffered no permanent disablement. The only thing he lacked was a faithful, affectionate wife rejoicing in his return and anxious to learn every detail of his achievements. War breeds infidelity and Lady Gort's thoughts were elsewhere.

As soon as he was fit to report for duty he was sent to the Horse Guards. There he made the acquaintance of Captain Basil Liddell Hart who, wounded on the Somme more seriously than

Gort, shared his passionate interest in the progress of military science and the development of new ideas. They also shared impatience with the conviction, by no means uncommon among soldiers, that what was old and well-tried must necessarily be best. Gort could offer greater practical experience in the field; Liddell Hart, invalided home, had had more leisure to contemplate the whole range of warfare objectively.

On 1st April, 1919, the Staff College at Camberley opened its gates to the first post-war course. The division between instructors and pupils, chosen by nomination and not by examination, was arbitrary because those selected to attend had had much the same practical experience of war. Colonels John Dill, Philip Neame, "Boney" Fuller and Harry Knox were instructors; and among the pupils were Gort, now promoted to the substantive rank of major, Alan Brooke, Maitland Wilson and Freyberg. They worked as one, on a shortened course, to re-establish the college and in January, 1920, after two terms of three months each, the students graduated. During this brief introduction to an institution which he later knew so well, it was noted that Gort was among the most enthusiastic, always prepared to get up and talk, to discuss tactical problems and to state his views on the innovations required. It was also noted that, while he naturally drew on his own experiences, he neither boasted of his exploits nor insisted too strongly on his point of view. Naval heroes are seldom immodest, but soldiers quite often are. It was said of one gallant general that publication of his book was delayed because the printer ran out of capital I's. Gort, for his part, was invariably modest, however little his modesty cloaked an ambition to reach the top of his chosen profession and an impatience with the slowness in promotion that had to be faced by young men, grown mature in the furnace of war but blocked by an apparently inexhaustible supply of senior officers still on the active list.

Rigidly correct when on duty, and generally disinclined to waste in frivolous pursuits hours that could be devoted to increasing knowledge or to maintaining physical fitness, Gort was nevertheless an incurable addict to ragging. In this respect he never quite grew up. At Camberley his riotous behaviour in the mess, where he organised some of his fellow students from the Household Brigade into a group which he christened the Red Guards, set a standard of disorderliness on which he improved still further when he returned eighteen months later as an instructor. Most of his contemporaries enjoyed his high spirits and were amused by even his more outrageous antics; but it was perhaps the memory of them that induced some of his brother officers in the years ahead to think of him as an overgrown schoolboy more notable for brawn than for brain.

This was a superficial judgment. Of course, in dangerous times the clever and the prudent, aware of their value to the community, sometimes seek shelter in work useful to the war effort but out of range of a machine-gun. A select and shining band of the finest flowering intellectuals took the opposite point of view in both world wars and many died fighting for their country; but there was nonetheless a belief, fostered by some popular historians and a few military rivals, that physical courage is the antithesis of intelligence. Thus, in less heroic days, a man who had shown outstanding bravery in the field came to be esteemed more for his past deeds than for the probability of future achievements. Gort's literary knowledge was confined to military history, biography and the works of his maternal grandfather, Surtees. He was, on the other hand, quick on the uptake, shrewd in judging both a man and a situation, possessed of a retentive memory and gifted with above average powers of concentration. It is a mistake to equate the intelligent with the intellectual, for it is perfectly possible to be the one and not the other, and a soldier's intelligence cannot be measured by his taste for the humanities or his interest in the arts. Decisiveness in action is vital to an officer and if he should rise to be a general, then the doubts and irresolution that so often beset an "intellectual" could prove a national disaster. In the days of conventional warfare at any rate, Surtees and Kipling were wholesome literary food for soldiers. Since, in those early years after the war, Gort's professional reputation stood high, accusations of stupidity were postponed until he had been sufficiently successful to breed detractors. His past acts of valour were temporarily condoned.

Graduation at the Staff College was followed by another year at the Horse Guards, where General George Jeffreys, incarnation of the model Grenadier, was commanding London District. During this time Gort began a correspondence with Liddell Hart, who had undertaken to rewrite the Infantry Training Manual and had found in Gort an interested and sympathetic critic. Liddell Hart's "Expanding Torrent" theory of attack was of much significance, but Gort thought it necessary to emphasise to him the vital importance of reserves in warfare. A torrent, he pointed out, will flow through a gap impelled by the force of the water behind it, but an army must have powerful reserves if it is to exploit a break-through. "Until you have exhausted the enemy's reserves in Static Warfare," Gort wrote in September, 1920, "you have little or no chance of a serious break such as occurred after August 8th, 1918." But he was impressed by Liddell Hart's thought and in his next letter he wrote: "I am confident your theories simplify tactics in the minds of those striving after knowledge." Throughout November the correspondence between them was concentrated on the details of tactical methods and Gort insisted that "the interchange of ideas helps me a lot," while Liddell Hart replied that he was "most keen for your comments and criticisms".

In 1921 Gort returned to the Staff College as an instructor for the first full two-year course since the war. He was raised to the rank of brevet lieutenant-colonel. His lectures on tactics, based on what he had seen and experienced, were considered by one and all to be the outstanding feature of the course. Men of great future distinction were assembled at Camberley. Fuller, the brilliant and original thinker on tank warfare, to whom Liddell Hart, Hobart, Martel and thus, indirectly, Guderian and the German panzer leaders of 1940 owed so much, was still an instructor. Wavell was there, too; and Montgomery, Alexander, Ronald Adam, Loyd and Platt were among the many officers destined for leadership in the next conflict who became Staff College graduates in the immediate post-war years. There were, by way of contrast, a number of instructors of the old school, whose views found disfavour with officers such as Martel and Frederick Pile for whom mechanised units rather than horsed cavalry seemed to hold the key to the future. The younger and the more impatient saw in Gort, Dill and Alan Brooke standard-bearers in the march against the entrenched forces of War Office obscurantism. They were critical of the General Staff on the Western Front and they believed that a revolutionary approach to the direction of war was a vital necessity. It is, however, improbable that many of them would have agreed wholeheartedly with the vicious indictments of Haig and his generals conceived by historians of a later age.

Each generation, conscious of its own defects, turns with relief to criticise those of its predecessor and in the process usually exaggerates them. Gort was acutely aware of the mistakes made by the High Command because he had seen them at first hand and had suffered from them. To the extent, therefore, that he

looked backwards to the First World War it was in eager enthusiasm to teach the lessons which could be learned from past
errors. He would certainly not have subscribed to latter-day
criticisms of Haig, a man whose straightforward honesty he
admired, and in this he was at one with most of his contemporaries.
It is a fact inconvenient to those delighting in the destruction of
reputations that Haig, who devoted all the strength left to him
after the war to the welfare of the maimed and to the dependents
of the dead, was loved and respected by the vast majority of the
men whose destinies he has since been accused of ruling so
callously.

The cross-fertilisation of ideas with Liddell Hart continued. In
November, 1921, Gort wrote from the Staff College that there
were "a lot of your works here which I refer to, as occasion
permits, in training discussions". That same month Gort, who
was convinced of the importance of closer co-operation between
all three armed services of the Crown, was well satisfied to be
involved in a combined naval, military and air force exercise at
Camberley. Partly, perhaps, because his own thoughts were considered to be racing too far ahead, and partly to comfort Liddell
Hart, whose Infantry Training Manual was running against
institutional brick walls, Gort wrote just before Christmas: "You
mustn't expect too much imagination in the Army – one is always
trying to come ahead of the times and like the proverbial snail in
the well, one is pushed down again."

In 1922 Major-General Sir Edmund Ironside took over
command of the Staff College. In February Gort was stricken
with scarlet fever, then a serious and sometimes fatal infection,
and it was not until June that he was fit to resume his duties. In
September he set sail for the harbours of Devon and Cornwall in
a seventeen-ton yacht, *Iolaire*, which he had recently bought, and
during the cruise he found time to send Liddell Hart constructive
criticisms of the latest proof of his Infantry Training Manual. It
was, he thought, of paramount importance to stress the role of
artillery in infantry training. As after every war, there was a great
and growing tendency in the army to forget it; and he feared, too,
that the major impact which the air was sure to make on future
operations might be overlooked. As regards the impetus of an
infantry advance he wrote that "when once men take to the
ground owing to the intensity of the hostile fire the sting is taken
out of the attack".

He remained at the Staff College till the end of March, 1923, and Ironside recorded that he was judged to be the most effective of all the lecturers. When he was speaking on a subject he knew, his words flowed easily and he could hold his audience in rapt attention. The wild rags continued: hoses were squirted under the bedroom doors of those who retired too early on mess-nights and Lady Ironside, hearing unaccustomed noises beneath her bedroom window, peeped out to see a torch-light procession headed by Gort and making for the tennis court, where Tutankhamen's tomb was recreated and one of the outgoing pupils, suitably trussed as a mummy, was solemnly interred with all his furniture and possessions. When Gort left, together with his fellow instructor and V.C., Philip Neame, Ironside recorded in his diary: "They are the most human of all the instructors and are in close touch with the students, who would do anything for them."

In the preceding autumn the War Office had set up an official inquiry into the phenomenon of shell-shock, a common affliction of the First World War about which many theories had been propounded. Gort was summoned from Camberley to be one of the witnesses before the committee. He was sceptical. Shell-shock was, he considered, nothing more or less than a nervous breakdown. He said that in a unit where the training had been right and an *esprit de corps* existed, shell-shock was practically non-existent. It was for the battalion commander to set an example which the troops would follow, and he believed that drill, which taught men to move in a mass rather than as individuals, combined with the teaching of regimental history, which gave them pride in their unit, were two efficacious methods of maintaining a spirit resistant to nervous disorders. So-called shell-shock was as infectious as the measles and the soldier should be taught to regard it as a disgrace; but if a man were really in a bad condition, this should be noticed by his commanding officer or the medical officer and he should be passed out of the line. "Officers," he said, "must be taught much more about man-mastership in the same way as horse-mastership. I think further care should be taken to teach commanders that at the Staff College, so that they do not overtax the men. It is all to a great extent a question of discipline and drill. The man with fourteen weeks' training had not been taught to control himself. He was probably a Yahoo before he was taken into the army and he could not get his nerves under restraint."

It may be deduced from this that Gort looked on some of the "other ranks" with a patrician contempt which would be intolerable to later generations. The division, and a wide one at that, between the classes from which officers and other ranks were drawn was accepted without question by Gort and his contemporaries, but his own "man-mastership" was superb and at all times in his career the men who served under his command regarded him with unfaltering devotion. He was, of course, right about shell-shock: in the Second World War, when there were no terrifying vigils in the trenches, few large-scale frontal attacks and a well-organised, watchful medical service, the expression was never used.

After the farewells at Camberley, he returned to 34 Belgrave Square, to a spell of regimental duty in London and to a thoroughly unsatisfactory home life, at any rate so far as his wife was concerned. During the next ten years his only domestic interest lay in watching his children grow up and, to a limited extent, supervising their education. The elder, Sandy, had many of his mother's characteristics. He was exceptionally good-looking, he was an agreeable companion, he loved Wagner operas and he painted well. Like his father before him, he went to Harrow. There he was popular enough, but it was noticeable that one of his principal objects of distaste was the Officers Training Corps. Anything to do with the army, anything that his father liked or represented, he almost automatically rejected; anything, that is to say, except his sister Jacqueline, to whom he was devoted. Subsequently, at Trinity College, Cambridge, he made few friends but many acquaintances, who regarded him with an affection tempered by misgivings. He was sociable, imaginative and sensitive; but he was not easy to fathom.

Jacqueline was every inch her father's daughter. Straight as a die, resourceful, energetic, shrewd, unflinching in adversity and endowed with a sense of duty from which nothing would deflect her, she loved her father deeply and was fanatically proud of him. She was his companion both in sorrow and in happiness. She was attractive, though less physically beautiful than her brother, and in the years to come a greatly beloved wife and mother. Yet it would have been more appropriate if Jacqueline had been born a boy and Sandy a girl. For Gort there was the compensation that in his daughter he found at one and the same time the characteristics he admired and understood and the feminine sympathy for which he was normally afraid to ask.

Before the children grew up, Lord and Lady Gort had parted. For many years the estrangement had been growing. Whether a more pliable and generous husband could have held her none can say. Gort with his disinterest in things intellectual, matter of fact approach to life, obsession with his career and carefulness sometimes amounting to meanness was certainly not the man to do so. She longed for gay society which he despised and she was highly sexed, which he was not. The true-lovers' knots on the bridal gown had long been forgotten. The trouble became serious when from 34 Belgrave Square she found it a conveniently short journey to the Spanish Embassy. It was not by any means the first of her infidelities and, much as he deplored the very thought of divorce, in 1925 he took the final and decisive step. He said to Lord Dalkeith, who was with him on the morning the case came forward, that for the first time in his life he felt ill at ease and afraid. And yet, since moral courage was as natural to him as physical courage and he was not prepared to run away from unpleasant reality, he remained on duty at Wellington Barracks and faced the ordeal of seeing his brother officers read with wide-eyed interest the lurid accounts of the case which appeared in the press.

As for Kotchy, she flitted from lover to lover, verses about her promiscuity circulated at the bar of White's Club, her closest relations ceased to see her and her children only occasionally visited her. She showed no signs of regret or remorse; and she passed out of Gort's life until the day, nearly twenty years later, when she was dying and he went to her bedside only to find her unconscious.

The vacuum was satisfactorily and platonically filled. Gort had taken to skiing and, inexpert though he was at most sports, climbing up Swiss mountains with skins attached to the bottoms of his skis had everything to recommend it. It required and induced fitness. After the Christmas of 1923 he accordingly took the children to Suvretta and he found staying in the hotel "Cis" Dalrymple Hamilton, formerly of the Scots Guards and a highly esteemed adjutant at Sandhurst, with his wife, Lady Marjorie. She and Gort immediately made friends and before long she succeeded in winning his entire confidence. She was, as Lady Morrison-Bell wrote, "like a fire to warm your hands by". In her presence Gort's least attractive characteristics, a certain lack of humanity, hardness towards those whom he judged to have failed in their duty and rigidity of outlook on matters he did not fully understand evaporated with the early morning clouds on the St. Moritz mountain tops. So did his shyness towards the other sex. He found her different in every respect from Kotchy: a clever and sympathetic listener, interested in people for themselves, unfailingly discreet, prepared and indeed anxious to know what he cared about and to care about it too. There were all the makings of a love affair, especially as Cis Hamilton, though much liked by Gort and engaging the permanent affection of his children, was by temperament able to offer but slender competition in his wife's esteem. However, this was not what either of them thought morally right, for they were both firm upholders of the Ten Commandments even where their own interests and inclinations were concerned. The friendship nevertheless flourished and deepened until Lady Marjorie supplied to Gort almost all the advantages that might normally be expected from a highly successful and affectionate marriage. There was the additional happiness that Sandy and Jacqueline loved her dearly and that her husband in no way resented or misinterpreted the relationship. As the years went by she occupied a place in the children's lives which their real mother could never have wished or contrived to fill, and the Dalrymple-Hamilton home at Bargany, in Ayrshire, became theirs. It also brought a close connection with Lady Marjorie's family, the Cokes, and for the next twenty years Gort spent much of his leisure at Holkham in Norfolk.

He was an early convert to the belief that a soldier should have first hand knowledge of the elements in which the other two services fight. This, combined with a genuine liking for the sea (especially if a gale were blowing) and his lifelong familiarity with the Solent, induced him to replace the small *Iolaire* with a slightly larger black cutter, *Carlotta*, of 28 tons, in which he took the enthusiastic Jacqueline and the somewhat reluctant Sandy cruising in all weathers. In 1925 he entered her for the Fastnet race and after 600 miles of struggle against heavy seas arrived soaked, cold, battered but happy at Plymouth. In 1922 he had been elected to the Royal Yacht Squadron, whose members rated his intrepidity as a seaman higher than his skill as a helmsman, and when at Cowes he preferred living in *Carlotta*'s cramped cabin to the spacious but uncongenial quarters of East Cowes Castle, where his mother and stepfather spent each summer in illtempered and inebriated solitude. After some years he disposed of *Carlotta* in favour of the white cutter *Thanet*, of 42 tons. She was his home, and an unfailingly happy one, during the summer months whenever he could escape to the Isle of Wight.

In 1932 he decided to master the other element too. He learned to fly and he bought a Moth aeroplane, which he named *Henrietta*. There were those who thought twice before accepting an invitation to accompany him, because weather conditions which his passenger or the meteorological experts might find discouraging presented no obstacles at all to Gort. Navigation, as he once explained to General Sir John Kennedy, was simple: if one lost one's way, one just flew on; something recognisable was bound to turn up sooner or later. All the same he was elected chairman of the Household Brigade Flying Club, and miraculously he and his Moth never met with the smallest mishap.

This, however, was the future. For the three years between 1923 and 1926 that he spent with the regiment life should have been agreeable enough, had it not been for the unpleasant episode of the divorce. The last clouds of war had vanished, a certain affluence had returned with the lowering of income-tax to 4/6d in the pound, and even though the General Strike of May, 1926, during which Gort acted as G.S.O.1, London District, suggested that all might not be well socially and industrially, the world was universally peaceful and it showed every sign of becoming increasingly prosperous. Gort continued his earnest studies of the military sciences and in November, 1923, he took part in a tactical course organised by the French army, with which he spent four industrious months. In April, 1924, he was once again aboard *Carlotta*, enjoying a few weeks' leave before returning to the regiment, and he was entrusted with the task of rewriting the Infantry Training Manual, which had endured such a long and frustrating gestation in the hands of Liddell Hart whose un-orthodox insertions were rejected by the War Office.

This did not deter Gort from consulting Liddell Hart about the ideas he himself proposed to incorporate in the manual. In April he wrote from *Carlotta* to say that he agreed "we need some drill reform as it is necessary in modern war to inculcate initiative in all ranks, which Prussianised drill kills". He added that he did not propose to show this section to General Sir George Jeffreys, whose ideas on the subject were somewhat old-fashioned. It was Jeffreys, commanding the 2nd Battalion in France who, when Winston Churchill had arranged an attachment to the Grenadiers before taking over command of the Royal Scots Fusiliers, received him with the chilling words: "Major Churchill, I want you to know that I did not ask for you." Nevertheless, Churchill shared Gort's admiration for Jeffreys as a soldier and referred to him with respect. In 1952 Sir George, who had by then served eleven years

in the House of Commons, was made a peer. Churchill, his gold
pen poised above the submission to the Queen, remembered and
repeated the story of his hostile welcome in Jeffreys' dugout.
Then, as he signed his name, he said: "This is my revenge."

Although the manual, revised and re-edited by Gort, was in
galley-proof by November, 1924, the War Office were so dilatory
in passing it for publication that it did not appear in print till
May, 1926, when Gort sent an early copy to Liddell Hart with
an invitation to review it. This Liddell Hart duly did in terms of
warm approval. "It is," he wrote, "distinguished by a crispness
and logical sequence familiar to us in French military writings
. . . Considered as a whole, it is probably the most nourishing and
digestible manual issued from the War Office for a generation."
By then Gort, no doubt on account of the reputation he had won
at the Staff College, had been sent, on promotion to full colonel,
as chief instructor of the Senior Officers School at Sheerness. His
arrival there may not have been wholly congenial to the high-
ranking students because he wrote to Liddell Hart in the early
summer of 1926: "We start a new course today week. We are
giving these fellows a good bit more to do now: I think it used to
be too much of a rest cure."

Subsequent courses had less to worry about. During the
Christmas holidays Gort as usual took the children to Suvretta
with the Dalrymple-Hamiltons, but he was summoned back to the
War Office a few days before the party was due to return home.
There, on Saturday, 22nd January, 1927, he was given forty-eight
hours' notice that he was to sail in the S.S. *Megantic* bound for
Shanghai.

CHAPTER 5

ASIAN INTERLUDES

THE despatch of a division to Shanghai, under the command of Major-General John Duncan, was a successful exercise of gun-boat diplomacy. In China, where competing war lords with numerous but comparatively harmless followers were natural to the landscape, a man with a beautiful Wesleyan wife had raised an army which was unacceptably dangerous. His name was Chiang Kai-Shek; he had a sinister Russian as political adviser and, in spite of the Wesleyan influence, underlying Bolshevik tendencies were suspected. Starting from Canton Chiang's men marched against the armies of northern China and in the process they seized and occupied the British Concession at Hankow. The far larger International Settlement at Shanghai was the next objective and there they menaced a port and trading centre of immense value and a large European community. Memories of the Boxer Rebellion welled up in the Chancelleries of Europe, with Chiang Kai-Shek playing the part of the Dowager Empress. Mr. Baldwin's Government took an instant decision while French, Dutch and Italian warships set sail for the threatened port. Deceptively myopic Japanese eyes had for some time been swivelling towards China, where anarchy presented enticing opportunities for an imperial power blocked elsewhere in the eastern hemisphere by British, Dutch and French colonial interests. So Japanese naval units were quick to join the Europeans in the harbour at Shanghai.

Thus it was that the S.S. *Megantic*, crowded with troops, steamed out of Liverpool on 25th January, 1927, with General Duncan on board and Gort as his G.S.O.1. They stopped at Malta to collect more men, while an additional brigade set sail from India. The Mediterranean Fleet lined ship and cheered them as they left Valetta harbour. Gort wrote home to the twelve-year-old Jacqueline that the ship was being driven full speed and shook from bow to stern continuously. He added, with the evasiveness common to all parents: "I must see what can be done about a Pekingese, but I am afraid they don't live round Shanghai. Still, I'll see."

On 28th February the *Megantic* docked at Shanghai and by the time the Cantonese troops arrived for the fray there were sixteen thousand British and Indian troops in the settlement as well as the naval complements of several foreign warships.

The Cantonese wisely paused. Gort wrote to Jacqueline: "Chinese generals are wonderful people and their work consists in being diplomats and bargainers. They always make their peace treaties before they fight their battles." He seemed a little disappointed and so, it would appear, was the robust British Consul General, Sir Sidney Barton. Almost immediately after his arrival Gort, who found himself quartered in an over-heated hotel packed with stranded American tourists and working in an office which had been created out of a derelict building, set off up the Whangpo River to inspect the friendly Chinese Northern Army. He judged them well-dressed but not in the least war-like. His judgment was quickly proved correct, for immediately the Cantonese came in sight the well-dressed northern warriors bolted, and on 21st March Gort wrote to his daughter: "We are just about to open in an hour or so the great battle of Shanghai."

That no such battle took place was partly due to General Duncan's skilful handling of a delicate situation and partly to the size of the British defending force. The Cantonese did, however, occupy the Chinese city of Chapei, lying on the northern side of the International Settlement, and there was a certain amount of firing. In Nanking they were more bellicose still and one of the British staff officers was seriously wounded. On 22nd March news reached British Headquarters that the nuns and children resident in a British convent in Chapei were surrounded and in danger. Gort invited Sir Sidney Barton to accompany him to their rescue and he succeeded in persuading two Red-Cross Ambulance men to join them in the expedition. The area had been continuously under fire for thirty-six hours and a French Jesuit who attempted to reach the convent had been shot. Sir Sidney and Gort, in full uniform, left their car at the barricade which had been erected at the entrance to the Chinese city and walked into the hostile area of the town. The Chinese snipers, lodged along their route, held their fire, but after they had covered three-quarters of a mile they were stopped by a detachment of Cantonese infantry who searched them roughly and announced that they were prisoners. Sir Sidney convinced his captors that he was the British Consul General with diplomatic immunity and, bewildered by his and Gort's surprising behaviour in attempting to rescue the nuns without the smallest display of force, the Cantonese allowed them to return to their own lines. Shortly afterwards the nuns and the children were released to safety. Gort did not report the incident in his letters home, but the newspapers did and Jacqueline wrote an indignant letter of protest. Her father replied: "I am amused to see you think I am foolish to go for harmless walks and then to find myself being forced 'to bunk back home'. Well, I have had no chances for any more walks and I am now like a bird in a cage unable to stretch my wings at all!"

The excitement died down, the Cantonese sullenly withdrew a few miles and Chiang Kai-Shek's main threat was deflected away from Shanghai northwards. All the same it was necessary to maintain the defending force. In May General Duncan, having sent Gort to accompany Admiral Tyrrwhit on an expedition to the fallen British Concession at Hankow, wrote home to his wife: "He is a bit too intense for peace time soldiering. He is a very fine soldier and extremely able, but he is in a class by himself and works himself to death. It may be the result of his domestic troubles, but if he was like this before I can quite imagine his wife leaving him." The Hankow mission, which lasted ten days, was safely and diplomatically completed. Gort had already made a reconnaissance of Soochow and Nanking, and in June he visited Tientsin and Peking to report whether the British Legation could, if necessary, be held against the Cantonese army. He found the travelling, in verminous trains, at least preferable to life in Shanghai, which in a letter home General Duncan described as socially boring, but added "I am not, like Gort, a woman hater." Had he seen the wistful letters Gort was writing home to Lady Marjorie and Jacqueline, he would have been forced to admit that Gort at least made two exceptions.

The social ordeal did not last long. There were trying occasions, as when General Duncan took his G.S.O.1 to a luncheon party given in their honour and in dripping heat by the Japanese navy. They were obliged to sit for nearly four hours on cushions, eating raw fish, peas and rice with chopsticks, each attended by a Geisha girl who insisted on holding their hands and feeding them. Duncan was amused and gratified but for Gort, who was in-veigled into dancing with his Geisha, the experience was altogether too exotic. Returning from a feast provided by the French to celebrate the 14th July, Duncan wrote: "This morning a telegram came ordering Gort to go home as G.S.O.1, 4th Division, Colchester. He is not at all keen on going as he wants to see this thing through. He is so conscientious that although he hates this place even more than I do, and never speaks to a woman if he can avoid it, yet he puts duty first. I wish I were so disciplined."

In August he sailed for England, and on his return was summoned separately by the King and the Prince of Wales to give a first hand account of his activities and of the situation in China. He wrote for the War Office an account of the difficulties the Shanghai defence force had encountered and of the lessons to be learned for future reference. He even went so far as to prepare and deliver a lecture on "The Chinese".

The posting to Colchester lasted three years, the last before the clouds again began to gather. The 4th Divisional Headquarters were responsible for the establishments at Dover and Shorncliffe. Gort's responsibilities included the preparation of training programmes for the gravely undermanned units stationed there and of schemes for their exercises in the field. There was plenty of time for sailing, and there was an absence of urgency on military matters by no means unnatural in days when the possibility of another war was far from anybody's thoughts. In 1928 Gort renewed his contacts and correspondence with Liddell Hart, to whom he offered to show his programmes for the September training schemes. By July, 1929, he was complaining bitterly of the "farcical state of affairs" with which the preparation of that year's manœuvres confronted him. His largest battalion counted 350 men and his weakest only 185. Some companies were only six to ten strong. However, he did his best to work out a scheme with token forces and based it, he told Liddell Hart, "on a situation analogous to that in the summer of 1918 when L.G., etc., still thought a raid possible and insisted on keeping large forces at home". He was bringing the mock battle right back into barracks so as "to practise actual house to house fighting, which is always overlooked in peace training. We have no tanks and the units are so weak that aircraft will be of no value . . . we are endeavouring under great handicaps to be as original and as realistic as we can and to break away from the usual hackneyed type of scheme." As he wrote some years later: "I think those post-war years were more than disheartening for everybody."

In 1930 he achieved the ambition of every soldier: command of his regiment. He was also given command of the 4th Guards Brigade, a skeleton unit which nevertheless provided useful tactical training opportunities. His conduct of its activities did much to enhance Gort's reputation. In the spring of 1931, the mumps struck in a most delicate area, but by July he was fit enough to devise a scheme for the brigade based on guerilla warfare. "I have," he wrote to Liddell Hart, "been keen on this type of war for some time as I think it is the true British war and one which has been rather forgotten in the chase after European war and the Shibboleths of 'Fire Plans' etc. I feel that little has been done in recent years to develop the tactical conceptions of 'leading' in the battalion commanders and below: so long as they conform to well-recognised formulae in preparing a fire plan in attack all has been considered to be well." He went on to give the details of one of his schemes: "Opposite us is a native state, under the influence of a Soviet state, and on our flank is another small native state whose Sheikh follows the usual policy of his kind in watching which way the cat jumps before deciding on intervention." It was at least more imaginative than most military exercises and Liddell Hart was glad to be invited as a spectator.

The depression which struck America like a hurricane in 1929 crossed the Atlantic slowly and it was not until September, 1931, that its full force was felt in the British Isles. With millions unemployed and Hunger Marchers processing southwards from Jarrow and the other badly hit areas, there was talk of civil disturbances such as had not been heard since the General Strike. A small cut in service pay produced trouble in the Royal Navy. There was an incident in the fleet at Invergordon extravagantly described by the press as a mutiny; but the army was unruffled and the general public accepted the lowering of living standards with surprising equanimity. Like every other professional soldier Gort now recognised with distress that any increase in the exiguous army vote, which the Labour Government of 1929 had not reduced in spite of their declared pacifist principles, was now out of the question. In 1931 and 1932 the army, like the country itself, lived on a shoestring and all that Gort could do was to maintain with what resources he had the discipline and training of his three battalions of the Grenadiers and continue the skeleton operational practices of the 4th Guards Brigade. In spite of everything, a Government directive, first issued in 1919, renewed by Churchill in 1928 and since then reissued annually, that planning for the armed forces should proceed on the assumption there would be no major war for ten years, was discarded by the National Government elected in October, 1931. This did not, however, discourage the Treasury from continuing to act as if the directive were still in force.

In the summer of 1932 Gort, on promotion to brigadier, was posted to India as Director of Military Training. He disliked leaving the regiment and his long weekly letters home show that the charms of the east were little compensation for the absence of Lady Marjorie and his children. He sailed early in September expecting a four-year exile with one interval of two months' home leave. During this late autumn of the Indian Empire the Congress Party, resolved to achieve self-government, was increasing its passive resistance to the Viceregal administration; but in most visible respects the life and attitude of the British official community in India were little different from those of their late Victorian predecessors. Gort wrote to his daughter: "Once you pass through the Gateway to India in Bombay, you have to realise that topis, chota pegs, sunglasses and an atmosphere of indolence are the real things that count in life besides smells and flies."

For him indolence was never an acceptable convention. At Delhi he settled into a bungalow with three senior officers. The gates of the compound had to be barred nightly against hyenas and jackals as well as against sacred cows which nobody was allowed to molest as they roamed aimlessly through the streets of Delhi, but which made short work of any garden into which they successfully forced an entry. He rose every morning at 6.0 a.m. for a ride, worked all day and devoted the evenings to preparing lectures and to learning Hindustani. The hot summers were spent in the constricted atmosphere of Simla and the cooler months of winter were the time for long journeys, often necessitating two or three days in trains, choking with dust and ill provided with food, to inspect training establishments, inaugurate schemes and deliver lectures. One successful ploy was an annual course of lectures to officers who aspired to enter the staff colleges preferably at Camberley or, if that failed, at Quetta. They were not, Gort discovered, the brightest of candidates, but his flair for lecturing on tactics, which had won him renown as an instructor at Camberley, produced remarkable results: after his first course almost three times more of those who had attended his lectures, and whose studies he had directed, passed their examinations than in previous years.

In the loneliness of Indian army life, far from the familiar and congenial surroundings of Birdcage Walk, Aldershot and Camberley, he was impatient with the speed of promotion. In October, 1933, Ironside wrote in his diary that after a dinner party "Gort was full of complaints of the length of time the older Generals go on serving"; and General Sir Frederick Morgan has written: "In expansive moments he had been wont to quote his own case as illustrating the bankruptcy of army policy. There he was, with as notable a fighting record as could be gained, drifting gently up the promotion ladder no more quickly than if, as he said, 'I had spent the war in the canteen.' " Gort, who thought boastfulness a close competitor of the Seven Deadly Sins, would not have staked any claim for consideration on account of his courage; but his professional ambition was powerful enough to induce him to make sure that his record and experience as a fighting soldier were not forgotten.

When he looked at a wood, his primary concern was its place in a tactical scheme; but he saw no reason for failing to scrutinise the individual trees. A saying he frequently quoted, and wrongly ascribed to Napoleon, was that genius is an infinite capacity for taking pains. In 1934 he wrote to Jacqueline that he had read of a remark by Joseph Chamberlain that "luck is careful attention to detail", and he then sent her an exhaustive list of articles to be ordered, in the most economical manner possible (and specifically *not* at Fortnum and Mason), for their projected summer cruise in *Thanet* during his forthcoming leave. The list included the number of pots of marmalade, recommendations about tinned peas and "one, or possibly two, bottles of sherry". He took advantage of the occasion to insist on the importance of method which, he assured Jacqueline, is "the great keystone in success in life".

There were some compensations for the drudgery, the heat, the insects and the mainly uncongenial company. There was the Delhi Flying Club. There was the excitement of visits to the North-West Frontier, where sniping tribesmen were still taking a small but regular toll of the Indian army, to Kabul, to Kandahar and to the jungle on the banks of the Tapti river where he shot, in exciting circumstances, a panther and a tiger. The tiger had been wounded by a general on an elephant and, as might be expected, Gort pursued it on foot through the thick grass to administer the *coup de grâce*. His marksmanship had evidently improved although back in Delhi irreverent junior officers averred that the tiger had died of fright.

After a short but happy summer's leave cruising in *Thanet*, he returned to India in the autumn of 1934 and was joined by both his children, by Lady Marjorie and by other visitors who occupied the bungalow which he had now secured for his sole occupation. On 9th October, far away in Marseilles, there took place an event which had further reaching consequences than was realised at the time. King Alexander of Yugoslavia, arriving on a state visit to France, was assassinated by a Croat terrorist. One of the more solid pillars on which the French had built the Little Entente, to contain Germany on the eastern front, crashed to the ground and in the King's place a régime was established which ultimately became pro-German. An equally important by-product of the tragedy was that a courageous French Foreign Minister, Monsieur Barthou, died with the King and General Georges was gravely wounded. Georges was the favourite candidate for the post of commander-in-chief of the French armies, but his enforced removal from the scene while he recovered from his injuries left the field open to General Gamelin, who was duly chosen for the post.

Gort was alive to the threat developing in Germany since Hitler had come into power, and on her return to England at the end of 1934 Jacqueline received from her father a memorandum on the dangerous implications of Nazi rule and policy. The decline of Britain's military strength, by which the Governments of Ramsay MacDonald and Stanley Baldwin did not seem perturbed, was a source of constant worry and indignation to an officer who had had, in his recent commands, first hand proof of the national deficiencies in men and equipment.

In 1935, while Mussolini used mustard gas to conquer Abyssinia and to confirm the impotence of the League of Nations, Gort continued his routine duties as Director of Military Training in India, increasingly anxious about the stagnation in the British and Indian armies. After a conversation with Gort, Ironside wrote: "We came to the conclusion that the health of the senior officers of the Army was not good enough for active service." There was another officer serving in India, as Commandant of the Staff College at Quetta, who held the same view: Colonel Bernard Montgomery. However, he and Gort were not mutual admirers. Montgomery found Gort more interested in lecturing on the previous war, and talking with admiration of Marshal Foch, than suited his taste. Gort, for his part, wrote to Jacqueline after the disastrous Quetta earthquake (during which Mrs. Montgomery was conspicuous for outstanding courage and resource): "Your friend Pandit Montgomery Karnel Sahib is once more holding forth pontifically on the rostrum while the unfortunate students below catch an odd forty winks. He fancies himself more than ever now, I expect." It would be difficult to conceive two soldiers with more opposing virtues than Gort and Montgomery and neither of them succeeded in understanding the other's merits.

Gort's time in India was cut short by his appointment at the age of 49, with the rank of major-general, to command the Staff College at Camberley. When Lady Marjorie's husband, Colonel Dalrymple-Hamilton, heard the news, he remarked: "He will have all the beds made of concrete and hosed down with cold water nightly." Such was the Spartan reputation he had acquired even among his closest friends and acquaintances. He arrived home in March, 1936, having been refused by the Chief of the Imperial General Staff, Field Marshal Sir Claud Deverell, permission to delay his return by one week so as to qualify for relief from income-tax during his last whole year spent abroad. Since he was convinced of his poverty, whatever his bank-account might indicate to the contrary, this was a disobliging act which Deverell lived to regret.

While Gort was away in India, Britain's economic strength had been largely restored, at least on the surface. Prices and the pound were stable, even though unemployment was still at an unacceptably high level. But in spite of the bright red danger signals flashing from Germany and Italy, the youth of the country were gripped by pacifism. Recruitment for the armed forces was dangerously low and, in the autumn of 1933, when the Government had decided that a small measure of rearmament was necessary, a by-election fought on the issue at Fulham resulted in a swing of nineteen thousand votes to the Socialist/Pacifist candidate, who was triumphantly elected. This convinced Mr. Baldwin that rearmament was not an electorally profitable policy. In 1934 the Army Estimates were for the moderate sum of £40 million. They were cut to £20 million. The little extra money that was made available, in spite of sustained opposition from the Labour Party, was fortunately devoted to the Royal Air Force for which new fighter aircraft, more effective than any others in the world, were already approaching the production lines. This merciful dispensation was not one which even a soldier who believed that close inter-service co-operation was essential could be expected to applaud. The Navy, for traditional reasons, was favoured; now the R.A.F. were being treated as the spoilt youngest child. The Army felt neglected and aggrieved.

Gort returned to England in the same month that Hitler, contrary to Germany's treaty obligations, reoccupied the Rhineland to the sound of military bugles on the one hand and carefully drafted protests from Britain and France on the other. As Commandant at the Staff College he did not, of course, have any say in high policy; but he was once again in touch with his army contemporaries, to many of whom he appeared a standard-bearer of new ideas and a representative of youth against the entrenched powers of the old time-worn generals. There was a new King on the throne too, and deeply as George V had been loved, the advent of the energetic, unconventional Edward VIII seemed, for a few brief months, to coincide with a new era in which youth would return to the helm.

In the comparatively unclouded summers of 1936 and 1937 there were visits to Holkham and to the Dalrymple-Hamiltons at Bargany, and uninterrupted cruises in *Thanet*. Jacqueline, who had "come out" under the auspices of Lady Marjorie while Gort was away in India, was hostess for her father at Camberley and Sandy was invited to act as unpaid private secretary to the Secretary of State for War, Mr. Alfred Duff Cooper. The impression Gort made on the students at Camberley was less forceful than before. His suggestion that officers might use their leisure hours more profitably by joining the Flying Club than by following the Drag was not calculated to win him popularity in all circles. When General Bertie Fisher, commanding the Royal Military College at Sandhurst, attended lectures given by visiting speakers at the Staff College on subjects outside the curriculum he noted the inadequacy with which Gort summed up the discussions. The eloquence he could display on subjects he knew and had studied was not extended to matters about which he did not consider himself an expert. He thought it dishonest to pretend knowledge he did not possess. Whatever the effect he made during the eighteen months he commanded at Camberley on the officers attending courses, he certainly left his mark on the visitors, military and political, who came into contact with him. By the early summer of 1937, Gort's reputation as a coming man stood high with the army, with Whitehall and with the gifted military correspondent of the leading national newspaper, Captain Basil Liddell Hart.

Part 2

Rapid Ascent

CHAPTER 6

PROMOTION

WHEN Gort assumed command at the Staff College, the Secretary of State for War was Mr. Alfred Duff Cooper. He was clever, cultivated, lovable, gay and, as a Minister, notoriously id e. Although rearmament had begun on a limited scale in 1935, the War Office, under the auspices of Duff Cooper and his C.I.G.S., Field-Marshal Sir Archibald Montgomery-Massingberd, was beset by apathy and frustration. Nevertheless, the Secretary of State, whose courtesy to subordinates was unfailing, and who reserved his asperities for those who were in a position to answer back, was well liked by the generals and, since he had fought as a Grenadier was particularly congenial to Gort.

Duff Cooper, for his part, had a high opinion of Gort and with Sandy Vereker as his private secretary he was unlikely to forget his existence. Indeed, Liddell Hart records that as early as the autumn of 1936 Duff Cooper had, with Lord Trenchard's strong approval, mentioned the desirability of Gort's immediate appointment as C.I.G.S. Such a palace revolution – for Gort was scarcely 50 and but recently appointed a major-general – would have been totally unacceptable to the military hierarchy and Duff Cooper, imaginative though he might be, was not the man to force through a measure of that kind. Moreover, Field-Marshal Sir Cyril Deverell had been chosen to succeed Montgomery-Massingberd.

In February, 1937, Mr. Baldwin's Government, unable entirely to disregard the disturbing trend of events in Germany, Italy and Japan, produced a White Paper on Defence proposing that over a five-year period some £1,500 million should be made available to the armed forces. In the same month the French Chamber of Deputies voted to extend their series of strong fortresses, known as the Maginot Line, northwards to the sea: it remained, however, a decision on paper alone. Gort wrote to Liddell Hart: "It is most inspiring to have some money for the army at last, as the cheese-paring era has broken the spirit of a large number of the younger generation." In May King George VI was crowned and enthusiastic crowds showed their affection for Mr. Baldwin as he drove to Westminster Abbey, leaning forward in a Clarence, his symbolic pipe held casually in his hand in spite of the Privy Counsellor's uniform he was wearing. When the festivities were over, Baldwin left 10 Downing Street and a new Prime Minister, Neville Chamberlain, reformed the Government. Duff Cooper was moved to the Admiralty and the much advertised Minister of Transport, Leslie Hore Belisha, was appointed Secretary of State for War.

Hore Belisha believed himself to have the makings of a second Disraeli, whose bust occupied a prominent position in his library. Perhaps he might have achieved this ambition, or something approaching it, if his wisdom had matched his intelligence. He was a hard worker and, though not a good administrator, an orator of high quality whose eloquence was as notable in debate as in a set speech. He was a man of contradictions: lovable to those who knew him well and an irritant to those who did not, personally ambitious but public spirited, oriental in his love of splendour and his craving for high society but genuinely touched by the plight of the humble and the poor. He was dynamic in his energy, fertile – sometimes to the extent of being ludicrous – in his imagination and a reformer of untiring zeal. On the other side of the balance sheet there were defects which were damaging to his reputation and popularity with senior officers. In a position of authority he could be rude and overbearing. An impatient manner, an intolerance of generals or civil servants with minds slower than his own, an appearance of devious insincerity (although he was deeply sincere), a tendency to mistrust those with whom he worked, a conviction that the generals despised his Jewish race and middle-class background, a faith in the importance of publicity and self-advertisement which were widely held to be vulgar: all these outward characteristics, occasionally served up in a dish of mysticism, combined to disguise his real virtues and his passionate desire to be worthy of his responsibilities. Of immediate significance were the facts that he knew nothing at all about the army, that he had been told by the Prime Minister a new broom was required and that since he believed this must involve an infusion of new blood he required an independent counsellor to tell him where it might best be found. Neville Chamberlain advised him to read one of Liddell Hart's books; Duff Cooper asked him to luncheon to meet Liddell Hart; he convinced himself that there was nobody else outside the War Office with comparable knowledge or experience; and he adopted Liddell Hart, military correspondent of *The Times*, as an intimate adviser. With conspicuous lack of wisdom he began his reign by circulating to all concerned at the War Office an eighteen-page paper written by Liddell Hart and entitled: "The British Army: Considerations on its Scale, Form and Functions". Amongst other things this paper contained a dissertation on the excessive age of serving generals with which Gort would certainly have been in agreement but which might with advantage have been conveyed more tactfully to the members of the Army Council.

In July the new Secretary of State visited the Staff College and he also had a long-drawn-out luncheon with Gort in London. Their acquaintance had been short; in fact it only dated from a collision on skis at St. Moritz during the previous Christmas holidays. Hore Belisha was impressed by Gort's vigour and in August, displeased with the Military Secretary whom he had inherited from Duff Cooper and whom he considered the mere mouthpiece of the Army Council, he invited Gort to accept the post. It meant acting as the Secretary of State's personal liaison officer with the General Staff and in particular it carried the responsibility for advising him on the appointment of senior officers. Hore Belisha went so far as to hold up all the appointments submitted to him by the existing Military Secretary until Gort should arrive to vet them. Gort was in a quandary. He felt enthusiasm for Hore Belisha's declared intention to revitalise the army, stimulate recruitment and dispose of the military deadwood; but he had many personal reservations about the man he was asked to serve, he disliked the thought of working in the War Office, he had hoped for command of a division and he was advised against acceptance both by the C.I.G.S., Sir Cyril Deverell, and by that paragon of the military establishment, General the Hon. Sir Francis Gathorne-Hardy, until recently Commander-in-Chief at Aldershot and brother-in-law of a former Secretary of State for War, Lord Derby. Perhaps they thought, like Gort himself, that a fighting soldier was ill-suited to the War Office; perhaps, too, they suspected Gort of being somewhat too revisionary in his professional views.

Jacqueline was loth to leave Camberley, but she persuaded her father to accept and on 23rd September, 1937, the appointment was announced with the accompanying promotion to acting lieutenant-general. It was received with acclaim by Gort's own generation of army officers and by some of his seniors. General Ironside, now G.O.C. Eastern Command, wrote in his diary:

"This is the best piece of news I have heard for many years. We shall now have one of the best officers we have in the Army, a man of human parts who is not finished as regards the Service. He will not deal with men as if they were so many pieces of paper with figures on them." In the course of a letter to Lady Marjorie Dalrymple-Hamilton, written on his last day at Camberley, Gort recognised that he was "in for a very difficult time for a while" and would be unpopular with "some of the older disappointed people who find the ship of ambition torpedoed under their feet." He added that he felt "qualms of conscience because people may say I am looking out for myself. Actually, if they are fair they will know that I never asked for it and tried to avoid it. It will be a pointer of how Belli's ideas on promotion run and of the clearance he intends to carry out on top." The unattractive nickname Belli was one which Gort and Lady Marjorie had devised for their own use and is indicative of a certain hostile prejudgment.

By now, at 51, Gort had behind him as varied an experience as any officer of his age. He had received a thorough staff training in war and far more intensively in peace. It is true that he was not, even in the judgment of friends and fellow Guards officers such as the future Field-Marshal Alexander anything like as good a staff officer as General Dill; but he did know about fighting, which it was beginning to seem might once again be necessary. There were few staff officers who had commanded actively and successfully in the field, even at battalion level. Gort had served overseas and attended a special course with officers of the French army, thus increasing his knowledge of the mentality, organisation and methods of Britain's most likely allies. He had shown an unwavering interest in new military developments, was mechanically inclined, experienced in training men and, however much disposed to hark back to the lessons learned from the last war, impatient with old-fashioned conventions except in so far as they were conducive to discipline or required for ceremonial purposes. He had shed much of his shyness, at any rate socially, and with his clear light blue eyes, pleasant expression and military moustache he attracted those he met by his appearance and by the strength of his personality. A Puritan by conviction, with a hard and sometimes unforgiving streak in his character, inclined to be obstinate, occasionally but by no means always imaginative and with an exaggerated reverence for detail, he was none the less one to whom men were glad to listen and his views, always modestly stated, commanded attention. He would not stoop to any kind of intrigue to further his own interests and he disdained those who did so. Indeed, there was no more honest man than Gort and if none would have called him brilliant, his integrity, experience, shrewd common sense and that most worthy of all qualities, true simplicity (which the undiscerning sometimes mistake for stupidity) were a combination that was certain to attract loyalty and might reasonably be expected to achieve success.

In the middle of September Hore Belisha was invited to the French manœuvres in Normandy and was attended by the British Military Attaché in Paris, Colonel F. G. Beaumont Nesbitt. Since British ministers are expected by all foreigners, and by the French in particular, to be well dressed and correct in every respect, the fact that Hore Belisha received the War Minister, Monsieur Daladier, in his bath was at least original; but it is his conversation with Beaumont Nesbitt in the course of a drive to Paris after the manœuvres were over that demonstrates his least admirable habit as Secretary of State. In his thirst for information about the qualities of the leading soldiers, he could never resist the temptation to ask comparatively junior officers what they thought of their superiors. In any profession this is to be deplored; in the armed forces, where loyalty to a superior officer is an unbreakable law, such behaviour by the Secretary of State was disastrous to his reputation. This was not an isolated instance, but it did have a particular significance at the time because Hore Belisha, exasperated by the obstructiveness which Deverell and the Adjutant General, Knox, were displaying towards his and Liddell Hart's reforming zeal, was moving towards a decision to remove them.

General Macready, the Deputy Director of Staff Duties at the War Office, had warned Beaumont Nesbitt to expect embarrassing questions, so that when on the evening of the last day of manœuvres Hore Belisha asked his opinion of Deverell, Knox and other members of the Army Council he was not entirely taken aback. Next day, in the car, Hore Belisha spoke with admiration of the firm way in which Winston Churchill, on becoming First Lord in 1911, had dealt with the Board of Admiralty and in particular with the First Sea Lord, Admiral "Tug" Wilson, whom he had dismissed. He implied that he might take a leaf from Churchill's notebook. Beaumont Nesbitt was an old friend of Gort and a Grenadier companion of the First World War. Troubled by what Hore Belisha had confided to him, he travelled to London as soon as he reasonably could and went to break the news to the newly appointed Military Secretary, now working at his desk in the War Office and established in a flat at 98 Mount Street. Gort did not seem entirely surprised: he took down the Army List and examined the seniority of Major-General Archibald Wavell, who had just been appointed Commander-in-Chief in Palestine.

For the short period of his Military Secretaryship, Gort's relations with both the Secretary of State and Liddell Hart were unclouded. There was much reorganisation to be done and, amongst other things, Gort altered and simplified the system of selection for staff appointments and the promotion of senior officers. He accepted one of the Hore Belisha/Liddell Hart proposals, which Deverell had tried to thwart, that a Territorial officer, Brigadier Claud Liardet, should be promoted to major-general and given command of the London Territorial Division. He also agreed wholeheartedly with the Secretary of State in finding poor Deverell, who had done his best and had been a great improvement on his predecessor, increasingly obdurate and ill-tempered. On the other hand, he was faced by a division of loyalties, as Ironside was one of the first to discover. When he had to present to the Secretary of State the Army Council's recommendations for appointments, he told Ironside that "he was in the bad position of having to sell him unsound horses and Belisha was too clever to buy duds". He had never been in a comparable predicament. Hore Belisha had made him Military Secretary to serve a purpose with which he was largely in sympathy; and yet by all the standards he had been taught and accepted he could not act contrary to the orders, or even the expressed wishes, of his military superiors.

According to the Psalmist, some put their trust in chariots and some put their trust in horses. In the British army of the twenties and early thirties the charioteers were still in a minority. Those who put their trust in horses did so mainly for sentimental reasons. Since every well brought up child knew by heart the Charge of the Light Brigade, it was not necessary to be a Hussar or a Dragoon to be convinced that the cavalry had a specially romantic role to fill in the Order of Battle of the British army. It was true that they had played little part in the First World War, except when they dismounted and acted as infantry, and that they could not charge machine-guns. They might have had their chance at Cambrai in November, 1917, but the orders had come too late. However, the next war, if there ever was one, would be quite a different affair, probably fought against Italians in Africa or the Middle East, where tanks and armoured cars would sink into the sand; and in any case cavalry were essential to keep the Indians and other colonial peoples under control in the much more likely event of some Fuzzy-Wuzzy war breaking out in a distant part of the Empire. Horses, after all, required no spare parts, were easy and cheap to produce and could usually be supplied with fuel by local requisition. The whole thing was well summed up by one distinguished observer of army manœuvres who wrote in *The Times* that while Salisbury Plain was littered with broken down vehicles, he had not seen a single lame horse. This rang a sympathetic bell even with officers of the Guards who, in accordance with long established tradition, received several weeks' hunting leave every winter in addition to their regular entitlement.

By 1937 the cavalry were fighting a losing battle, but their susceptibilities were strong and Deverell felt that the regiments which had exchanged their horses for armoured cars and were now part of the so-called Mobile Division would be humiliated if an expert in mechanised warfare rather than a cavalryman were given command of the division. This was too much for Hore Belisha since, like Gort, he was deeply disturbed by the lack of equipment for modern war and he was of the opinion that a step in the right direction would have been to include the Tank Brigade in the Mobile Division, thus converting it into a genuine Armoured Division. Gort was principally an expert in infantry tactics and training, but he was acutely conscious that the Germans already had four fully fledged Armoured Divisions and that others were in the process of formation. That the C.I.G.S. should try to insist on giving the only British mechanised force to a cavalryman indicated a wholly unacceptable attitude to the drastic changes which had now become essential to the safety of the country.

Furthermore, Deverell was obsessed with the British responsibility for India and unwilling to agree to changes in the organisation of the Indian army which both Liddell Hart and Gort considered necessary for the good of the British army as a whole. For these and similar reasons Hore Belisha, encouraged by Gort, concluded at the end of October that a change could not be delayed: Deverell must go and the adjutant-general, Knox, who was even more conservative in his outlook, must go, too. The search for a successor to the C.I.G.S. began.

Gort's selection for the new C.I.G.S. would have been Wavell, but Hore Belisha considered him too inarticulate and had also been irritated by some of the demands he had made on accepting the command in Palestine. Dill was an obvious choice and one which would have been widely approved: a brilliant staff officer, a man of unsurpassed personal charm, a good diplomat, the perfect type of soldier-civil servant required for the post. But Dill had had a serious accident, from which he was slow in recovering, and adverse accounts of alleged weakness and vacillation reached Liddell Hart, who duly passed them on to Hore Belisha. Then there was Ironside, the only full general with possible qualifications; but he had never served in the War Office, loathed the idea of an office job, was known to be outspokenly critical of all Ministers and, like Gort, had set his heart on command in the field. Two other names were discussed by the Secretary of State and his unofficial adviser: one was Colonel Pile, an expert in mechanical warfare but too junior in the Army List even for Hore Belisha to contemplate; the other was Gort's successor at Camberley, Major-General Sir Ronald Adam, whom all admitted to be a man of outstanding intelligence and ability.

There remained Gort himself. Hore Belisha, in recommending his name to Neville Chamberlain, said that he was the most dynamic personality he had met in the army. Colonel Pile, who had long been one of Liddell Hart's closest associates and was subsequently commander-in-chief of Anti-Aircraft Command during the war, wrote that Gort's appointment would meet with universal approval. His claims had already been supported by Duff Cooper and Trenchard, whom in one of his more fantastic flights of fancy Hore Belisha momentarily considered as a possible candidate himself.

Gort was by no means keen. It was not the job for him and he knew it. His ambition was to command the British army in battle and not to wrestle with endless committees in Whitehall. He accordingly suggested both to Hore Belisha and Liddell Hart that he should be appointed Inspector General, with a seat on the Army Council, direct responsibility for the activities of the Director of Military Training and with the reversion to command of the forces at home, and subsequently abroad, in the event of war. Moreover, as he had been so closely involved with the recent disagreements in the War Office he did not, as he frankly admitted to Liddell Hart, want it to be said "that I had pushed out Deverell and then Liddell Hart had made me C.I.G.S.".

He had not forgotten Deverell's meanness to him on his return from India and had certainly not grown to admire or respect him in the last two months. Thus he did nothing to soften the tone of Hore Belisha's letter of dismissal nor to alleviate the somewhat shabby financial treatment which the War Office accorded their fallen chief. Liddell Hart considered that Gort would be more suitable as Deputy C.I.G.S.; but he fell in with Hore Belisha's strong preference for Gort as being the man of action he required, especially as the Secretary of the Cabinet, Sir Maurice Hankey, though initially supporting the claims of Dill, had come to the conclusion that Gort was the man for the post. Hore Belisha therefore told Liddell Hart, on 24th November, that he proposed to make him C.I.G.S. with Sir Ronald Adam as deputy "to be the thinking head while Gort provided the drive". He said that he thought this "a better arrangement than the idea of making Wavell C.I.G.S. and Gort Inspector-General, even though Gort favoured the latter arrangement. H.B. wished he were not so inclined to fear taking power."

In all matters affecting the command of the armed forces the King had the right to be personally consulted and so Hore Belisha took his proposals to Buckingham Palace. The King agreed to the appointments with enthusiasm, encouraged no doubt by his private secretary, Sir Alexander Hardinge, who was a close friend of Gort. A communiqué was issued to the press for publication on 3rd December, Hore Belisha having taken the wise precaution of preparatory talks with all the leading newspaper proprietors and editors. The dual role of Gort and Adam was acclaimed; the infusion of comparative youth into the High Command received favourable comment; and with Major-General C. G. Liddell succeeding Knox as adjutant-general and Wavell transferred from Palestine to Southern Command, it seemed that Hore Belisha's team for rejuvenating the War Office and reforming the army was established in control. The Old Guard were disgruntled. "How on earth," wrote Field-Marshal Sir Philip Chetwode, "a man of Gort's standing and calibre is going to criticise and direct the training of men [with] five times his experience, and much older, I do not know."

It had been a rapid and triumphant progress to the top. Less than two years previously Gort, a mere brigadier, had been pursuing the weary routine of his Indian duties, depressed by the solid block of slow thinking and even slower moving officers at the head of his profession who were apparently destined to stay for

M.V.—F

ever in the seats of power while the country's defences became increasingly inadequate in the face of parsimony at home and aggressive preparations abroad. Now, at bewildering speed, he had risen to the pinnacle; but not to the pinnacle he would have chosen nor that for which he recognised himself, either by training or by temperament, to be suited. It was, at least in part, to his early friendship and association of ideas with Liddell Hart that he owed the smoothness of his passage in the last months, but this was in itself galling to a man for whom the army and its properly constituted leaders must be the arbiters of military destiny. He had indeed contributed to the removal of those who held this position, and he felt justified by the overriding claims of the country's needs; but as a soldier, and now as C.I.G.S., he could scarcely accept as tolerable the strong influence on appointments and policy of an *éminence grise*, however brilliant, knowledgeable and public spirited, who was at the same time correspondent of a newspaper. Feeling on the subject within the War Office was rising dangerously and Gort, much as he had formerly admired Liddell Hart's questing and modernising spirit, soon allied himself with the rapidly growing number of malcontents in his own service.

For the next two years Gort settled down to a routine life in his Mount Street flat. He walked each day to and from the War Office for exercise, found diversion at week-ends with the Moth *Henrietta* at Heston, avoided all official entertainments but those which the C.I.G.S. was obliged to attend and spent the evenings and early mornings in reading military history or the latest publications on tactics, strategy and training. Colonel Ian Jacob, working with General Ismay at the Committee of Imperial Defence, was astonished to be told by Gort, as they walked together across St. James's Park, that he tried to devote four hours every day to the reading of books on military affairs.

The road to success had been comparatively smooth. From now on it became a steep and rugged pathway so that for the remainder of his life he needed all the strength and resolution he possessed to drive him on his way. He was welcomed to the Chiefs of Staff Sub-Committee of the Committee of Imperial Defence on 9th December, 1937, and was at once involved in the consideration of such diverse problems as the reinforcement of the garrison in Egypt, the military consequences of the Government's proposal to withdraw the British garrisons stationed in southern Irish ports and the defence of the Dutch East Indies. He was also promoted to full general and consequently overtook in seniority men such as Dill, Wavell and Alan Brooke, who had hitherto ranked ahead of him in the Army List. But the new era began in earnest when, on the Wednesday before Christmas, he found on his desk the draft of a submission to the Cabinet on the future role of the British army.

CHAPTER 7

THE OBSTACLE RACE

THOSE who wish to navigate the twisting currents of policy and events in the First World War find no better pilot than Major-General Sir Edward Louis Spears. One of his books, "Prelude to Victory", written shortly before the outbreak of the Second World War, contains this indictment of an earlier generation, composed with intentional allusion to the situation existing as he wrote: "If the cadres of our army were insufficient, if our trained staff officers were few and our commanders lacked the experience of handling large masses of men, does not the blame rest with Parliament and successive Governments, who, knowing we might be involved in war, starved our tiny army in peace-time, allowing it to train with skeleton forces at inadequate manœuvres? . . . The small B.E.F. had been superbly equipped: Haldane had served the country well by creating an effective territorial force, but statesmen had indulged in the pleasing illusion that there is such a thing as a limited liability war, one in which we need not engage more than the small force it suited us to maintain in peace-time. Surely no great foresight was required to realise that, when there was a possibility of having to fight a great European war, the result of defeat might be our extinction as a nation? . . . The valour of British soldiers on the battlefield was being expended to compensate for the lack of courage in England's political leaders, who, in fear of the electorate which they found it not easy to enlighten, allowed her to embark, inadequately prepared and bewildered by the effort she had to make, on the greatest war in history."

At the beginning of 1938, the General Staff would have found these sentiments distressingly apt; but the Cabinet, the House of Commons and a majority of the politically conscious would have dismissed them as warmongering, arguing that history does not repeat itself and that, whatever the soldiers might think, the situation was totally different from that prevailing in 1914. Experience of the horrors of world war was too recent for any Government of any nation to contemplate a repetition. What the senior members of the Cabinet and the heads of the Civil Service did consider vital was the maintenance of a strong economy, a stable currency and a healthy balance of payments. Unless these were to be jeopardised, the country could not afford more than the bare minimum required for the defence of the British Isles and the overseas empire, a defence which depended primarily on the Royal Navy and the Royal Air Force. The rapid development of air power was admittedly disturbing and even the most placid recognised that London was uncomfortably close to the Continent as the bomber flew. If, contrary to all probabilities, war did come, the fighters of the R.A.F. would be unable to cope with night raiders, so that there was a case for spending money on anti-aircraft guns. The Home Secretary, Sir Samuel Hoare, was strongly of this opinion; so were Hore Belisha and Liddell Hart; and so were those millions who had seen the film of H. G. Wells's book, *The Shape of Things to Come*, which opened with a scene in Trafalgar Square, a few minutes after the declaration of some future war, and showed the tower of St. Martin-in-the-Fields crashing on the terrified populace. Only the soldiers thought differently.

The Minister for the Co-ordination of Defence, Sir Thomas Inskip, had spent the summer recess of 1937 wrestling with the demands of all three services and he had cut their respective coats to fit the inadequate amount of financial cloth available to him. He must be given credit for deciding to allocate the largest ration to an increase in the fighter strength of the R.A.F. and for postponing the more extravagant elements of naval construction. When he came to apply what was left to the least important of the three services, he realised that the only course open to him, apart from a demand for larger funds involving increased taxation, was to ensure that the role of the army fitted the finance he could provide for it. It was on this practical but injudicious basis that Gort was required to prepare a paper for Hore Belisha to submit to his colleagues in the Cabinet.

The first priority was the Air Defence of Great Britain. It was, indeed, a matter of urgency for the army as well as for the R.A.F., because although a new anti-aircraft gun, the 3.7 inch, had been ordered, only a few incomplete prototypes were actually available and the defences were equipped with an outdated model used in the previous war. As so often happens, once the priority had been accepted, it became an obsession and Hore Belisha, persistently prodded by Liddell Hart, was initially among the front runners in the race to provide anti-aircraft guns and gunners at the expense of other forms of equipment and man-power. Churchill, too, in the process of goading the Government, was among the insistent; and it was not until some years afterwards that he acknowledged the emphasis placed on the destructive and perhaps decisive power of air forces to have been premature. The second task of the army was the defence of British shores, ports and trade routes. The third was to defend the empire. Last, and certainly least, was the provision of a Field Force ready to go overseas wherever it might be required.

The General Staff were far from enthusiastic about the order of priorities and the relative division of the available funds. To them war meant a certain demand for the despatch of a British Expeditionary Force to the Continent. Brigadier Henry Pownall, who became Director of Military Operations and Intelligence at the beginning of 1938, expressed the view that support of France was in fact home defence, and he told Hore Belisha that he believed sooner or later British troops would have to fight on French soil. Unless this were recognised and the essential preparations were made in peace time, the Expeditionary Force would go untrained and ill-equipped, with dire results. Gort thought the same, but it was his duty to prepare the paper for which the Cabinet had asked on the lines they had laid down.

It was the function of the Chiefs of Staff to represent their views to the Government through the Committee of Imperial Defence, a combined civilian and military body established before the First World War, of which the principal Ministers of the Crown as well as the Chiefs of Staff were members. Once a decision contrary to their advice had been taken the Chiefs of Staff could but obey their instructions. If there was one immutable axiom it was the subordination of military to civil authority.

The paper was drafted. Gort amended it and inserted so much detail that it was unreadable to all but military experts. Pownall tried his hand but equally failed to find favour. Finally, Hore Belisha and Liddell Hart between them produced a shorter and more persuasive document which was privately greeted by Gort, Pownall and Dill, now commanding at Aldershot, with a scorn that was ill-deserved since it at least provided an intelligible basis for Cabinet discussion and War Office planning. The estimated cost of the new proposals was £347 million to be spent over five years. With this hurdle apparently surmounted, Hore Belisha presented the Army Estimates to the House of Commons on 9th

March in a speech which fully merited the congratulations he received. In preparing it he had referred constantly to notes, provided by Liddell Hart, which he kept in a half closed drawer of his desk but which were clearly visible to General Ronald Adam, the newly appointed Deputy C.I.G.S. who sat with him in his room at the House of Commons during the period of gestation. Seeds of discontent were germinating fast in the War Office.

While the Cabinet and the Treasury, with a majestic disregard for realities, were withholding the financial support which alone could make rearmament effective and were refusing to consider the establishment of a sorely needed Ministry of Supply, the War Office was dividing its functions and its activities. Since he first took office, the Secretary of State had been devoting much of his energy and imagination to the task of popularising and modernising the army. New barracks were built, conditions and pay were improved, all Hore Belisha's skill in advertisement and public relations was deployed, with the gratifying result that recruits, both officers and other ranks, flocked to the colours and signed on as Territorials to a degree which would have appeared incredible a few years previously. Meanwhile Gort and Adam allocated the principal functions of the General Staff. Adam was entrusted with training and with the many administrative problems arising from the reorganisation of the army. Gort and Pownall concentrated principally on operational planning. On the military side all worked smoothly: Gort might sometimes be at a loss at the Committee of Imperial Defence when he was called upon to give ready answers to questions addressed to him by the agile politicians who attended it; he might stumble in debate with Hore Belisha at meetings of the Army Council; but in the military hierarchy he was liked personally and respected both for his qualities of leadership and for his straightforward handling of affairs. During their close association, lasting almost two years, he and Adam never had a serious difference of opinion.

The three Chiefs of Staff formed the most important of many sub-committees of the Committee of Imperial Defence and their advice was therefore given at one remove from the Cabinet, to which they did not normally have direct access. Their deliberations were, however, followed with great attention by Sir Maurice Hankey, Secretary not only to the Chiefs of Staff Sub-Committee but also to the Cabinet and to the C.I.D., and by his deputy with the C.I.D., Colonel H. L. Ismay. Gort's colleagues as Chiefs of

Staff were Admiral of the Fleet Lord Chatfield, First Sea Lord, and Air Chief Marshal Sir Cyril Newall, Chief of the Air Staff. In the two countries of the Berlin–Rome Axis, Germany and Italy, demands of the armed forces on industrial production were being given overriding priority and the civil populations, especially in Germany, accepted their consequent deprivations with masochistic enthusiasm. Spain, where civil war had been raging since July, 1936, provided facilities for trying out new weapons and training the armies and air forces of the Axis powers in real warfare. The British Chiefs of Staff, for their part, had to consider how, without conscription and with a population unwilling to be deprived of consumer goods or to work anything but normal hours, they could plan the reinforcement of Egypt, the provision of troops to keep the peace between Arabs and Jews in Palestine, the organisation of home defence and the strengthening of bases in Singapore, Hong Kong and Malta. The British Empire covered almost one third of the world's surface and its protection, with such small help as the Dominions might afford, was the duty of the exiguous forces for which these three men had direct responsibility.

If Lord Chatfield had his worries, more particularly the Government's decision to withdraw from the naval bases in Southern Ireland necessary for the protection of convoys in war, Lord Gort had even more. The navy at least had ships and guns and men. For the army it was difficult to know where to start. Moreover, the effort must be spread. On 19th January Gort agreed with Chatfield in voicing "the gravest misgivings". The Italians, with whom Chamberlain wished to have talks in the hope of detaching them from Germany, were about to form a new Army Corps in Libya. The British had a mere handful of troops in the Nile Delta, and Gort felt sure that if Egypt were lost, Germany's opportunity to attack in the west would have arrived. "It might almost seem," he said, "that the importance of the Air Defence of Great Britain has been over-stressed in relation to our other vital commitments." There had been no switch of industrial output to defence requirements and Gort complained that the factories producing munitions were only working at two-thirds of their capacity owing to the shortage of skilled labour. His insistence on a more balanced attitude to the priorities influenced Hore Belisha, who, on 17th March, told the Committee of Imperial Defence that an absolute priority for the air defence of Great Britain was "placing a terrible responsibility upon the War Office" since "the Field Force had no proper guns at all at the present time". Gort underlined this statement by explaining that the existing field guns were of a 1905 pattern, a fact which was well known to potential allies and enemies alike. "It would," he said, "be murder to send our Field Force overseas to fight against a first-class Power."

Staff conversations with the French might be thought helpful, but the British had nothing whatever to offer and, besides, it was the Government's policy to reach a peaceful understanding with both Germany and Italy. The Foreign Office had declared that while it would be useful to arrange "the technical conditions" in which, if France were ever attacked, British obligations under the Locarno Treaty could be fulfilled, such talks should not lead on to "any political undertaking nor to any obligation regarding the organisation of national defence". In other words the ultimate extent of British armed assistance, or the means by which forces could be provided, were banned as subjects for discussion. Gort could but agree that in view of this attitude, and the decision that a Field Force for the Continent should take such a low priority, full staff conversations would be futile, although informal discussions at Military Attaché level were to be encouraged. On 4th February the Chiefs of Staff, required, as they were, to implement but not to question the Cabinet's foreign policy, recorded their view that: "it would be more appropriate frankly to inform the French of the new situation, rather than to contemplate re-opening staff conversations upon which we, for our part, could only embark empty handed. We feel certain that the opportunity of turning such conversations to their own political advantage would be seized upon by the French with avidity. The temptation to arrange a leakage of the information that such collaboration was taking or had taken place would, in our opinion, prove irresistible to them in order to flaunt an Anglo-French accord in the face of Germany. Apart from the deplorable effect of such a leakage upon our present efforts to reach a détente with Germany, it is most important, from the military standpoint, that at the present time we should not appear to have both feet in the French Camp."

This last sentence reflected the anxiety of the Admiralty not to risk a breach or, worse still, a denunciation of the Anglo-German Naval Treaty which limited the size and number of German capital ships. A denunciation would have necessitated heavy additional expenditure on naval construction.

It was not for the Chiefs of Staff to comment on the Government's efforts for appeasement, but they would have failed in their duty if they had not drawn attention to the weakness of the base from which it was possible to negotiate, let alone to fight. On 11th February, they submitted a paper emphasising their conviction that the British Empire was in greater danger than ever before in peacetime. Britain was competing in her rearmament with nations which had been mobilising their whole financial, social and industrial system on a war footing for at least three years.

The approved rearmament programme was already falling behind and was in any case inadequate for the country's safety. The navy lacked skilled labour; so did the army, which was also short of essential steel supplies. At the then rate of production important items of equipment, such as anti-tank guns, would, by April, 1939, be 60 per cent. below the target and there would be a 45 per cent. deficiency in tanks. Only one out of three new shell-filling factories would be ready and even 3-ton lorries were two years behind. As for the R.A.F., unless factories worked on the basis of more than one shift a day, a quarter of the fighter squadrons would still be equipped with obsolete machines in April, 1939, and the bomber squadrons would be short of reserve aircraft. Existing factories were working far below capacity and they quoted as an example the new Vickers plant at Scotswood where seventy skilled men were employed against a total of 522 required for full production.

Gort was worried about the proposed negotiations with Italy, the issue on which Mr. Anthony Eden and Lord Cranborne resigned from the Government. Early in March he expressed to the Chiefs of Staff his fear that if, as appeared possible, the Italians were treated with greater frankness than the French or the Turks, the British Government might justly be accused of flirting with the dictators and disdaining its allies. He recommended that if there were to be talks with Mussolini's government, the military element should be restricted to a limited exchange of information through the Military Attachés in London and Rome. In a paper dated 21st February the Chiefs of Staff had already pointed out that the Abyssinian War had converted Italy from a traditional friend to a potential foe and that an attack on Egypt from Libya offered Italy an opportunity for an easy, spectacular success. In addition, and in the course of a lengthy survey of the dangers confronting Britain, they made two observations which might well have been taken to heart. The first was that even if French industry were undamaged by war, that country's manufacturing capacity was inadequate to support the forces she could mobilise. The second was that war against Japan, Germany and Italy combined was "a commitment which neither the present *nor the projected* strength of our defence forces is designed to meet, even if we were in alliance with France and Russia."

The applause given to Hore Belisha's presentation of the Army Estimates was still ringing in his ears when on 10th March Hitler ordered the occupation of Austria. It now required an unusual degree of myopia to disregard the possibility of European war. Yet, once the usual spate of elegantly phrased diplomatic protests had been despatched, and some effort had been made to play on Mussolini's dislike of his friend's Austrian venture, the Cabinet illogically decided to reduce by £70 million the sum of £347 million required to enable the army to fulfil its proposed responsibilities. The Field Force was now to consist of four regular infantry divisions and one mobile division, but these were to be equipped as reinforcements to the garrison in the Middle East rather than for war in Western Europe. The Territorial Army of twelve divisions was to be allotted £9 million and this was to be spent on peace-time training equipment. The provision of war equipment for two of its divisions, included in the estimates originally presented to the Cabinet by Hore Belisha, was refused, and his request for an element of industrial mobilisation sufficient to arm and maintain the Regular and Territorial Armies was accepted only to the extent necessary for the Air Defence of Great Britain and the regular Field Force of five divisions. Even this was difficult to implement in practice. When the Board of Vickers informed General Adam that once the existing order for anti-aircraft guns had been completed, they would be compelled to disperse their specialised labour force unless they knew for certain that a further order would be placed, Adam was unable to obtain the requisite Treasury sanction.

Slowly, as the weeks went by, illusions began to evaporate although there was still no disposition to provide more money. The General Staff considered that the politicians, and Hore Belisha in particular, laid too much emphasis on defence. All the same, after the Nazi seizure of Austria it began to dawn on many people, including some Cabinet Ministers, that what Gort considered a certainty, namely the commitment of a British army to the Continent in the event of war, was indeed a disagreeable possibility. However, at the Committee of Imperial Defence on 11th April Sir Samuel Hoare expressed his opposition to the idea of despatching a Field Force abroad, adding that at any rate in the initial stages all available troops would be required to assist in the defence of the United Kingdom. The Prime Minister supported Hoare since he could not see "into what strategical plan our small Field Force would fit". He favoured telling the French that "we could not commit ourselves to the despatch of any military force to the Continent, except such formations as were required for the lines of communication and the protection of our Advanced Air Striking Force". Officially the Field Force, which was in any case only the fourth priority for men and equipment, remained destined for the Middle East; in practice Gort, in his capacity as C.I.G.S., took pains to ensure that it could equally well be sent to Europe, although Pownall ruefully noted that "since it is financially last, it means that the troops we send will be ill provided for their task".

Once Austria had been incorporated in the Reich, it was evident that Czechoslovakia, whose south-western flank was now exposed to German attack, was next on the list. In case any should doubt it, Hitler himself proclaimed the fact, and the Chiefs of Staff met on 21st March to consider the military implications. Meanwhile Gort had additional worries. A Royal Commission under the chairmanship of Lord Peel had proposed that the Arab-Jew problem in Palestine should be solved by partition. The prospect of policing the corridor between the two states, running from Jaffa to Jerusalem, meant a man-power commitment and Gort expected it to be a long one, prophesying that "the Jewish and Arab states might for many years remain at logger-heads". Gort proposed to establish at Sarafand a Middle East Reserve which would serve the dual purpose of keeping the peace in Palestine and standing by to reinforce Egypt in the event of Italian aggression, as well as being available for employment farther eastwards, in Iraq, Persia or even India, should the necessity arise. Then the extensive Japanese garrison on the Chinese mainland meant that the defence of Hong Kong must be considered; and as if all this were not sufficient Hore Belisha, who could never resist duchesses, even red ones, was persuaded by the Duchess of Atholl, M.P., that the British Government should encourage the French to intervene in Spain on the anti-Franco side. Hore Belisha, after dilating on the subject at length to the unenthusiastic audience of Gort and Adam, put this proposal to the Cabinet and in consequence Hankey was instructed to ask if it reflected the opinion of the General Staff. Gort assured him it did not.

The War Office could only press forward their preparations to the extent that resources allowed. With such poor fuel available, no amount of pressure on the accelerator would make the machine go faster; but after the seizure of Austria it was natural that the desirability of staff conversations with France and Belgium should again be mooted. Gort and his colleagues discussed the question early in April and again on 13th May. Gort had authority to tell the French that *if* a British contingent were sent to the Continent it would consist of two infantry divisions and Line of Communication troops to serve the force as a whole. The French had already asked that the divisions might at least be motorised. They would be sure to inquire what and when the follow up might be and if a truthful answer were given the bareness of the British cupboard would be alarmingly exposed. There would be two more divisions available for despatch by the early summer of 1939 and the Mobile, or Armoured, Division would be ready in April, 1940. The Territorial Divisions could not be fully trained and equipped for embarkation until a year after the outbreak of a war. As regards the Belgians, the Military Attaché in Brussels had been given confidential information about their plans and that was sufficient for the time being, especially as the hostility of Flemish nationalists to any sort of Franco-Belgian accord made triangular talks impossible.

The Admiralty were opposed to staff conversations for quite different reasons: they were so much the senior partner in naval affairs that the French contribution at sea seemed to them of only slight importance and, with a misguided sense of honour, they were resolved to keep from the French the information which the Germans had in secrecy imparted to them after the signature of the Anglo-German Naval Treaty in 1935. The Prime Minister, with his unfailing integrity in such matters, thought it disloyal to the French to keep them in the dark about the measure of assistance they could expect from Britain: if they were going to receive a shock, then the sooner the better; and he was in favour of telling the Germans frankly that staff conversations were proposed. However, the Cabinet, frightened that talks might lead to commitments and conscious that in the past the communication of secret information to the French had resulted in leakages, decided on 12th April that conversations should be undertaken by the Air Staffs alone. The recommendations of the Chiefs of Staff, after their meeting on 13th May, were not such as to encourage the enlargement of this proposal, but on 27th May the Prime Minister and the Foreign Secretary, Lord Halifax, alarmed by the German threat to Czechoslovakia, asked the Cabinet to agree that if the French Government so desired, the army as well as the air force should be the subject of staff conversations. The French Government did so desire and, as foreseen by the General Staff, they immediately leaked the decision to the newspapers. The conversations themselves were slow to start and barren of results.

On 20th May news had come that German forces were concentrating on the frontiers of Czechoslovakia and there was a week-end of anxiety. The Cabinet, summoned to meet on the Sunday afternoon, were faced with a catalogue of deficiencies which the Chiefs of Staff had produced six weeks previously and which they now presented again. The Field Force of two divisions had neither tanks nor Bren guns nor modern field artillery; of the twenty-seven serviceable fighter squadrons, twenty were equipped with obsolete aircraft, slower than the majority of German bombers; the bomber squadrons, of which nearly one third were armed with obsolete, short-range light aircraft, could not reach Germany unless refuelled on the Continent, and no arrangements had been made with the French to this end; the productive capacity of the British aircraft industry was insufficient to replace normal wastage and the French factories were in a deplorable state; the balloon barrage and the Air Raid Precautions Organisation existed on paper but not in practice; by the end of March none of the new 3.7 inch and 4.5 inch anti-aircraft guns had been delivered and only 252 of the old 3 inch guns were available; the French had based their whole military philosophy on the defensive strength of their Maginot Line and would be neither able nor willing to take the offensive; the allied air forces had a combined bomb lift of 575 tons as against an estimated 1,825 tons credited to the Germans. As a final touch to this depressing scene, the Chiefs of Staff advised that there was nothing to prevent the Germans dropping bombs on Britain at the rate of 400 tons a day and sustaining this effort for two months. In March the military advisers to the Government had ensured that the writing was plainly visible on the wall of the Cabinet Room; in May the inscription was in larger letters still.

There was a rapid easing of the week-end tension for which the press, at home and abroad, gave firm British diplomacy the credit. The French, too, had been firm in public. Monsieur Bonnet, the Foreign Minister, declared that France would honour the Treaty which bound her to defend Czechoslovakia, but in private he hastened to reassure His Majesty's Ambassador that if the Czechs were unreasonable the French Government might feel obliged to reconsider the matter. The British Government, for their part, exhorted the service departments to expedite the rearmament programme; but they did not suggest the provision of supplementary estimates nor any fiscal deterrent to civilian consumption and expenditure. The estimates had been debated and approved. The Budget speech had been delivered. Any further measures must await the appropriate season in the following year.

Throughout June and July the time, strength and energies of Hore Belisha and the General Staff were consumed by internal squabbles, although they did take some useful decisions, in particular to establish a "Preparations Section" in the War Office, placed under Adam's authority and charged with the task of making administrative plans for the despatch of a British Expeditionary Force to the Continent. Sir Henry Wilson had formed a similar section before 1914, and when the time came Gort had been a personal witness to the smooth and successful results of its endeavours. Now, a generation later, the movement of an Advanced Air Striking Force had to be included in the preparatory scheme and provided with maintenance services by the army. Planning went on, slowly but methodically; and the problems of the Indian army, the Hong Kong garrison and the deteriorating situation in Palestine competed with the urgent necessity of attending to recruitment and the re-equipment of the army at home. Interest, however, was centred first on the disagreement between the Secretary of State and his official advisers and subsequently on an ill-judged battle in the House of Commons with Mr. Duncan Sandys and his formidable father-in-law, Mr. Winston Churchill.

The quarrel between Hore Belisha and the generals, with whom the Permanent Under Secretary, Sir Herbert Creedy, was in sympathy, arose partly from a clash of temperaments but more specifically from Hore Belisha's continuing dependence on the advice and assistance of Liddell Hart. With equal lack of success, Hore Belisha tried to handle this explosive problem by alternating frankness and subterfuge. He began by being frank: on 2nd February he delivered a panegyric on Liddell Hart's merits to the unresponsive audience of Gort, Adam, Creedy and Pownall. Gort had, at Hore Belisha's suggestion, lunched with Liddell Hart ten days previously, but he had concentrated on details of comparative unimportance and had declined to discuss broad lines of policy. When Liddell Hart telephoned a few days later to discuss War Office organisation, Gort dismayed him by insisting on the importance of not upsetting "the people in the clubs" by going too fast. This remark has been quoted as evidence of Gort's innate conservatism and excessive deference to the military and social establishment. Since he was never notably deferential to either, it is at least as likely that he made the first excuse that came into his head for declining to discuss matters which fell more properly into the competence of the General Staff. He had been an admirer of Liddell Hart's ability and revolutionary zeal, but a notable characteristic both of revolutionaries and their admirers is the readiness with which they replace impatience by circumspection once they occupy the seats of power. Perhaps if Liddell Hart had resigned his appointment with *The Times* during the early months of his "partnership" with Hore Belisha and an official position had been found for him in the War Office, as Adviser on Research or something comparable, he might have been accepted, with however ill a grace, and have become a licensed official gadfly. In such a capacity he would have been part of an integrated machine, able to assess more readily than was possible from an office in Printing House Square the extent to which interference was wise and practicable. He and Hore Belisha did discuss such an appointment in the spring of 1938, but by then it was too late. Implementation would have brought with it the wholesale resignation of the General Staff and as a consequence the downfall of Hore Belisha himself.

As things were, officers, serving and retired, were saying openly that the army was being run by Liddell Hart. Field-Marshal Sir Philip Chetwode had written to General Ironside on 3rd January: "The way Belisha is over-riding the Selection Board is very dangerous indeed, and I fear the real secret is that Liddell Hart is behind him all the time. Geoffrey Dawson, the Editor of *The Times*, told me that he had him in his pocket." The C.I.G.S. felt that his advice and that of the Army Council or the Permanent Under Secretary were subject to subsequent private endorsement by Hore Belisha's unofficial counsellor. Moreover, Liddell Hart had friends and disciples, such as Colonels Pile, Broad and Hobart, with whom he was constantly in touch and whom, because they were exponents of mechanical warfare, he sought through his influence with Hore Belisha to place on the commanding military heights. Finally, in spite of his brilliant exposition of the expanding torrent theory of attack, and his advocacy of the aggressive use of armoured divisions, he was regarded as the leading exponent of the theory that in future wars advantage must lie with the defence. Much blame was attached to him for the "Maginot mindedness" of those in Britain as well as France who were sure that an attacker would falter and finally break before the unquenchable fire power of modern defensive positions. Gort, on the contrary, believed that wars could only be won by taking the offensive and that even if inferiority of manpower and equipment determined the necessity of an initially defensive posture, this should be regarded as a temporary and regrettable expedient.

The frank approach having fallen on stony ground, Hore Belisha turned to subterfuge. The close association must be disguised. It was thus that Liddell Hart's notes were kept in half-open drawers, that Hore Belisha suddenly produced bright ideas which not even the most gullible general believed to be his own and that he spent long hours at his house in Stafford Place discussing clandestinely with Liddell Hart questions of policy and personnel which were properly the domain of the C.I.G.S. and the Army Council.

Already in February Gort had spoken to his intimate colleagues of resigning if this state of affairs continued. Already he and the other senior officers in the War Office were beginning to feel an almost automatic prejudice against measures and men if Liddell Hart was suspected of recommending them behind the scenes. Things came to a head at the end of May, a few days after the first Czech crisis had been surmounted. Hore Belisha disregarded the War Office proposals for reorganising the Anti-Aircraft Command and decided to appoint a controller with a seat on the Army Council who would, in effect, usurp some of the functions of the C.I.G.S. himself. Holding, as they did, that Hore Belisha placed too great an emphasis on the priority of anti-aircraft defence, and constantly critical of his weakness for self-advertisement, the General Staff suspected that he was hoping to impress the House of Commons and the press by a striking reform and thus deflect too searching an investigation of his recent public statement that 100 new 3.7 inch guns were available. In fact there were only eight complete guns in existence and enough people knew this to make Hore Belisha's over-optimism politically dangerous to him. Gort guessed, rightly, that Liddell Hart was behind the demand for an Anti-Aircraft Controller in the Army Council and that he had in view for the job his close friend, Colonel Tim Pile, whose substantial merits were wrongly but by now almost inevitably distorted in the eyes of Gort and his colleagues by the mere fact of his association with Liddell Hart. Hours which might more profitably have been spent on tasks of real urgency were lost in argument, and not only Gort but Adam and the Adjutant-General decided to resign if the Secretary of State pressed his case. The tempers of the General Staff were not improved by Hore Belisha summoning Sir Hugh Dowding, the Commander-in-Chief Fighter Command, and seeking his advice on the question at issue, an incident which culminated in Gort, who had never failed to show proper deference to the position and prerogatives of the Secretary of State, telling Hore Belisha in straight terms that he had no right to discuss internal War Office affairs with an airman except in the presence of the C.I.G.S. Hore Belisha bowed to the storm and dropped his proposal for an anti-aircraft member of the Army Council as well as for the selection of Colonel Pile, who was promoted to command an anti-aircraft division instead. A compromise was reached by the appointment of an additional D.C.I.G.S., in the person of Major-General James Marshall-Cornwall, who had been with Gort at Shanghai in 1927. Within a few days the second, still more time-consuming and still less relevant squabble arose, this time with the House of Commons.

Mr. Duncan Sandys, M.P., was a second lieutenant in a Territorial anti-aircraft unit. He obtained from the adjutant, Captain Hogan, disturbing information about the inadequacy of the defences, including details about their deployment which were regarded as highly secret. Towards the end of June he wrote to Hore Belisha stating his intention of putting down a question in the House unless he received satisfactory reassurances. Hore Belisha handled the affair with the maximum ineptitude, invoking the support not only of the Prime Minister but of the Attorney General and the Official Secrets Act. He proposed to suspend Sandys and Hogan and their commanding officer, but was dissuaded by Gort from so doing. He then agreed to the establishment of a Court of Inquiry and though he had done so in the presence of Gort, Sir Herbert Creedy and Sir Frederick Morgan, he subsequently told the House of Commons that the decision had been taken in his absence. For a man of basic integrity, with a deep desire to do right, he could be surprisingly untruthful when faced with an awkward situation; and this was a characteristic that lowered him in Gort's esteem more than any other. The question of Parliamentary Privilege arose; Churchill entered the fray vigorously on his son-in-law's side; and this in turn aroused the animosity of those in the Government, such as Hoare and Simon, who thought Churchill a menace to peace and good government. For six weeks the battle raged, to the detriment of work in the War Office. A Select Committee was established by the House of Commons and a Committee of Privileges assembled.

Hore Belisha spent hours confronting the Select Committee so that, as Pownall complained, he had no time to attend to his essential duties. Gort, too, was summoned before the indignant parliamentarians, some of whom found a petty enjoyment in their unaccustomed authority and particularly relished an opportunity to act as inquisitors of the General Staff. In the second week of July Gort spent nearly three hours before the committee. He was summoned again a fortnight later and was treated as a hostile witness, especially by the three Labour members of the committee, throughout the proceedings. One of the first questions put to him was: "I suppose you dislike politicians?" It was assumed, before he began to speak, that he had a personal animosity against Sandys and Hogan whereas, according to Pownall, his advice had from the start of the affair been to show and exercise moderation. Doubts were cast on his veracity and the infuriated Pownall wrote in his diary: "The fact is that he is a plumb-honest straightforward gentleman quite incapable of telling lies. . . . I wish the S. of S. were of the same category." Hore Belisha had been too busy to confer with his military advisers. On 28th July Gort wrote to Ironside:

"My dear Tiny,

I have been waiting to answer your letter hoping I should get a chance to see H.B. This has proved a vain hope as, except at meetings of the C.I.D., or banquets at the F.O. or Mansion House, I have not set eyes on him, much less had a chance of a talk.

This foolish Sandys case has put him out of stride momentarily and I can't help feeling he has been knocked round the ring in a wholly unnecessary way by the Select Committee. . . ."

That July, while the House of Commons consumed its own and

the War Office's energies in the sacred cause of Privilege, Messer-schmitts and Heinkels, tanks and field guns were emerging in hundreds from the German assembly plants. The British generals were anxiously calculating that given two years more peace the armed forces of the United Kingdom might, with much luck, more money and many more men reach a minimum state of preparation for European war. They recommended that the Foreign Office and the Government should bear constantly in mind the necessity of keeping diplomatic initiatives in step with the country's actual military potential. Before escaping from their labours and long hours for a brief summer holiday, the three Chiefs of Staff debated the probable situation in the event of war breaking out the following April. Gort gave his view that either Germany "would attack to the East and hope that we and the French would not intervene, or alternatively endeavour to knock us or the French out by a swift blow in the West . . . Germany had learned her lesson from the last war regarding the dangers of fighting on two fronts."

Fully conscious that the storm was gathering, and that Dr. Goebbels's noisy propaganda campaign against Czechoslovakia must lead to a grave confrontation between Germany and the western powers, Gort decided to take three weeks' leave before the Continental harvests were gathered and the traditional cam-paigning season arrived. In April his son, Sandy, had married Miss Yvonne Barnett. Apart from that he had had no time for domestic affairs nor opportunities to relax, save for week-end flights in his Moth, during a gruelling and by no means enjoyable eight months at the head of the British army. Now, accompanied by the Dalrymple-Hamiltons and Jacqueline, he left for Cowes and set sail in *Thanet* for a cruise in the therapeutic waters of the Solent and the English Channel.

CHAPTER 8

APPEASEMENT

———

THE events leading to the Munich Agreement are recounted in every book which covers this period of history: how Hitler used the nationalist emotions of the German speaking Sudeten minority as a convenient *casus belli* against Czechoslovakia; how their leader, Conrad Henlein, was at first prepared to settle for autonomy in local affairs until he received orders to the contrary from Berlin; how Dr. Goebbels invented atrocities which he alleged the Czechs had perpetrated on his patient Sudeten brothers; how Neville Chamberlain, grasping the nettle, danger, flew to Berchtesgaden and Godesberg in search of the flower, safety; how Hitler always asked for more each time the British and French had succeeded in browbeating the hapless Czechs into accepting his successive demands; and how at the end, when Hitler's final ultimatum was on the verge of expiry, he graciously received Chamberlain, Daladier and Mussolini, but not the Russians, at Munich in order to receive the surrender of the democracies to *force majeure*.

What is less clear, and will perhaps always remain in dispute, is whether Hitler was staging a gigantic bluff or whether he would in fact have gone to war. At the Nuremberg trial of the Nazi leaders the impression was given that had Hitler decided on war, the generals would have overthrown him and that only Chamberlain's willingness to consider a deal at the expense of Czechoslovakia deterred them. It is also on record that in June, 1938, Hitler had told General Keitel he would take no action against Czechoslovakia unless, as in the cases of the Rhineland and Austria, France and Britain remained passive. Hitler was prone to change his mind and he was no less unreliable in the undertakings he gave internally than in those he gave to foreign powers. At Nuremberg the German military chiefs, on trial for their lives, were seeking to convince their judges that all that had happened was Hitler's fault. Moreover, German generals proved themselves singularly incompetent at staging a *coup d'état*. It may, on the other hand, be that faced by a war on two fronts and disturbed by the mobilisation of the French army and the Royal Navy, Hitler would in fact have withdrawn from the brink if his opponents had stood firm and if Russia had been invited to take a hand. There will always be those who agree with Churchill's verdict that a year's grace was paid for with dishonour and that *except in the field of aircraft production* the postponement was of greater material and moral value to the Germans than to the allies. It is, however, an important exception. The Air Ministry, Gort and most of the British military leaders considered that war with Nazi Germany was sooner or later inevitable, but from their point of view the longer it could be postponed the better. The British Government hoped and even dared to believe that it might be averted altogether.

During this period neither the Service Ministers nor the Chiefs of Staff and the departments in which they served had any control of the course of events. They were, indeed, scarcely consulted. The French were far from anxious to sound or listen to clarion calls, although it was they who, next to the Czechs themselves, were most immediately implicated. As for the Russians, they were deeply distrusted, not only by France and Britain but with still better cause by the small and vulnerable states whose geographical misfortune it was to lie between Germany and the Soviet Union. It was the British Prime Minister who made the dangerous choice of joining Hitler alone in the centre of the stage.

Great Britain was in effect governed by a Cabal composed, like the original seventeenth-century instrument, of five men on whose opinions the actions of Gort and his fellow Chiefs of Staff were dependent. They were Mr. Chamberlain, Sir Horace Wilson, Lord Halifax, Sir John Simon and Sir Samuel Hoare. All highly intelligent, they were much more public spirited than Charles II's notorious advisers. Strikingly dissimilar in taste and temperament, they were alike in their lack of any close personal experience of war, the very thought of which they abhorred, and united in their belief that patient diplomacy could prevent it. When, some months after Munich, they began to realise they might be mistaken in their optimism, they clung to the hope that economic blockade and the unchallengeable power of the Royal Navy, combined with the strength of the French defences and the deterrent skill of the R.A.F., would suffice (some hoped sooner and others feared later) to induce a famished German people and a discontented officer caste to overthrow the Nazi régime. The leadership of the Cabal or Inner Cabinet was undisputed: its members gave their advice freely, but decision rested with the Prime Minister alone.

Neville Chamberlain, whose lot it was to be first the object of his countrymen's hysterical gratitude and then the victim of their disenchanted bitterness, was a determined, masterful man with a tireless sense of duty and, during his brief apotheosis, an almost mystical belief in his mission. Lord Birkenhead had said of his brother, Austen: "He always played the game and he always lost it." Neville had a lesser intellect than his brother, but he was a subtler politician. His motives were invariably high and nothing would ever have induced him to put his personal interests or those of the Conservative Party before what he believed to be the advantage of his country. He was courageous, in and out of the House of Commons, and if he cannot be acquitted of vanity he was none the less impervious to the risk of unpopularity. Once he had decided that a cause was just, it became for him an article of faith and he found it difficult to sympathise with, or even to respect, those who took an opposite view. Deeply sensitive to the beastliness of war, he was determined that the new generation should, at any cost, be spared the fate of his own contemporaries. He was cold in outward manner, but when glimmers of warmth appeared they won the loyalty of those towards whom they were directed more readily than the welcoming smiles of more obviously attractive men. It was thus that, poor speaker though he was, he established an apparently unassailable domination of the large Conservative majority in the House of Commons. He was respected, too, by senior civil servants and by the military leaders, who, whatever their antipathy to politicians in general, saw in the Prime Minister a man whom they trusted and whose calm efficiency they admired.

Chamberlain inherited from Stanley Baldwin, as Chief Industrial Adviser to His Majesty's Government, Sir Horace Wilson, formerly Permanent Under Secretary at the Ministry of Labour. He was subsequently created one of history's leading scapegoats. He has been a long-suffering one because, true to his conviction that the civil service should be a silent service, he has not replied to his detractors or sought to defend himself in public. His move to 10 Downing Street was originally due to his exceptional skill as a negotiator. He was totally unselfseeking and held that while it was the duty of a civil servant to guide his master, he must also identify his policy and his interests with those of the Minister he served. Nobody was more adept at smoothing the ruffled feelings of Permanent Secretaries, at suggesting the ideal choice for a civil appointment and at saving the Prime Minister time and effort by mastering the details of intricate social and industrial problems. By September, 1938, he was already indispensable, seated in an office leading out of the Cabinet Room and available for consultation on matters great and small. Chamberlain had a mind of his own, and an incisive one, but he was a lonely man, with political associates, admiring acquaintances and scarcely any friends. Horace Wilson's quiet manner and grave demeanour suited him admirably; he became Chamberlain's *alter ego*. His influence exceeded that of the politicians in the Inner Cabinet. It was not an evil influence: indeed, it was in many respects a wholesome influence; but on foreign affairs and defence his advice should neither have been sought nor followed. Perhaps, with his limited knowledge of other lands and their inhabitants, Wilson supposed that the language and attitude which succeeded so well with a recalcitrant Permanent Under Secretary should be equally effective with the Nazi leaders. It is because he was unsuited, by training and temperament, for the task with which he was entrusted at a moment of gravity in the history of Great Britain, a task in which the most experienced diplomat would have been equally unsuccessful, that he earned the obloquy not only of the Foreign Office, whose members resented a home civil servant trespassing in their preserve, but also of all the politicians and men in public life opposed to the Munich settlement. No historian has yet attempted an objective assessment of Sir Horace Wilson nor rendered him the critical justice which is his due. Churchill, at least, much though he disapproved of Chamberlain's dependence on Wilson, was unwilling to blame him for accepting the responsibilities which the Prime Minister had imposed on him and was sufficiently convinced of his abilities and loyalty to retain him in office as Secretary of the Treasury and Permanent Head of the Civil Service after the change of Government in May, 1940.

Whenever they think they will be believed, the Foreign Office insist that their Secretary of State is a wise and lovable hero, although they have occasionally made exceptions. In March, 1938, the loss of Anthony Eden, whom they and many others regarded as the hope of the nation, left a scar which almost any successor other than Lord Halifax would have found it hard to heal. He succeeded in the task in spite of the fact that, unlike Eden, he accepted the Prime Minister's policy of dealing personally with the Dictators, a policy abhorrent to all the members of the Diplomatic Service. Halifax was lifted respectably close to the top of the heroic pedestal which the service expected its chief to occupy, and in subsequent years, as Ambassador in Washington, he fully justified their faith. As a Fellow of All Souls and former Viceroy of India, who was also a Master of Foxhounds, he was one of the last examples of that phenomenon in English politics, the well-educated nobleman with catholic interests and tastes, which astonished but frequently captivated Europeans and Americans in the eighteenth and nineteenth centuries. Deeply religious, intelligent and honourable, he was not, however, a strong enough man to restrain the Prime Minister from some of his less well advised excursions in the field of foreign policy and he thought an excess of zeal indicative of bad taste.

Sir John Simon, Chancellor of the Exchequer, and a survivor of Mr. Asquith's Government, was unloved because he was indecisive, appeared ungenerous and was often contemptuous in manner and speech. He was erudite both as a classicist and a mathematician. His idea of making himself socially agreeable was to quote Homer at length and follow it up with an exposition of the Binomial Theorem. A brilliant advocate, he had been as unpopular at the Bar as he later became in the House of Commons; nor did his own colleagues trust him. Yet, effectively though he disguised the fact, he could show humanity; he displayed it in marked degree to his ailing second wife and with cold but unwavering detachment to others when he had reason to believe there had been a miscarriage of justice. He was socially and politically ambitious, but personally ungrasping, and he was convinced it was his duty to defend the nation's patrimony against the military squander-bugs who had so little conception of the economic and financial difficulties with which the Treasury was faced. In the summer of 1938 he rightly refused to meet the demands of the Government of India when they sought a subsidy from the British Exchequer for their military establishment which included among other luxuries sixteen regiments of cavalry.

Sir Samuel Hoare had been Secretary of State for Air, for India and for Foreign Affairs, as well as First Lord of the Admiralty. He was now Home Secretary. He was widely mistrusted and almost universally known as "Slippery Sam". His reputation rose on account of his masterly handling of the Government of India Bill, but fell sharply in consequence of the notorious Hoare-Laval Pact, made at the expense of Abyssinia during the Italian invasion of that defenceless country. He bore little resemblance to Laval, with whom his name will for ever be linked on account of that distressing incident, and he would never have shirked his duty nor sold his country to Hitler even though he might not have been among the first to fight on the beaches. He was a fluent speaker and a brilliant political manipulator. If, early in 1940, Chamberlain had died there would have been a movement in the Conservative party in favour of Hoare as Prime Minister, and a number of influential men canvassed the possibility. Having once been Secretary of State for India, and so renowned as an architect of the Government of India legislation, his ambition was to end his career as Viceroy, and after the fall of Chamberlain's Government he maintained, to Churchill's mystification, that he had received a promise of the reversion provided he first served for a year or so as Ambassador in Madrid. In the event he had to be content with a peerage and he remained in Spain throughout the war, exercising his skill as a diplomat to the great benefit of his country.

These were the five men, four politicians and a civil servant, who ruled the country. Sometimes included in their councils and sometimes not, was Sir Thomas Inskip, Minister for the Co-ordination of Defence. He was as devout and practising a Low Churchman as Halifax was a High one; he was by profession a barrister, less brilliant but better liked than Simon; he was esteemed by the Conservative Party, but he was not, like Hoare, a born manipulator. The office allotted to him provided some responsibility but no power; he was not Minister of Defence and he had no departmental authority. He was, however, regarded by Chamberlain as wise and experienced, and since he had no prejudices, at any rate in matters affecting this world, he tried to be fair in his adjudications between the three services. Unfortunately, war and the armed forces of the Crown were among the subjects on which he was least qualified to exercise his judgment.

There were several important changes in Whitehall during the summer of 1938. Lord Swinton, the energetic Secretary of State for Air, who had done much to improve the operational capacity of the R.A.F. and bring the "Spitfire" off the drawing board on to the production line, was dismissed in May and replaced by Sir Kingsley Wood; at the end of July Sir Maurice Hankey retired, his joint tenure of the Secretaryships of the Cabinet and C.I.D. being divided between Sir Edward Bridges on the civil side and Colonel Hastings Ismay on the military side; and in August Lord

Chatfield was succeeded as First Sea Lord by Admiral Sir Roger Backhouse.

Although the Prime Minister and other members of the Inner Cabinet attended the Committee of Imperial Defence from time to time, and Chamberlain had for some years been genuinely convinced that limited rearmament was necessary provided it did not dislocate industry or disturb the export trade, they saw no reason why the Ministers responsible for the three service departments and their Chiefs of Staff should be allowed to exert any decisive influence on questions of policy even when these might involve war or peace. The plea of the Chiefs of Staff, endorsed by Hankey, that diplomacy should be closely allied to military capacity was not, indeed, disregarded because the main objective of British diplomacy was to avoid war at almost any price; but the Government's military advisers were only on the circumference of the circle in Downing Street where so many anxious deliberations were taking place that August and September. War might be imminent, but those on whom the main responsibilities would then fall were confined principally to discussions among themselves and to the preparation of lengthy assessments and anticipations. It occurred to nobody, for instance, to consider who might be selected to command the small British Field Force if it should be required to embark for the Continent in support of France.

It would have been irresponsible to sail far from the Solent during that brief yachting holiday, and on 23rd August Gort returned to the War Office. The German "war of nerves" against Czechoslovakia was becoming daily more vicious and in Palestine, where the Grand Mufti was believed to be in the pay of the Axis powers, the threat of riot and civil war had increased to such an extent that the Governor and the Commander-in-Chief, with eleven battalions and a cavalry regiment already at their disposal, were demanding another whole division precisely at a time when detailed plans had to be made for the despatch to the Continent of the only two divisions available in the United Kingdom for service overseas. The British Government would shortly be expected to reach a decision about the publication of a new report on the partition of Palestine. The Foreign Office, traditionally well-disposed to the Arab cause and profoundly disturbed by the implications of Arab hostility in the event of war, was itself waging a private war with the Colonial Office, which was resolutely determined to pursue the accepted British policy of establishing a Jewish National Home. The influence of the Foreign Secretary, Lord Halifax, was, of course, greater than that of the Colonial Secretary, Mr. Malcolm Macdonald, and the weight of the War Office was, on severely practical grounds, thrown into the scales on the side of the Foreign Office. All this was time consuming, and it was a distraction from still more pressing demands in Europe and at home.

Czechoslovakia was well-governed and prosperous, but within the body politic lay all the seeds of disintegration, fertile and ready to germinate. The efficient Czechs and the more backward Slovaks regarded each other with distaste. The Sudetens were intolerant of Czech domination even before the prods from Berlin began to exacerbate nationalist prejudices. The Ruthenians, residing in the far eastern tip of the country, felt no brotherly sentiments for the compatriots imposed on them by the Treaty of Versailles. There were Poles and Hungarians who looked nostalgically towards Warsaw and Budapest. In the event of war against Germany the temptation of the minorities to stab their Bohemian rulers in the back might prove irresistible.

Britain had no direct treaty obligation to Czechoslovakia, but France had; and if France honoured her undertaking, the Soviet Union was pledged to march in support. Was Britain to be dragged into a world conflict because of a French commitment made fourteen years previously? Was it, on the other hand, conceivable that Britain should stand by and watch France fight alone with the knowledge that if she were defeated the Germans would be in control of the Channel ports and the aerodromes of northern France? The Czechs had a well equipped army of twenty-one divisions, totalling over a million men. They had an admirable mountain defence line in Bohemia and, at the Skoda works, one of the most modern and extensive armament factories in the world. But in the previous March the Chiefs of Staff had approved a report, submitted to them by the Joint Planning Staff of the three services, which had reached this carefully considered conclusion: "No military pressure we can exert by sea, or land or in the air can prevent Germany either from invading and overrunning Bohemia or inflicting a decisive defeat on the Czechoslovakian Army . . . In short, we can do nothing to prevent the dog getting the bone, and we have no means of making him give it up, except by killing him by a slow process of attrition and starvation."

The situation had not changed at all since March and as Gort

had been one of the foremost in opposition to military talks with
the French at any level above that of military attaché, the War
Office had no clear idea of the French army's intention in the
event of war. What they did have was an exaggerated view of its
strength and efficiency. They knew, however, that the French
could not reach Bohemia in time to help the Czechs; that the
Russians, many of whose senior officers had been shot in Stalin's
recent purges, would have to force their way through Poland or
Roumania in order to reach the Czech frontier; and that the
aircraft industry in France had been so weakened by strikes and
disorganised by nationalisation that the French Air Force would
be useless for an aerial offensive in support of Czechoslovakia.
The leaders of the British army also knew the capacities of their
own service; and the knowledge gave them no satisfaction. All
they could usefully do was to make sure that the plans for utilising
the available forces for home and imperial defence were polished
and re-polished, and to leave the issue to the politicians and the
diplomats.

It would have been wise to discover, at whatever level was
thought desirable, what the French military authorities had in
mind. Such little information as was received in London was
indirect. The British Ambassador in Paris reported on 4th
September that he had heard, second-hand through the Quai
d'Orsay, that "General Gamelin is convinced of his ability, if the
worst comes to the worst, not only to contain the Germans, but to
wear them down by a system of carefully executed offensives.
The fortifications in the Rhineland are far from equalling the
Maginot Line." General Gamelin, on whose wisdom as Commander-in-Chief of the French army so much depended, went on
to say he thought the role of aviation apt to be exaggerated and
that after the first few days of war the air forces would be confined
to acting as accessories to the armies. Shortly afterwards Monsieur
Daladier declared that if German troops crossed the Czechoslovak frontier, "the French will march to a man". He promised
to consult the British before taking action, but he gave no indication precisely what that action might be.

The Chief of the Air Staff, Sir Cyril Newall, suggested that
since "if France gets embroiled with Germany, it is quite obvious
that we shall not be able to stand out," it was important not to be
committed to a French plan of campaign about which nothing
was known in advance. It was at least desirable to have an
opportunity to comment. It does Gort little credit that he held

obstinately to his view that discussions with the French should be avoided. In his reply to Newall he wrote: "I am doubtful whether it would be considered politically opportune to discuss military plans at this juncture with France nor, indeed, do I consider that there is any advantage to be gained at the moment since the French General Staff would be extremely unlikely to discuss any plans except in the guise of a 'project' couched in very general terms." It is difficult to justify Gort's rejection of Newall's sensible proposal because he was certainly wedded to the idea of co-operation with the French and even at this stage he was personally convinced that, as in 1918, a British army fighting on the Continent should be subordinated to a French commander-in-chief. His previous fears of exposing the inadequacy of the British contribution and of French security leakages were no longer valid on the eve of a potential European conflict.

He escaped by air to Holkham, in his Moth *Henrietta*, for the night of 28th August, and Ironside, who was a fellow guest, described the scene thus: "Gort had come up in an aeroplane and we went to see it at Bircham Newton. A small two-seater absolutely open to the wind and rain. Gort told me that he had lost his way coming up and then found that he hadn't a map marked with the latest aerodromes. He was most annoyed because the R.A.F. charged him 5/- landing fees and 4/- garage fees for one night. He went back on Sunday evening and lost his way again." During the weeks of crisis which followed, Gort found time, late at night or early in the morning before he set out for the War Office, to write reassuring letters to Lady Marjorie, so recently with him on board *Thanet* and now far away in Ayrshire. On 8th September, after complaining that Hore Belisha had suggested his flying out to Palestine that day, as if there were no European crisis, he wrote: "He is really quite hopeless and not in the least bit interested about the present situation. All he talked about yesterday was changing the name 'Infantry battalion' to 'Light Machine Gun battalion' as he had talked about the latter in his speech on Estimates in the spring!! What can one do with him? If the worst happens it would be quite impossible to work with him in a crisis as he is temperamentally unfitted." It was all too clear that relations between the Secretary of State and the C.I.G.S. had not been improved either by the holidays or by the crisis. Later in the same letter, Gort continued that Hitler was like a perverted Joan of Arc: "he follows no recognised lines of conduct but listens to the voices". This was a perceptive comment: the unpredictability of the Führer's moods are among the reasons why it would have been dangerous to assume he was bluffing.

All Europe waited for Hitler's speech due on 12th September at the end of the Nuremberg rally. Such was the tension that sighs of relief greeted the absence of an actual announcement of a move against the Czechs. On 14th September the Chiefs of Staff forwarded to the Cabinet through Inskip their revised version of an "Appreciation of the Situation in the Event of War against Germany". After stating that they had no knowledge whether the French intended to stand on the defensive in the Maginot Line or to attempt an offensive across the German frontier, they raised their estimate of the potential daily German bomb-load which could be dropped on Britain to 500–600 tons a day for two consecutive months, and they concluded by restating their conviction that neither Great Britain nor France could take any action whatever to save Czechoslovakia from total defeat. It was the echo, almost identical in words, of what the Joint Planning Staff had written in the previous March.

This time it arrived at 10 Downing Street the day before Chamberlain set off to meet Hitler at Berchtesgaden, a meeting at which he was presented with an uncompromising demand for the incorporation in the Reich of all Sudeten areas in which half or more of the inhabitants were of German origin.

On 19th September Gort's normal equanimity was all but shaken when, in the midst of many cares and activities, he was obliged to waste an entire morning with his Secretary of State, who was accustomed to go late to bed and incapable of early rising. He wrote to Lady Marjorie: "This week-end I was unable to do any flying as I was too busy one way and another and then found when I got in that I had a telephone message to ring up Belli at Wimbledon. It was to ask me to come down in the morning today so as to drive up with him and so save him any work. The object was that I should discuss with him the problems likely to arise at his meeting this morning. It was maddening as I had to leave by car at 9.20 a.m. and found he was not downstairs until just after 10 a.m. when he went in and had breakfast and Haydon and I had then to talk to him while he ate it. The net result was that my whole morning was wasted and it is not my job to run off down there but rather his to come up to the office. When he arrived up, instead of going straight to Downing Street like everybody else he stops the car at the Horse Guards end so that he can get the photographers all to himself and he sits on in the car until he sees them all assembled and then he emerges. Too childish for words. He undoubtedly is very jealous that the big four can get on without him as he is missing so much publicity thereby and he ill conceals his feelings on that score." Nobody could accuse Gort of an exaggerated sense of his own importance; but this was not the way for a Secretary of State to treat the C.I.G.S. even if personal relations had been excellent and mutual respect had been firmly established.

Gort's assessment of the political situation in mid-September was that there would be no war that autumn, but that Hitler would lead Europe from crisis to crisis until either the régime collapsed or there was war. It must therefore be fatal to relax for one instant the preparations which Britain was belatedly making to meet the threat. The previous war had been fought to rid the world of autocracies (so, at any rate, Gort believed), but the last state was now much worse than the first. The Nazi Party extremists were, as he put it, "bound to produce a new affront next year of some sort or another", and the peoples of Europe could not continue to live in such intolerable conditions.

On 21st September the Government saw that some preparatory measures must be taken. Trenches were dug in the London parks as refuges from the bombs expected to drench the capital immediately war was declared. Inskip summoned the leaders of all three services to Admiralty House and, in the Government's name, authorised most of the preliminary measures apart from mobilisation. On the 23rd the Chiefs of Staff recommended that, if hostilities were considered imminent, immediate mobilisation should be ordered; but if the Government feared such an order, publicly announced, would provoke an attack, then the order itself must be postponed for forty-eight hours after the decision had been made so that vital defensive measures might first be taken. On the 24th, the day Chamberlain, dispirited and unsuccessful, flew back from Godesberg, the Chiefs of Staff had been required to report on the military action Britain could take to bring pressure on Germany. Their answer was: effectively none. If the two divisions earmarked for the Field Force were sent to France they could embark twenty-two days after the orders were given and would be ready for action eighteen days after that; but they would be deficient in modern equipment, including tanks and medium artillery. Gort was one of the few who had not by now decided that war was inescapable. In his letter of Sunday, the 25th, to Lady Marjorie he told her he detected a few signs of cold

Secretary of State for War and C.I.G.S.
Hore Belisha and Gort in the War Office 1938

Gamelin and Gort in the Champs Elysées, 14th July 1939

Georges and Gort, January 1940

feet in Hitler's latest actions. "Also you see, or will see, that the nauseating propaganda from Berlin started to cool down on Saturday and the Berlin press keeps on announcing agreement has been reached. Even so we must not relax our efforts to rearm as it is only a postponement . . . I still believe *if* we show our teeth the bully will falter."

On the morning of the 26th, with the temporary collapse of hope following the Prime Minister's return from Godesberg, Gort ordered the despatch of the telegram "Cromwell" to all military establishments. It was the code word initiating "the precautionary period". That afternoon "Haig" was sent, calling out the Territorials and others required for the air defence of Great Britain. It was followed by "Marlborough", placing the coastal defence units on the alert. The same evening Duff Cooper, First Lord of the Admiralty, asked (but did not yet receive) permission to mobilise the fleet and Lord Halifax agreed to the issue of a statement that if France went to war, Great Britain and Russia would do likewise. Since the Russians had not in fact been consulted, this statement of their intentions was presumably based on the obligations arising from their treaty with Czechoslovakia.

To Gort's satisfaction all the precautionary measures were put smoothly into effect and the dress rehearsal was afterwards seen to have been a useful exercise. He was ceaselessly occupied: there were long and frequent meetings to attend; two battalions and a cavalry regiment, on loan from Egypt to Palestine, had to be moved back urgently for the protection of Mersa Matruh; a battalion was despatched from Shanghai to reinforce Hong Kong; transports had to be diverted and redirected; troops were ordered to leave India for Singapore and Egypt; the whole defence of the empire, against not only Germany but Italy and Japan, was reviewed and activated.

There were some people in Britain, by no means Fascist in outlook and undoubted in their patriotism, who had long been foolish enough to admire Hitler and his much vaunted regeneration of the German people. They disbelieved or closed their ears to the stories of concentration camps and the persecution of the Jews. Some of them were socially important, some sat in the House of Commons, some occupied high positions in industry and commerce. They believed Soviet Russia to be a greater danger than Nazi Germany. None of them were included in the Government or among the Government's principal advisers, but when Lady Marjorie reported what such people were saying, Gort wrote to dispute the suggestion that the trouble had been stirred up by Russia. "Hitler has caused it all and it is only a stage of 'Mein Kampf', which he follows religiously." He went on to give Lady Marjorie Chamberlain's own impression of Hitler as told him by the Prime Minister on his return from Berchtesgaden: "One must be impressed with the power of the man; he is extremely determined. He has thought out what he wants and he means to get it. You can see he would not brook opposition beyond a certain point." He ended his letter: "A sad state of affairs for us momentarily, but we will be able to sing a very different tune in a year's time. Our nation went pacifist mad and now has no armaments. You can't walk about a jungle, which holds a man-eating tiger, unarmed. You have always to be ready to swarm up a tree!"

On the same 26th September, after the British Government had resolved to reject Hitler's Godesberg terms, the French Prime Minister and the Minister of Foreign Affairs, Daladier and Bonnet, came to London where they unenthusiastically confirmed France's obligation to fight for Czechoslovakia. As Gort put it: "The French could not see why they should be stiff so long as such a simple problem could be possible of solution by negotiation." Sir Horace Wilson, sent to Berlin with a letter to Hitler from the Prime Minister (to the impotent fury of the Foreign Office) was abused by Hitler and achieved nothing. Indeed, Hitler added to the general depression by telling Wilson that he would invade Czechoslovakia on 28th September, and not on 1st October as he had previously said, unless the terms he had dictated at Godesberg, involving occupation of the Sudeten areas by German troops, were accepted. All was set for the explosion. General Gamelin, too, had crossed the Channel on the 26th and Gort, who had not been able to go to bed till 2.30 a.m., was at Croydon at 7.0 a.m. to meet him. He found little to encourage him when Gamelin explained that the great French plan, the carefully executed series of offensives, would consist of advancing towards the Siegfried Line and then withdrawing to the Maginot Line. This manœuvre would no doubt be repeated at convenient intervals. The Grand Old Duke of York evidently had a twentieth-century imitator.

Hardly had the French ministers returned to Paris when they sent a message demanding to know if the British would mobilise simultaneously with them, if conscription would be introduced in the United Kingdom and if the economic and financial resources of the two countries might be pooled. It was now the eleventh hour and Gort's letter to Lady Marjorie began: "To-day twenty years ago I went into action for the last time in 1918 and to-day, twenty years later, it seems one is preparing to start a new campaign in circumstances which find us far less prepared than in 1914." He would still, he said, only wager even money on war although he thought the more prudent would be laying odds-on.

The Munich Agreement, which seemed a last minute miracle to most people, was signed in the early hours of 30th September. There was one Minister, Duff Cooper, who resigned in shame; Churchill and the increasing band of his followers in Parliament considered that their country was dishonoured and debased; most of the members of the Foreign Office were shattered by the ignominy and no less worried by the evident irresolution of the French Government, opposed as it was by strong anti-war parties on the right and on the left. Sir Orme Sargent, Deputy Under Secretary, stood on the balcony of the Foreign Office gazing with distaste on Chamberlain's enthusiastic reception in Downing Street when he returned from Munich. "You might suppose," he remarked, "that we had won a major victory instead of betraying a minor country." So saying he turned on his heel and closed the french windows behind him in order to blot out the sight and the wild cheering in the street below. Gort, however, had no doubt that the Munich respite was essential. A war against Nazi Germany was certainly not abhorrent to him. "It will be fun," he remarked to General Haydon, Hore Belisha's Military Assistant, "to see those field grey coats again." But the fun must be postponed. Late one night, while the crisis was at its height, he and Adam paced round and round St. James's Square, unwilling to go home to bed until they had resolved the problem in their own minds. Adam, acting as devil's advocate, argued for taking up the Nazi challenge; Gort maintained that to go to war in such nakedness would be an act of irresponsible folly. Adam, in his heart, knew that Gort was right because it would be two years before either the Air Defence of Great Britain or the Field Force were ready for action. During the entire emergency Gort had used to the best advantage his ability to inspire other men. Pownall noted in his diary: "The War Office has played up and together extremely well, led by a natural leader in Gort."

Chamberlain really did believe it might be "Peace in our time" and he even convinced himself it was "Peace with Honour". By his exertions, and by keeping his temper in the face of abuse and duplicity, he had saved his country and the world from war. He thought, too, that in signing his Anglo-German declaration of future peaceful intentions, which Chamberlain dramatically produced from his pocket after the signature of the main Munich Agreement, Hitler meant to keep his word. Hitler did indeed exclaim "*Ja, ja*", as each sentence was read aloud to him, but his thoughts were on the dismemberment of Czechoslovakia and he regarded the declaration as an unimportant scrap of paper to be signed in order to keep Chamberlain happy. Just over a year later Chamberlain was driving back to Downing Street with the author of this book, consumed with anger at an attack made on him, as he considered offensively, by an Opposition Member of Parliament. Perhaps the Member in question was sincere in his mistaken beliefs? What, replied Chamberlain, was the good of that? Hitler had been sincere at Munich: he had really meant what he signed and said; but he had changed his mind later. He was, Chamberlain went on (forgetting the cause of his original indignation) a man who believed his own words at the time he uttered them but was totally inconstant in his subsequent views and intentions.

It is, however, possible to present an apologia for Munich on other grounds and there is no doubt that Gort, for his part, would have endorsed at least three of them. He would not, perhaps, have agreed with Chamberlain, and many others who were cheering at the time, that a war postponed might well be a war averted. Whether or not Hitler was temporarily sincere in his protestation that he had no further territorial claims on Europe – and what is seen to be false now was less obviously so then – there was the possibility of his death, assassination or overthrow. However long the odds, it would have been difficult for any statesman to disregard an outside chance when the alternative was world war. To Gort war with Germany, the later the better from Britain's point of view, seemed an eventual certainty. He would, however, have agreed with the other good reasons for a settlement. First and foremost the country was undefended: only the navy was well prepared. The air force was making rapid strides and whereas for another few months even its first line planes would be obsolete, it would in eighteen months or two years be a formidable power, both offensive and defensive. The army would never again be strong without conscription and industrial mobilisation; but at least it could in two years' time be a useful appendage to the eighty-five divisions which the French were expected to put into the field. The small British army of 1914 had, after all, grown into one of nearly five million men by 1918. As things were that September, the British medium tanks were fourteen years old and there were insufficient Bren guns even for the two divisions it was hoped to mobilise.

Secondly, the Dominions had made it clear they had no intention of fighting for Czechoslovakia. General Smuts, devoted though he was to the imperial theme, let it be known that South Africa would not come in. Canada was almost equally negative, Australia was doubtful, De Valera had said that he would declare Ireland's neutrality. India and the colonies would, of course, do as they were told; but of the self-governing Dominions New Zealand alone seemed sure to help. War, then, would mean the weakening, and perhaps ultimately the dissolution, of what every right-thinking Briton knew to be the world's greatest power for good: the British Empire.

Finally, the British people themselves would have fought without enthusiasm, uncertain that their sacrifice was a necessity. When a year later they did go to war, it was as a united nation, convinced that no policy of further appeasement and no amount of patience would save them from ultimate destruction or from slavery to what they had at long last been forced to recognise as an atrocious, world-devouring tyranny. This was Mr. Chamberlain's achievement.

On the day the Munich Agreement was signed Gort wrote to Lady Marjorie: "Obviously it can only be a respite, though a most valuable one . . . we are nowhere near ready and it is foolish not to make supreme efforts now to put our house in order, cost what it may."

CHAPTER 9

RESPITE

THE respite gained at Munich was the signal for increased activity in the three Service Departments, convinced as they all were that war was now certain and, after the dress rehearsal, more conscious than ever of their unreadiness for the final raising of the curtain. All the same, such concessions as Hitler, without a flicker of sincerity, had given at Munich had to be treated as if they were part of a permanent settlement. There was to be an international commission to delimit the new Czechoslovak frontier and, in the meanwhile, an international force to police the disputed areas. Gort was a realist. Drawing on an apparently inexhaustible supply of tiger-shooting metaphors derived from his Indian experiences, he wrote: "Now they all think in this country that it is possible to ignore another well-known rule of the jungle and that is that, having killed your tiger, you always throw stones at him before you descend from your machan to make sure he is really dead. They all seem to think all precautions can be relaxed at once with no further thought." "They," however, did not include the Secretary of State for War and the General Staff, nor the Admiralty and Air Ministry.

Gort's first duty was to provide the British element of the international contingent for Czechoslovakia. It was, he wrote, believed "that the British Legion and the *Anciens Combattants* would be more acceptable to the Czechs than actual troops, but I hope that will die as nobody will be received with open arms there and it is more than likely that unarmed legionaries 'doing policeman' will get embroiled with Communists and others out to make rows". He proposed instead to send a contingent of the Brigade of Guards, the Gordon Highlanders and the King's Own Yorkshire Light Infantry, under the command of General Andrew Thorne, since "I wanted battalions that would look smart and also that were up to strength, so as to impress the Germans that we have got some troops." The Germans, for their part, continued by a series of skilful delays and prevarications to ensure that no international contingent or commission set foot in

the disputed area, and Gort was soon left free to prepare his
battalions for more arduous duties.

Nothing could be done until the extent of their task had been
firmly established and the requisite funds provided. There were
still political and administrative battles to be fought. Towards the
end of October the War Office submitted to the Cabinet a clear
statement of the essential requirements for a British Field Force
equipped to fight on the Continent. The Cabinet immediately
referred this distasteful subject to a Special Sub-Committee. The
Special Sub-Committee felt that some of the matters under discussion were outside its terms of reference and remitted the
problem to the Committee of Imperial Defence which duly failed
to reach any conclusion and passed the papers on to the Chiefs of
Staff. Meanwhile, late in November, the Prime Minister went to
Paris with Halifax in order to discuss these and other matters with
the French Government, but he omitted to consult the Cabinet
Sub-Committee, the C.I.D. or the Chiefs of Staff before setting
off on his journey.

Hore Belisha fought gallantly for approval of the General
Staff's demands both at the Cabinet and the C.I.D. There was no
equivocation. The Cabinet were told that "The General Staff
wish formally to call attention to the fact that present arrangements will not permit the Army to meet satisfactorily or safely the
responsibilities it may be called upon to discharge in accordance
with its approved role". This did not prevent Hoare from declaring that it was wrong to draw any distinction between units
employed on anti-aircraft defence and the rest of the army, or
Simon, in his capacity as watchdog of the country's financial
resources, from proposing niggardly economies. Hore Belisha
eventually found an ally in Halifax who, especially after his visit
to Paris with the Prime Minister, was aware that the promise of a
British contribution on land was an essential factor in maintaining
the morale and determination of a French Government already
demoralised by internal dissensions, by rising Fascist sympathies
on the right and by Communist disaffection on the left. It was,
however, left to Gort to conduct the main battle for the future of
the army, a battle which opened at the meeting of the Chiefs of
Staff on 21st December.

He asked his colleagues to recommend to Ministers a Field
Force of two mobile divisions and four infantry divisions fully
equipped for war in western Europe. Two of these divisions
should be ready to embark in fourteen days, instead of twenty-one

as hitherto proposed, and two more fourteen days later. War equipment and reserves should also be made available to four Territorial divisions, prepared to leave for the front four months after mobilisation, and a more realistic scale of armament should be supplied to all the remaining Territorials. The First Sea Lord, Sir Roger Backhouse, after stressing his opposition to unlimited commitments and maintaining there were neither sufficient men nor productive capacity to build up all three services, finally supported Gort's proposals provided the Field Force was limited in size. The Chief of the Air Staff, Sir Cyril Newall, scenting that additional funds coveted by the Air Ministry might be diverted to the War Office, spoke strongly against the scheme. If four divisions were despatched initially, the country would be committed to unlimited land warfare, a prospect unacceptable to the people. He was therefore opposed to equipping the Territorial Army for offensive war. He went too far when he expressed doubt whether a German occupation of the Channel ports and the airfields of northern France would necessarily be fatal. This heresy was roundly condemned by the First Sea Lord, who remembered that in the previous war there had been an anti-submarine net stretched across the Straits of Dover and firmly anchored in allied territory at Calais.

In reply Gort quoted Kitchener's statement that no country could wage "a little war". If hostilities broke out, the very existence of the British Empire would be at stake and it would be a fight to the finish. A definite undertaking to support France with land forces might induce the French authorities to dispose some of their troops, perhaps ten divisions, for the defence of Holland and Belgium, both of vital strategic importance to Britain. If the British gave no such undertaking, the French would merely defend the Maginot Line on the German and Belgian frontiers. It seems that at this stage he had little idea of the weakness of the French defence preparations north of the Maginot Line.

Gort made a spirited defence of his proposals, refusing to be diverted to the discussion of other potential areas of hostility, since he asserted that Germany itself was "the keystone to the enemy's arch", and emphasising the folly of maintaining the existing plan under which two fully equipped divisions would alone be sent to assist the French army. How could such a force stand up indefinitely to hammer-blows without relief from home by units fully trained and armed? If the Territorials were given only training equipment, it would be fully ten months after mobilisation before they were ready to fight.

With little sense of urgency as far as the needs of the army were concerned, Newall, in his capacity as chairman, adjourned the discussion until after Christmas. Gort seized the opportunity for a brief skiing holiday at Suvretta, the last he was ever to enjoy, but he returned before the middle of January to pursue his vital objective and continue arguing his case. His demand, he said, was a moderate one when seen against the background of £2,000 million granted for all defence purposes and only £277 million of this vast amount allotted jointly to the army and A.D.G.B. Indeed, of the army's comparatively small allocation, only £78 million was intended for the Field Force which he was striving to form and to train and which was by any standards "a very modest affair for an Empire like ours".

By the end of the month he had, with increasing support from the Admiralty, won his battle and the whole issue was referred back to the Cabinet where Hore Belisha fought valiantly for his department, encouraged still further by the fact that the C.I.D. were showing signs of recommending approval of his project to establish a Ministry of Supply. Lord Halifax, declaring that he would prefer bankruptcy to defeat by Germany, was a potent counter-weight to Simon and Hoare, however much the latter might keep on repeating that the money demanded, some £80 million in all, would be better spent on still more anti-aircraft guns and searchlights. Now, for the first time, Hore Belisha obtained agreement to equip even the first two divisions of the Field Force on a full war standard, and in mid-February, more than four months after Munich, the Regular Army and the Territorial Army were given at least the major part of the funds they required to prepare for the tasks confronting them. For the sake of financial decency some economies were imposed, even at this stage, by postponing planned dates of embarkation, by slightly reducing the standard of equipment for the Territorials and by refusing to authorise more than one "Colonial Division" for the reinforcement of overseas territories. However, a further £55 million were made available for the Field Force and Hoare was kept happy with £33 million more for the Air Defence of Great Britain. The German army was in the fourth and final year of its rearmament programme; the British army was effectively entering on its first with the grant of an additional sum equivalent to much less than the cost of one week's full warfare.

The task was made no easier by a temporary relaxation of international tensions in the new year. On 10th March Chamberlain incurred the wrath of the Foreign Office, and evoked a private letter of remonstrance from Halifax, when he told the lobby correspondents about his expectations of a peaceful future and his hopes for a general disarmament conference in the autumn. However, five days later Hitler, having first promoted an attempted breakaway by the Slovaks from their Czech partners, occupied Prague and the whole of Czechoslovakia. On 21st March he seized the Lithuanian port of Memel, which had always been on his long list of intended acquisitions. Then on Good Friday, 7th April, Mussolini, anxious not to seem backward in the game of grab, occupied Albania and at a single blow knocked down the card-house of Anglo-Italian goodwill which Chamberlain had been sedulously building in the hope of keeping the Axis powers divided. In the course of three weeks the cloud-capped towers of Munich had dissolved.

Poland was next on Hitler's list. The neighbouring Free City of Danzig was known to be occupied by a well-trained band of German "tourists" who would, on instructions, perform services comparable to those of Henlein and his Sudetens in Czechoslovakia. Adjacent to Danzig, the Polish Corridor, the country's only access to the sea, was a creation of the Treaty of Versailles and as such an object of particular hatred to Hitler. By fastening like vultures on the corpse of Czechoslovakia, and ripping away Teschen, the Poles had earned the disapproval of the Western Powers; but they at least had an army. It was nothing like so modern as the Czech army and its generals had a well known penchant for cavalry charges against whatever odds; but it presented the last measurable obstacle to Germany's designs in eastern Europe short of the Russian frontier. If neither the Polish method of Government nor their recent activities endeared them to the British, their long endurance and past misfortunes did. The recreation of a Polish state had been one of the few constructive results of the world war. Like the Cavaliers in "1066 and All That", the Poles were widely held to be "wrong but romantic", whereas the Czechs, like the Roundheads, had been "right but repulsive".

Two days after the occupation of Prague, Chamberlain, depressed and disillusioned, had made a speech to the citizens of Birmingham which announced his conversion to the belief that appeasement was at an end. There is no zeal to equal that of a

convert. *Monsieur J'aime Berlin*, as the French had irreverently
and unfairly nicknamed him, did not lose hope, but he did resolve
that Hitler, unfaithful to the trust Chamberlain had put in his
word, should be left in no doubt that Britain would resist the
seizure of any other independent states by the German army.
Poland was threatened, Roumania was threatened and once the
Italian imitator had digested Albania he might turn hungry
eyes on Greece. It should never again be said, as it had been in
August, 1914, that Germany went to war in the belief that the
British Empire would remain neutral.

Conscription in Britain would hearten the French, who had
asked for it before Munich, and might be a deterrent to the
Germans. However, such a measure in peacetime would be
unprecedented, shocking to deeply held convictions and resisted
by the Trade Unions. Even an unofficial "go-slow" would
dislocate the rearmament programme. Therefore, without so
much as consulting Gort or Adam, Hore Belisha proposed to
Chamberlain as an alternative to conscription the doubling of the
Territorial Army from thirteen to twenty-six divisions. Gort was in
France, deep in discussions with Gamelin, when the measure was
announced on 29th March and he must have had difficulty in
explaining to the French his failure to inform them of this welcome
proposal. It was indeed welcome, except to those who were
already struggling to find instructors, arms, equipment and
accommodation for the existing thirteen Territorial divisions.
Even Lord Chatfield, who had succeeded Inskip as Minister for
Co-ordination of Defence, first heard of the decision at a Cabinet
Meeting on the day after it had been taken.

Determined to prove the British Government were in earnest,
Chamberlain next announced a guarantee to Poland. It has in all
seriousness been suggested by some post-war writers that this step
drove Hitler to resolve on war. The implication that Hitler would
have rested content with his existing booty is a curiously ludicrous
one. The guarantee did make Britain's intentions clear and it was
received with general acclaim, especially in France. It was
followed by the creation of a Ministry of Supply, for which Hore
Belisha had long been pressing, and by guarantees to Roumania
and Greece. Churchill, though supporting the guarantee to
Poland, pertinently inquired in the House of Commons whether
the General Staff had been consulted about the means of implementing it. They had not been consulted: if they had, they
could only have advised that it would be just as impracticable

to give active military support to Poland as to Czechoslovakia.

Hitler's reply to this catalogue of challenges was to denounce the Anglo-German naval treaty and to tear up unilaterally the Polish-German Pact of Non-Aggression. He took these steps on 28th April. Next day Chamberlain, without any prior consultation with the Labour Party, the Liberals or the Trade Unions, and contrary to a number of previous pledges given in the House of Commons, authorised Hore Belisha to announce the introduction of conscription. It was a measure restricted in scope, but it was a dramatic declaration of new principle in the face of an approaching emergency so grave that past undertakings, given in different circumstances, faded into insignificance. Praise has justly been given to Hore Belisha, who saw that the temporary dislocation of a War Office mechanism already strained to the limit by the doubling of the Territorials was outweighed by the political significance at home and abroad.

The most determined admirer of the British system of Parliamentary Government must pause for reflection when he considers that after Hitler's ruthless intentions had been made clear beyond further dispute, after scores of Jewish and Liberal refugees had poured into horrified British ears their accounts of concentration camps and Gestapo methods, after the size and efficiency of the German war machine had been patently exposed, two such undoubted patriots as Mr. Attlee and Sir Archibald Sinclair, both men of truly noble character, smarting no doubt from Chamberlain's discourtesy in failing to consult them in advance, should have put the call of party solidarity before that of national safety and urged their followers in the House of Commons to refuse support of Hore Belisha's bold proposal for this limited measure of conscription. To their discredit they did so; nor is there reason to suppose that an opposing vote by the Labour Party or abstention by the Liberals were based on kindly consideration for the administrative difficulties facing the War Office. That was a problem for the generals.

The teeth of the British lion, though sorely in need of attention, had at last been bared. It was now vital to concert action with the French. The Front Populaire government, which had welded left wing Radicals, Socialists and Communists into one overtly enthusiastic but covertly disunited coalition, had ruled with increasing ineptitude and had in the name of democracy permitted strikes and demonstrations which brought French industry, and in particular the companies producing tanks, armaments and aircraft, into disarray. Daladier had at last rid himself of the Communists, but he was bitterly opposed by the parties on the right. However, the French army under the calm, too calm, leadership of Gamelin, stood aloof from these undignified wrangles. It was proudly conscious of its past glories, although an analytical observer might have noted that these glories stemmed principally from the era of the first Napoleon and from superb interludes in the First World War.

The British, with rare exceptions, looked upon the French army as invincible. Gort's personal admiration of the French was epitomised by Marshal Foch, whose command of the Anglo-French forces in 1918 seemed to him a model of military excellence and whose offensive philosophy appealed to him more than the fashionable creed in the superiority of defence preached by Liddell Hart. He was therefore determined that from the start a new British Expeditionary Force should be placed under French command; nor, indeed, would it have been sensible to suggest that so small a British contingent should act independently of the vast French armies with which it must co-operate. The experiment of independent command had been tried in August, 1914; but it was inconceivable that the early errors of the last war should be repeated. He did, however, point out to the Chiefs of Staff Committee that a cause contributory to the success of the Foch experiment had been a close personal relationship with Haig. The misfortune was that Gamelin was not Foch. Gort had no reason to doubt his ability, nor much evidence on which to assess it, but he had a personal preference for General Georges.

Gort's recommendation of a French commander for the allied armies was discussed with Gamelin in Paris, agreed by the Chiefs of Staff and brought before the Committee of Imperial Defence on 2nd May, 1939. He informed the committee that the proposed instructions to the British commander-in-chief were based on those given to Haig in 1918. The Minister for the Co-ordination of Defence, Chatfield, expressed the hope that the British army, which was no longer to be a Field Force of six divisions but eventually, since the events of March and April, an army of thirty-two divisions, would not in any circumstances be subordinated to the French political authorities but would be under the orders of a French supreme commander, himself subject to direction by an inter-allied council. The instructions issued to Haig by Lord Milner on 21st June, 1918, were produced and examined. In consequence the C.I.D. agreed on 24th July that the British commander should be subordinated to the French commander-in-chief provided that he "will be at liberty to appeal to his own Government before executing any order which appears to him to imperil the British Army".

Meanwhile full staff conversations had been authorised. Even before the Cabinet had agreed to any form of Continental commitment Adam, with Gort's full approval, sent Brigadier Hawes to Paris to make detailed plans for the movement by boat and rail of a British Field Force to France. This was the first Anglo-French contact on a practical military basis since 1935, when war had seemed a possible result of the sanctions imposed on Italy as a punishment for her unprovoked attack on Abyssinia and Adam had been sent to Paris for conversations with Generals Gamelin, Georges and Coulsen. They had been hampered by the discovery that the maps in the French War Department stopped short at Switzerland: there was none of the Franco-Italian border. By March, 1939, the appropriate maps were fortunately available and some agreement was reached about the scope of useful exchanges of information. In the light of events, Gort dropped his opposition to disclosing the weakness of the British contribution, and such was the urgency of the situation that the Cabinet and the C.I.D. were obliged to suppress their fear of the Field Force being committed to employment in accordance with French plans which the British General Staff were uninformed.

Gort himself went over to France in March. His visit included a stay at Rheims, where the French spent more time showing him the Cathedral and the Pommery wine cellars than in discussing military matters, but where he did meet the commander of the 1st Light Mechanised Division, which he subsequently inspected in detail. At Metz he was introduced to General Giraud, an officer whom, then and later, Anglo-Saxons tended to find more impressive than did some of his own compatriots. He was taken on a tour of the Maginot Line, interrupted by a splendid ceremonial tattoo at Nancy, and was duly satisfied as to the strength of the defences, although he observed that no provision had been made against concentrated aerial attack. He was not shown the slender defences in the north, between the extremity of the Maginot Line and the sea.

Before setting off to meet Gamelin in Paris he advocated complete frankness, even to the extent of telling the French about the new British inventions of RADAR and the ASDIC anti-submarine device. On 26th April he wrote to Gamelin giving him formal

notice that it would in eighteen months' time be practicable
to despatch six regular divisions to France within six weeks of the
outbreak of war, and that these would be followed by ten
Territorial divisions during the fourth, fifth and sixth months
while the remaining sixteen divisions would be ready to embark
between the ninth and the twelfth month. If war broke out earlier
it would still be possible to send two divisions abroad in three
weeks and eight more within five months. Anglo-French conversations now proceeded at an accelerated pace, not only in
Paris and London but also in Rabat, where the North African
scene could be more readily inspected. The French were unwilling
to disclose the intended use or location of the British contingent
on its arrival in France. There was much discussion of the employment of the Advanced Air Striking Force, which the British were
to send to France with their Expeditionary Force but which the
Air Ministry were not prepared to submit to the control of either
the British military commander or of his French superior. The
Air Ministry were also invited to consider making the full strength
of Bomber Command available to stem a German advance, an
invitation which was coldly received in Whitehall. Finally the
British Chiefs of Staff ventured to lay emphasis on the importance
of retaining an adequate number of divisions in reserve, both to
resist a potential invasion of Holland and Belgium and to provide
the means of counter-attack. History gives no account of General
Gamelin's reaction to this recommendation.

Considering that it had been laid down, as recently as January,
1938, that equipment justified solely by a hypothetical Continental
commitment should not be provided, the speed with which the
army's rearmament programme began to be effective was commendable. As late as January, 1939, Gort complained that only
30 per cent of the engineering industry was employed on the
production of armaments, but the events of March and the
subsequent creation of a Ministry of Supply induced a notable
acceleration. In March the projected Field Force was still to be
protected by 3-inch anti-aircraft guns of the First World War
pattern. During the summer 3.7-inch and 4.5-inch guns began to
flow from the factories and 2-pounder anti-tank guns were also
becoming available. British industry had, by no means for the
last time, been hampered by its own perfectionism. Tanks, guns,
equipment of all kinds, which might well by now have been in
ample supply, had been withheld from the production lines
because of some new and improved design. Now, however, mass-

production was seen to be urgent and the perfectionists were obliged to hold their peace when the number of divisions to be equipped had been so greatly increased. The acute shortage was tanks: there were to be two mobile, or armoured, divisions and there was a need for heavy or medium tanks in addition to the light tanks in which the planners had put their main faith. To expedite production one of the leading tank experts, Martel, had concluded that an all-purposes cruiser tank, with armour as heavy as it could carry, should be developed in preference to two separate designs, one heavy and one medium. Gort encouraged this proposal, and with his strong support it was approved in 1938; but it was too late to be of significant value in 1940. Britain went to war with two designs of heavy infantry tank: the Mark I, armed with nothing more than a machine-gun and already obsolescent; and the Mark II, with its improved design and 2-pounder gun, but only just in production.

Gort had disturbing preoccupations in foreign fields. In February he visited Palestine and Egypt, where only eighteen thousand British troops were available to face Mussolini's Libyan hosts. He was contemptuous of the Italian army and in any case they could not be expected to throw their whole force against Egypt while they were threatened by the French on Libya's western frontier; but it was none the less evident that Egypt was inadequately defended. Arrangements had to be made, in the face of some political opposition at home, to despatch reinforcements from India and Palestine. Moreover, the choice of a new and more dynamic commander-in-chief, Middle East, was more than a routine necessity. The Japanese, too, were showing signs of hostility and it was impossible to disregard the facts that in Manchuria, which they had invaded in 1931, they were aggressors comparable to the Italians in Abyssinia and the Germans in Central Europe and that they were openly declared adherents to the Berlin-Rome Axis. Now, in 1939, they seized and maltreated a number of British subjects in Tientsin and there were indications that they might be preparing for active support of their fellow Axis miscreants in Europe. Hasty consideration had to be given to improving the security of Singapore, Hong Kong, Australia and New Zealand against Japanese attack, so that all three Chiefs of Staff were obliged to devote much time and many meetings to Far Eastern affairs.

These diversions from the European scene added to the general strain, but without direction of labour there was nothing further

Commander in
Chief, British
Expeditionary Force

A Pride of Field Marshals, March 1940 (left to right: Deverell, Birdwood, Duke of Gloucester, Jacob and Montgomery-Massingberd

that could be done to expedite the output of arms, and at the working level Anglo-French staff conversations were now pursuing a somewhat languid course. Since Gort had been shown the tattoo at Nancy, it was desirable to prove that the British could do still better at Aldershot. Dill, who was in command there, gladly invited Gamelin and it was arranged that, in case the Aldershot Tattoo was insufficient, he should see the Trooping of the Colour as well. He duly came to London at the end of the first week in June. There was a reception at the French Embassy during which the Military Attaché, General Lelong, who was well informed of Gamelin's views and was also disposed to talk to Hore Belisha behind the backs of the General Staff, came up to Beaumont Nesbitt, now a brigadier working in the War Office. He pointed to Gort and said in a somewhat peremptory manner that when the time came to despatch the British Field Force to France, there was a man who would be acceptable to the French as its commander. General Ironside, he added, would not. There can be little doubt that either Lelong or Gamelin himself made a similar communication to Hore Belisha.

Gamelin had discussions with Gort while his personal adviser and assistant, Colonel Petibon, talked to Pownall about such matters as the British military missions to be attached to the French headquarters, the role of the British air forces, the likely place of the British Field Force "in the line" and the possibilities of "irregular warfare", a subject to which the British had given much consideration and the French had given none. It was important to clear the air with Colonel Petibon because he had recently told the British Military Attaché in Paris that in the event of the Germans attacking in the east and merely holding their line in the west, the French would, as Gamelin had said the previous September, undertake offensives "well prepared but with limited objectives", by which, of course, he meant skirmishes in front of the Siegfried Line. If, Petibon added, the Germans attacked in the west, the French would make no positive suggestions to the Poles but would warn them against being too ambitious and trying to reach Berlin in a day. It was reported that the Poles were, not surprisingly, "a little disappointed that the French were not prepared to go bald-headedly for the Germans".

The 14th July, one hundred and fiftieth anniversary of the Fall of the Bastille, presented another ceremonial opportunity for visiting France and for holding serious discussions in the intervals of taking the salute, side by side with Gamelin, at the Champs

Elysées parade and attending official receptions. Gort set off for Paris, taking Jacqueline as well as Pownall and his deputy, Brigadier John Kennedy. Now, for the first time, agreement was reached on the exact concentration area, north-west of Amiens, for the British Field Force. It was suggested that the British should be on the left of the line, with their flank on the sea, unless the Belgian army were also engaged. In that event the Belgians would be next to the sea and the British placed between them and the French. Both for ease of communications and because the British, to whom the Channel ports appeared particularly vital, should have the task of defending them, this arrangement seemed entirely logical both to Gort and to Gamelin, though the latter did at one point mention the possibility of French forces joining the Belgians on the British left. Since enemy aircraft must not be allowed to hinder disembarkation, the British army would land at Cherbourg and at west coast ports far from the scene of action. There was to be a British Military Mission, under Brigadier Swayne, at the headquarters of General Georges, who would be in command of all the armies in north-east France, and another mission, directly representing the C.I.G.S., at Gamelin's own headquarters.

With these and many other details settled, Gort flew home on the night of 15th July. There was little more that could be planned or decided by the soldiers alone: it was up to the politicians to declare war or peace and to give the marching orders if the time came.

CHAPTER 10

CLIMAX

In January, 1939, Gort told the Chiefs of Staff Committee that "it was dangerous to imagine it would be sufficient for the French to hold the Maginot Line to win the war"; but in April the French stated bluntly that the principal aim of allied strategy should be to maintain the integrity of French territory. If the Low Countries were invaded by Germany, then a front should be held as far forward as circumstances permitted and the prospective lines of defence must be examined. The difficulty was how to honour the guarantee to Poland if, as was now generally expected, the Germans attacked eastwards and merely retained sufficient troops in the west to hold their Siegfried Line from Switzerland to Luxembourg.

The recommendation laid before the Chiefs of Staff was that France and Great Britain should in that event "exert all possible pressure on Germany by sea, land and air". This would mean a naval blockade, liable to be weakened if Italy remained neutral and imported goods on Germany's behalf; an assault by the French army on the Siegfried Line, which aroused no enthusiasm in Paris; and an air attack on Germany, principally by Bomber Command of the R.A.F. since the French air force was out of date and under strength.

The British and French Governments, conscious of Germany's air superiority and of the speed with which the Luftwaffe might be transferred from the Polish to the Western Front, were opposed to opening an air offensive against military targets, oil installations or armament factories in Germany. It was, they thought, wiser to conserve their own striking force and not to invite powerful and almost certainly indiscriminate retaliation, at least until allied bombers could be used with maximum effect. It would be folly to risk the piecemeal destruction of their limited bombing strength in raids which could have no practical influence on the course of a German campaign against Poland. As the crisis approached, the French let it be known that they intended to bomb communications behind the Siegfried Line and they hoped the R.A.F. would assist in this task. Newall gave a flat refusal: such action would result in heavy casualties and would bring no relief to the Poles. He indignantly protested that the French request amounted to using the R.A.F. in support of a land campaign on the western front. Gort found this proposal much less shocking than Newall. It would, he insisted, be important to reduce the weight of attack on Poland. The subject of an aerial offensive had been under discussion with the French for many months, but by 29th August, 1939, no policy decision had been made or recommendations forwarded to the Cabinet.

Only Russia could provide material assistance to Poland, but there were doubts in western minds whether the Russian army was much more efficient than it had been in 1914. As late as 22nd June, 1941, Sir John Dill, by then C.I.G.S., said at Chequers that he did not believe the Russians could hold out more than six weeks against the German attack which had begun that morning. This was a false estimate in the summer of 1941, but it can scarcely be doubted that in August, 1939, the overpurged Russian army was incapable of taking the offensive against Germany. However, the moral effect of a war on two fronts would have been as important as the practical and Gort believed that the mere threat of it might preserve the peace. The Chiefs of Staff favoured a treaty of mutual assistance between Great Britain, France and Russia and on 16th May they had recorded their conviction that failure to achieve such an agreement would be a diplomatic defeat, would encourage Hitler to further acts of aggression and might ultimately throw the U.S.S.R. and Germany into each other's arms. They considered it important to obtain something more substantial than the bare neutrality of Russia.

A Foreign Office mission under Mr. William Strang was sent to Moscow in June and over the weeks of negotiation he was authorised to surrender point after point to meet Soviet demands. The mission was not, however, prepared or empowered to concede to Russia a free hand in Finland or the Baltic States of Lithuania Latvia and Estonia, small anti-Communist republics which Stalin had every intention of devouring. Nor was its task made easier by the Polish conviction that Russian troops on Polish soil would be every bit as dangerous to the country's independence as an invading German army. This fear was shared, with equal foresight, by the Roumanians who knew that Stalin looked covetously on their province of Bessarabia.

The Russians kept their options open. They negotiated secretly with the Germans at the same time as they were talking to the western allies. The belated arrival in Moscow of a British Military Mission under the leadership of Admiral the Honourable Sir Reginald Plunkett-Ernle-Erle-Drax, whose name was longer and more distinguished than his instructions, failed to impress them. The Soviet Ambassador in London, Ivan Maisky, later told Lord Boothby that his Government had expected a mission headed by Gort and Gamelin. Maisky, during and after the war, devoted much time and thought to justifying the unjustifiable, perhaps in an endeavour to atone for his earlier activities in favour of an alliance with the western powers and his intimate discussions with Winston Churchill. Entire credence should not therefore be given to his statements. It cannot be supposed that a visit to Moscow by Gort and Gamelin, unless they had been instructed to renounce all interest in the liberty of Finland and the Baltic States, would have altered the course of events. A rebuff to them would, however, have been more serious than to Admiral Drax and his French colleague. It would have provided Dr. Goebbels with a rich propaganda feast. The replacement of Litvinov, who was a man of some idealism, by Stalin's dour, time-serving henchman, Molotov, had already removed any small hope that motives other than *raison d'état* could marginally affect the Kremlin's choice. The Russians were frightened: they might later speak disparagingly of Munich and hint that if they had been approached at the right time they would have thrown in their lot with the western powers, but this was to excuse a *volte-face* made without the smallest consideration of right and wrong, and so calculated as to bring them substantial territorial acquisitions in payment for giving Hitler a free hand to make war. They chose appeasement with an eye to the main chance.

It was recognised in London that there must be some Anglo-French machinery for the higher direction of the war. Ismay, who was Hankey's successor at the C.I.D., was despatched to Paris to discuss the matter with Gamelin. There was a major difficulty because whereas in London each step in the Anglo-French staff conversations had been endorsed by Ministers, in Paris the French General Staff had withheld all strategic plans from their political chiefs for fear of leakage. French military policy had thus been settled by Gamelin alone, and a British proposal that Chamberlain, accompanied by one other Minister and the three Chiefs of Staff, should form a Supreme War Council with their equal and opposite French delegates was not immediately practicable. However, Gamelin agreed that if war actually broke out there should be a Council empowered to make recommendations to the two Governments about the higher conduct of the war.

Still more curious than this failure to establish, well in advance, allied machinery for the conduct of the war was the absence of discussion in British Government circles about the choice of a commander of the Field Force. This was because the ruling cabal was utterly divorced, in interest and experience, from military affairs. The command would be of vital interest to the nation: yet, subject to the Cabinet's final endorsement, Chamberlain was content to leave the decision to the Secretary of State for War. Hore Belisha did give thought to the question and in May he consulted Liddell Hart. He did not mention Gort, of whom he hoped to dispose by appointing him commander-in-chief in India; but he sought Liddell Hart's comments on Alexander, Dill, Maitland Wilson, Wavell and Ironside and concluded that the best would be Ironside in spite of Liddell Hart's preference for Adam and high recommendation of Pile or Hobart. He accordingly brought Ironside back from Gibraltar where Gort had persuaded the Colonial Office to send him a year previously with an important additional responsibility as overseer of plans, forces and strategy in the eastern Mediterranean. Ironside was appointed Inspector General of Overseas Forces, but he was based in the United Kingdom and he had, or assumed he had, direct access to the Secretary of State. He believed that the reversion to command of the Field Force was his, since Sir John French had briefly held the same appointment in 1914, and Hore Belisha, openly or tacitly, encouraged him in this conviction. Sir John Dill had succeeded Wavell as Commander-in-Chief, Southern Command. He also had some reason to believe that he would be considered the appropriate choice for command of a British Expeditionary Force proceeding overseas. After the war Sir James Grigg, who was at the War Office from 1939 to 1945, first as Permanent Under Secretary and then as Secretary of State, maintained that Hore Belisha had led Dill to believe he would be chosen. Certainly in June, during Gamelin's visit for the Aldershot Tattoo, there were conversations between leading staff officers in which Dill's name was freely used as if he were the accepted nominee for command. One of the records included this sentence: "The French higher command intended to place French units and formations under General Dill's command in war in order to bring him up to the

status of an Army Commander from the start". In a subsequent
memorandum to the C.I.G.S., the Director of Military Operations
and Intelligence referred to Dill in a context which could only
imply that he was commander-in-chief elect. The natural
adviser to the Secretary of State in deciding this important matter
was the C.I.G.S.; but the relations between Hore Belisha and
Gort were by now so strained that Sir Ronald Adam was at times
obliged to act as the agent of communication between them.

This unhappy development was mainly due to a clash of conflicting and mutually unsympathetic temperaments. It was
exacerbated by the distaste and in many cases contempt which
Hore Belisha's mania for publicity, in the interests of the army
and coincidentally himself, had engendered in the Army Council
and in a high proportion of the other soldiers in contact with the
General Staff. One of the most vehement in his dislike was the
Director of Military Operations and Intelligence, Major-General
H. R. Pownall, a devoted admirer of Gort and one of his principal
lieutenants. The antagonism was immediately sensed by Sir James
Grigg, universally known as "P. J.", whom Sir Horace Wilson had
selected to succeed the quiet, competent but conventional Sir
Herbert Creedy as the principal civil servant in the War Office
and non-political head of the department. On 25th May, 1939,
Grigg, about to begin a few months' indoctrination, wrote to his
father: "Before we left London I saw Hore Belisha and had lunch
with Gort. I can see that the War Office is by no means a happy
family and that I shall have to tread warily if I am to have any
influence in keeping the show together. On a minor scale H-B feels
very much like L.G. did about the soldiers, and the soldiers
certainly feel about H-B what their predecessors in 1918 did about
L.G."

There was nothing quiet nor conventional about "P. J.". He
had been Principal Private Secretary to Churchill when Chancellor
of the Exchequer and he was subsequently Finance Member
of the Viceroy's Council in India. Brilliantly clever, honest and
indefatigable, he was outspoken to the point of rudeness and it
never crossed his mind to suffer fools gladly. He respected men for
their competence and not in the least for their position. If he
thought ill of the Minister he served, he said so to all and sundry,
including the Minister. He held truthfulness to be a cardinal
virtue, tact a social affectation. He was respected by all, feared by
many and loved only by the few who had experience of his more
sterling qualities. Hore Belisha, delighted by the prospect of such

a dynamic successor to Creedy, had little idea what a sea green incorruptible Tartar he was welcoming into the uneasy fold of the War Office.

In the last week of June "P. J.", to whom Creedy was in the process of handing over, wrote: "The civilian staff are jaded and overworked, and Hore Belisha is obviously encouraging the soldiers to brush them aside. All the same I get the idea that the machine, both civil and military, isn't a bad one and that the shortcomings are due partly to the absence of any coherent policy on the part of the Government and partly to H B being so much of a stunt-merchant. I haven't had any business to do with him yet and on the few occasions I have seen him he has spent his time blackguarding the rest of the office, soldiers and civilians alike."

Gort's indignation had been building up since the early days of his appointment as C.I.G.S. In recent months there had been a number of specific irritants, against which he insufficiently balanced the qualities Hore Belisha had displayed in battling for the army at the Cabinet, in the C.I.D. and in Parliament. Among Gort's understandable grievances was his Secretary of State's failure to consult him about appointments. Hore Belisha replaced Sir Clive Liddell, the adjutant-general, by Sir Robert Gordon-Finlayson, brought Ironside home and selected Sir Walter Kirke as Inspector-General of Home Forces without giving Gort due opportunity to reflect and comment, even though the last two of these appointments impinged on the authority of the C.I.G.S. He had talks with foreign military attachés, as well as with pillars of the British military establishment such as Field-Marshals Milne, Chetwode and Cavan, but did not disclose the subject matter to Gort. He attended a ministerial meeting to discuss control of the High Command in War without first talking the matter over with Gort, who was known to have firm views on the subject, or with Creedy. He made a decision about the new composition of the Army Council, consequent on the establishment of the Ministry of Supply, but did not so much as mention his intentions to its existing members. At the end of June, 1939, when activity in the War Office was at as high a pitch as it had ever been, Pownall recorded that during the whole month Hore Belisha had only sent for the C.I.G.S. on one occasion, and Gort's dislike for his Secretary of State was such that he declined to ask for interviews. Both Gort and Pownall thought that the selection of a new Commander-in-Chief, Middle East, at the end of June would be used as an opportunity to remove Gort to an overseas command, but in the event Hore Belisha accepted Gort's recommendation of Wavell and although relations only improved on the surface an open clash was avoided.

At the beginning of August, P. J. Grigg was installed in the seat of power at the War Office and quietly though he played his part in the early weeks of his appointment, the Army Council had in him a more powerful and persuasive ally than they had found in his sympathetic but less forceful predecessor, Creedy. When early in August Hore Belisha sought, for publicity reasons, to make the Deputy Director General of the Territorial Army a lieutenant-general, thus promoting him over the heads of officers holding more important appointments, Grigg sided with Gort and the new adjutant-general in opposing the promotion. He wrote to his father on 3rd August: "My first week at the W.O. is going smoothly so far. I can manage most of the soldiers, but Hore Belisha is going to be an awful trial and one or two of his soldier toadies will be a nuisance."

By no means a toady, and perhaps the most objective and unbiassed witness of the Hore Belisha/Gort antagonism was Major J. C. Haydon, military assistant to Hore Belisha until he left the War Office in the middle of July. He became deeply attached to Hore Belisha, although their association had started with a blazing row. He also respected and admired Gort, with whose military assistants he shared a room. There was nobody in a better position to observe the two men and he concluded that great as was the difference of character, outlook and method, a difference which evidently grated more on Gort than on Hore Belisha, they were by no means antagonistic in their attitude to matters of fundamental importance. However, they were never at ease with one another, even though both were modernisers, differing mainly in their views on timing, and both were fervent patriots united at least after Munich in their belief that war was a certainty.

On the other, less important side of the coin, Gort, for all his Irish blood, was English to the core, and he was the kind of Englishman who, while accepting genuine foreigners as a regrettable necessity, finds foreign touches and tendencies in a compatriot wholly repellent. To him the press was on a par of undesirability with professional politicians; Hore Belisha, once a journalist and now the most political of animals, found life blood where Gort found gall. Hore Belisha so mishandled the generals that characteristics which Haydon grew to accept as those of an engaging, colourful personality, were to them nothing but bad manners and lack of consideration.

It was because Hore Belisha, in some ways so artful, was in others incurably naïve that he failed to see where he gave offence and was surprised as well as distressed when he realised he was disliked. Gort was much to blame because he was incapable of providing Hore Belisha with the affection and understanding for which he yearned; nor did he allow him all the credit which was his due for making the army a career attractive to young men, for improving the conditions of service, for achieving conscription and the Ministry of Supply, for fighting the army's battles with his colleagues and, latterly, for exerting all his strength to help Gort obtain a modicum of fair treatment for the Field Force. A C.I.G.S. less formal in his official relationships, capable of over-looking or even, perhaps, laughing at obvious failings and willing to disregard petty irritations, might have gained Hore Belisha's confidence and been in a position to influence his decisions. Gort stood too firmly by his principles and it cannot be denied that he sometimes confused principle and prejudice.

Hore Belisha bore no malice. When he finally left the scene he told the House of Commons: "I did not select my collaborators upon the principle that they should be readily complacent or supinely acquiescent. I selected the strongest men whom I could find. I respected them most when they were most outspoken in council. It was not a dull or stagnant administration. If, from time to time, there have been differences of opinion, if there have been differences of outlook or temperament or understanding, they have been no deeper than must occur in any association of men engaged upon pressing tasks of more than transitory importance."

Parliament rose on 4th August, twenty-fifth anniversary of the outbreak of the last war. There was an international lull, only disturbed by the raucous anti-Polish propaganda from Berlin: but no lull before a storm has been more easily recognisable as such. The leaders of the British nation, dedicated to the precedent of Drake's famous game of bowls, set off on their holidays. After a superb spring the summer of 1939 had been grey, rainy and cold, so that some, including Hore Belisha, went abroad in search of the sun. Chamberlain entrained for the north of Scotland. The Chiefs of Staff, including a new First Sea Lord, Admiral Sir Dudley Pound, vanished from London and even General Ismay, who was the most conscientious slave of duty, found the Glorious Twelfth of August irresistible. Gort decided that a cruise in *Thanet* would be too risky and he therefore took Jacqueline to stay with Lord Leicester at Holkham and subsequently with the Dalrymple-Hamiltons in their yacht *Polar Star*. It was only for a few days and he spent them sailing in unfamiliar waters. As August drew on, the skies cleared and a hot, belated summer settled on the British Isles.

Hitler had fixed 3rd September for the annual Party Rally at Nuremberg, but in the middle of August British Intelligence ascertained that he had decreed priority for the movement by rail of additional troops for manœuvres near the Polish frontier where a large German army was already mobilised. It was known that the German railways could not, at one and the same time, transport large bodies of troops eastwards and the many thousands of storm troopers and party members expected at Nuremberg. By the afternoon of Saturday, 19th August, the news of troop movements was sufficiently disturbing to warrant the Chiefs of Staff being recalled to London. They met the following day, in stifling August heat, to prepare their list of defence requirements for the Prime Minister, who was hastily returning from Scotland. Writing late that evening to Lady Marjorie, at Holkham, Gort said: "I got up on time after travelling in a filthy dirty carriage such as only that Line could produce . . . we are in for a new crisis now, but actually I feel it is going to be far the worst we have ever been through. It seems almost impossible for Hitler to draw back now unless he is ready to lose some face, which is anathema to a dictator . . . Anyhow Hitler and Ribbentrop are now clear that further aggression on their part brings us in, which is all to the good."

On Tuesday, the 22nd, Hore Belisha came back from Cannes and the Cabinet approved a number of minor measures, such as the calling up of key men in Anti-Aircraft Command and Civil Defence; but that day there came, like the roar of a cannonade, news that Germany and Russia were about to sign a Pact of Non-Aggression. It was, Gort wrote, an action "beyond the pale of normal intercourse". The British and French missions were still in Moscow assiduously working with their Russian hosts on the details of a draft convention. Without a word of warning Stalin closed his other option and, at the expense of Poland, the Baltic States and the peace of Europe, supped with the devil. The Ribbentrop-Molotov pact was one of the most dramatic double-crosses in history; and it was one for which both parties paid with rivers of blood and the total destruction of large areas of their countries. Even those who still believed that Hitler was

bluffing and manœuvring for another Munich began to doubt
their own optimism: and yet on the following day the Cabinet
Committee on Defence Preparations refused Hore Belisha's
impassioned plea for authority to call up the Regular Army
reserves. Gort was bewildered by the news from Moscow. He
wrote to Jacqueline: "The Russian imbroglio is a real puzzle as
our Franco-British mission had another interview yesterday
afternoon. I fancy it is all a form of window-dressing and that
what Russia really wants is to stand clear of any European
struggle so as to be able to step in when everyone is exhausted."
It was a widely shared view.

The Cabinet hesitated to approve steps which the Chiefs of
Staff, and the War Office in particular, believed to be urgent.
Four days' notice was required for the evacuation of children to
the country, but Chamberlain feared that measures signifying the
imminence of war might provoke Hitler and drive him over the
brink on which he might be indecisively poised. Had he but
known, Hitler had given firm orders as long ago as 3rd April for
the invasion of Poland to be ready on 1st September. The Cabinet's
indecision, and more particularly the first weak and compromising
draft reply to a transparently dishonest letter from Hitler, offering
eternal friendship to the British Empire in return for a settlement
of the Polish question agreeable to himself, gave rise to suspicions
that Chamberlain and Sir Horace Wilson were indeed contemplating a second Munich. This was by no means true, but even
at this late stage Chamberlain, disillusioned though he might be,
hoped against hope that Hitler would draw back from the
precipice if he were not driven into one of his fits of ungovernable
frenzy by some ill-judged or provocative step. Hore Belisha, who
had been no wholehearted supporter of Munich, was opposed to
further appeasement but anxious to avoid going to war with an
unprepared army. He sought and received support for his usually
firm, but sometimes wavering, intentions from Gort, P. J. Grigg
and Pownall, and the coldness with which he had regarded Gort
throughout the summer began to thaw. If Gort reciprocated at all,
he effectively disguised the fact. "Belli," he wrote to Lady
Marjorie, "is hanging on to me like a leech at the moment and
indulges every short while in wishful thinking that war will not
come this year but will be certain next year. He then talked about
a General Election and whether it would be a good thing, etc –
hoping I suppose he would then get a less warlike post in the
next Cabinet." The last sentence was unfair to Hore Belisha, who,

according to his own lights, had fought so hard for his department.

On 27th August Gort set out his own simple views in a hastily scribbled letter to Lady Marjorie:

"A short line to say that in my opinion we have all to remain clear about our objective. It is to rid Germany of the present Nazi tyranny either (a) by war if necessary, which is an uneconomic method of achieving our aim or (b) by striking a blow at the régime in the diplomatic and political field. This latter can be achieved by bringing the issue at stake to the conference table either by direct contact between the two contestants or else under the guidance of say Roosevelt. Personally I would far prefer the latter as bringing the U.S.A. into the problem which in the end would be a good thing from our viewpoint. What must not happen is another Munich. . . . I can't disclose Hitler's letter beyond saying it contains much futile and cheeky muck, but that is only to be expected. He is in a jam and has to continue to bluff to the very last, even to war. The one thing I always fear is the resolution of your democratic leaders at the last, but we must do all we can to keep them up to scratch. . . ."

The War Office machinery revolved more smoothly than in the previous September. Soldiers and civilians alike knew what was expected of them. Their activities were restricted by an absence of decisions from 10 Downing Street, where hope of a settlement, perhaps through the good grace of Mussolini, still remained wanly alive. It was not till Thursday, 31st August, that authority was given to call up the Army Reserve. The evacuation of the children from London, which had been asked for on the previous Monday, was sanctioned the same day; and full censorship, agreed on Friday, 25th, and rescinded by Hoare on the 26th, was also put into force on the 31st. The roads and railways were subjected to an unnecessary strain by simultaneous evacuation and mobilisation because it was thought that any of these steps, if taken at an earlier stage, might have precipitated disaster. The British Ambassador in Berlin, Sir Nevile Henderson, had told Hore Belisha on 26th August that calling up the Territorial Army could make the difference between peace and war. It was important not to distress the highly excitable Führer.

In the early hours of Friday, 1st September, the German armies began their advance into Poland. It is noteworthy how distorted personal accounts can be in their record of details. Hore Belisha's diary states that Gort told him of the invasion by telephone at 5.30 a.m. Gort wrote that same day to Lady Marjorie saying he had been woken with the news at 7.0 a.m. Ironside records in his diary that he reached the Horse Guards at 10.0 a.m. and was informed of the event by a telephone call from Churchill, who had heard about it from the Polish Ambassador at 8.30 a.m. Ironside describes how he then rang up Gort, who said he did not believe it but, on being pressed, went to inform Hore Belisha. Many members of the British public, most of whom by 1939 had wireless sets, learned what had happened from the B.B.C. at breakfast time, long before Ironside arrived at the Horse Guards.

There could be no further hesitations as far as military preparations were concerned. All the forces of the Crown were mobilised and "the Precautionary Stage", for which the War Office had been clamouring for days, was officially authorised. In fact most of the preliminary necessities had already been arranged, without any detailed reference to Ministers, by a committee of Permanent Under Secretaries which had been meeting daily in Whitehall under the chairmanship of Sir Edward Bridges, Secretary of the Cabinet. The War Book, containing instructions for all immediate actions, military and civil, had been brought up to date well in advance of the emergency. There were, however, hesitations on the political front. The French were alarmed by the prospect of bombardment if an ultimatum were sent to Berlin while they were still completing their mobilisation and moving their divisions to the preordained assembly areas. Moreover, the Italians attempted to arrange a conference of heads of Government on the Munich model. Chamberlain was faced with a restive Cabinet and an increasingly suspicious, bellicose House of Commons, representing an electorate no less united in its determination, while he delayed the despatch of the fatal ultimatum which must mean the collapse of all his hopes and the failure of his long, deeply sincere struggle for peace.

On 3rd September war was declared on Germany. The millions who had cheered for Munich almost unanimously resolved that peace could be bought too dearly. The former members of the Oxford Union who had voted not to fight for their king and country volunteered to do so. The enthusiastic signatories of peace ballots and pledges became equally enthusiastic for battle. The Parliamentary Labour Party had sat approvingly behind Arthur Greenwood as, speaking for England, he led the cry for war at any price, war without even waiting to make sure the French were in line, war without stopping to think too hard about the country's ability to wage it. None of the expected and dreaded consequences occurred. It was indeed bewildering: the air raid sirens duly sounded, but no enemy air-craft appeared and the tower of St. Martin-in-the-Fields did not crash on the terrified populace. On the contrary, it was a calm and beautiful day and Whitehall was filled with conscientious officials who had overcome their reluctance to report for duty on the Sabbath but now found they had practically nothing to do. At 10 Downing Street, however, there was one important decision which still had to be taken: the appointment of a commander-in-chief of the Field Force, on which the 1914 title of "British Expeditionary Force" was now conferred.

Since Ironside had been brought back from Gibraltar with this appointment in mind, he had every reason to believe that it was reserved for him. The senior general on the active list, a man of impressive appearance and dynamic personality, a brilliant linguist who knew all Europe from north to south and east to west, an expert in military training and an enthusiast for mechanical warfare, he nevertheless had his detractors in the War Office and he could be outspokenly tactless to important politicians. He was, however, admired by Winston Churchill, with whom he had stayed at Chartwell shortly before the outbreak of war and who had now become not only First Lord of the Admiralty but also a member of Chamberlain's small War Cabinet. Ironside had been more or less promised the command by Hore Belisha and there were times in the summer of 1939 when Gort resented some of Ironside's initiatives which seemed to trespass on the prerogatives of the C.I.G.S. It is, however, difficult to blame Ironside: he believed that he must prepare himself for a job of the greatest importance in the shortest possible time, and since he served a Secretary of State who was in the habit of taking short cuts he saw no valid reason for not pursuing the same path.

However, in the course of the summer a number of factors militated against the choice of Ironside. According to De Guingand, who succeeded Haydon as Hore Belisha's military assistant, he lost favour by the directness of his approach to the Secretary of State, demanding personal consideration of matters which even Hore Belisha thought should first have been referred to the C.I.G.S. Then the French took against him and a few days before war broke out Gort told Lady Marjorie, who knew "Tiny" Ironside well, that he had received a strong hint to the effect that the French would prefer Dill as commander-in-chief. He duly informed Hore Belisha, but "Belli did not react very favourably as obviously any readjustment means eating his own words to

Tiny". Finally there was the powerful influence of P. J. Grigg, who wrote on the subject as follows:

". . . When war broke out in 1939 Mr. Hore Belisha was set on making Ironside either C.I.G.S. or C.-in-C. of the B.E.F. which by this time had grown to an immediate four divisions with of course more to follow. But he was uncertain which of the two he wanted. As Permanent Under Secretary of State I renewed my plea that he should in fact be given neither and that the best thing to do in the circumstances was to make Lord Gort C.-in-C. of the B.E.F. and Dill C.I.G.S. However the new War Cabinet decided otherwise, and though Gort became C.-in-C., it was Ironside who was appointed C.I.G.S. I had always supposed that Mr. Churchill had had a good deal to do with inducing the War Cabinet to arrive at this conclusion. Anyhow Dill, our most brilliant Staff Officer, was left to command one of the two British Corps under Gort, and so even the satisfaction which had earlier been promised him was withdrawn."

Dill, indeed, seemed to be the alternative choice, particularly as the French thought so highly of him, and the British General Staff had evidently assumed he would be appointed. Field-Marshal Alexander, a week before his death, told me that at the time he had hoped for Dill; but in retrospect he believed he had been wrong because, although a brilliant staff officer, Dill was neither a commander nor a fighting soldier. Alexander also learned, as time went on, that Dill was inclined to be a defeatist and he believed that had he commanded the B.E.F. in May, 1940, the consequences might well have been disastrous. Hore Belisha, whose recommendation counted most, had not considered Dill suitable to be C.I.G.S. and he did not now consider him suitable to command the B.E.F. He was, on the other hand, anxious to be rid of Gort from the War Office and though it would never have crossed his mind to use this vitally important command to achieve such an end, Gort's reputation as a fighting soldier, his great popularity with the army and the "build up" with the general public which, through no wish of his own but in the train of Hore Belisha's publicity campaigns, he had received from the press, all pointed to Gort as the best selection. For this Hore Belisha won the support first of his Permanent Under Secretary, then of his fellow service Ministers and finally, with complete unanimity, of the War Cabinet. On the evening of 3rd September Gort, to his surprise and immense gratification, was appointed commander-in-chief. The choice of Ironside to succeed him as C.I.G.S. met with opposition from Kingsley Wood and some other

Ministers, but with Churchill's puissant support the proposal was accepted.

Gort had been C.I.G.S. for exactly one year and nine months, the youngest soldier ever to hold the office. He had not aspired to it and even though he had, in 1937, seemed to Alexander "much the livest wire in the Army", and had been equally acceptable to the "modernisers" like Pile and Martel, he was not the ideal choice. Dill, insufficiently resilient by the time the office came to him in 1940, would have been a prudent selection in 1937. Gort had, however, done his conscientious best in work and surroundings that were uncongenial and with a Secretary of State he found even more so. Admiral Sir Harold Brown, responsible for the supply and production of munitions at the War Office from 1936 to 1939, made this comment: "I don't feel competent to say whether Gort was a good C.I.G.S. I can only say that his advent at the War Office was like a breath of fresh air so far as 'Production' was concerned, that he was helpful and that he did attempt to see that 'Production' was given details of the type of equipment required. He was always most helpful, too, in cutting down unnecessarily elaborate requirements and standards of finish which delayed production. I might add that at Munich when war appeared imminent, and the War Office was generally in 'a flat spin', Gort held the team together and got on with the work."

No C.I.G.S. could have provided the army with tanks in the quantity and of the quality necessary to face the German Panzers; but it may well be that Gort, who had always been an advocate of mechanisation, should have staffed the War Office with more tank experts and generated greater enthusiasm for armoured formations. Equally, no C.I.G.S. could have marshalled enough political support to force the R.A.F. to disgorge more of its bombers in the interests of the army; but Gort, in spite of his long-standing conviction that the three armed services must be interdependent in modern war, failed to make even a small dint in the defences of the Air Ministry or to insist on a workable plan for co-operation between a British Expeditionary Force and its supporting air forces. It would have been difficult, but it might conceivably have been possible, to win a Whitehall battle for the direct authority of a future commander-in-chief over the Advanced Air Striking Force for which the army was to supply labour, protection and manpower on French soil.

He would have been far out of his depth as C.I.G.S. under Churchill's wartime Government. The encroachment on the regular, well organised time-table by which he governed his life, already sufficiently dislocated by Hore Belisha, would have been unbearable to him. But Alanbrooke, who co-operated triumphantly, if resentfully, with Churchill and P. J. Grigg, could have made no greater practical impact than did Gort on the régime of agonising insufficiency which faced the Army Council in the two years preceding the war. At least, under Gort, the War Office machine worked efficiently and confronted by such parsimony and procrastination it was no mean achievement to land two army corps in France within a month of the outbreak of war.

At 53 he now commanded Britain's embryonic army, the tardily accepted and hastily equipped British Expeditionary Force. An abler and more experienced soldier than Sir John French, he stood in French's shoes, with a small well-trained regular army at his disposal and a territorial force which would grow in size and improve in quality as the months went by. Like French he was the junior partner in an allied army: unlike French he was, by his own wholehearted advocacy, subordinated to that ally's command. Within a year there would, if all went well, be two British armies on French or Belgian soil, each with its own general: for the time being he must double the role of commander-in-chief and army commander. Beneath him he would have two corps commanders, Dill and Brooke, both originally senior to him on the Army List and Dill, at any rate, swallowing his disappointment that Gort had been preferred to him, first as C.I.G.S. and now as commander-in-chief.

CHAPTER II

ANTI-CLIMAX

━━━

THE comparisons with August, 1914, were numerous but, except
that once again the country was unprepared for land warfare,
they were mainly coincidental. The differences were more important. The Germans left the western front alone and concentrated on Poland, where they advanced without difficulty.
They treated the Poles with the ruthlessness which had earned
them the unenviable name of Huns in Belgium twenty-five years
before, and they bombed Warsaw without regard for the civilian
population. The Polish cavalry charged tanks and machine-guns
with gallant folly and before September was out the Russians
advanced from the east to perpetrate a new partition of Poland.

In Britain the general public went wearily to work, their gas
masks slung over their shoulders, without the smallest hope that it
would all be over by Christmas. Keen recruits for the armed forces
were invited to return later when it might be convenient to
absorb them. There were no manifestations of enthusiasm, there
was no rationing and no shortage of customary purchases; but
there was a general feeling of irritation that nothing was happen-
ing. Whatever the Germans might do to Warsaw, the British and
French were righteously determined to bomb military objectives
alone and since even that might provoke retaliation, it was
thought wiser, apart from an ineffective foray against the German
fleet, to employ the R.A.F. in dropping leaflets over Germany
where the inhabitants were reported in a state of such low morale
and bodily inanition as to be susceptible to propaganda pamphlets
extolling democracy and embellished by an occasional improper
cartoon. It was, said Mr. Charles Ritchie, Secretary at the
Canadian High Commission, like sitting in the dentist's waiting
room, turning over the pages of some tattered 1914 magazines.

Gort left his illustrious office chair with relief. He moved out of
his room to make way for the new C.I.G.S., Ironside, but he
established himself in other quarters at the War Office and
collected together his senior G.H.Q. staff. He wanted Adam as

Chief of Staff, but Hore Belisha and Ironside reasonably objected to the simultaneous departure of both the C.I.G.S. and D.C.I.G.S. and he therefore selected his faithful friend and supporter, Henry Pownall, now a lieutenant-general, who wrote in his diary that night: "I can but do my best. I am happy indeed to be allowed to go on serving directly under so great a gentleman and so fine a soldier as is Gort."

Lieutenant-General Sir Douglas Brownrigg had been chosen as adjutant-general, Lieutenant-General W. G. Lindsell as quarter-master-general, Gort's old fellow instructor at the Staff College, Major-General Philip Neame, v.c., as assistant to Pownall, Major-General F. N. Mason-Macfarlane as head of Intelligence, and as G.S.O.1's Colonels P. G. Whitefoord, Gerald Templer and Viscount Bridgeman. Captain the Earl of Munster, until recently Parliamentary Under Secretary at the War Office, became his personal assistant and, during the months to come, his most helpful and intimate companion. The Duke of Gloucester was appointed Chief Liaison Officer on his staff.

Small advance parties began to leave for France the day after war was declared so as to be ready to receive the main body of the troops at Cherbourg and the stores and vehicles at Nantes, St. Nazaire and Brest. Gort collected his staff at Camberley on 13th September and on the following day he and Dill, commanding I Corps, sailed for Cherbourg in a destroyer, H.M.S. *Skate*. The assembly area for the B.E.F. was between the towns of Le Mans and Laval, a hundred and fifty miles from the ports where their supplies were unloaded. Nevertheless, I Corps, which began to arrive on 22nd September, was successfully concentrated and on the 26th the leading units of Brooke's II Corps disembarked. It was the first time in history that a mainly mechanised, or at least motorised, army had been transported overseas and the movement was flawlessly achieved. The enemy were too fully engaged in Poland for aerial intervention and the Royal Navy convoyed the transports to their destination without allowing an opening for any kind of submarine interference.

Gort meanwhile visited both Gamelin, the Supreme Commander, and Georges, Commander of the French Front of the North-East, under whose orders the B.E.F. as well as all the French armies from the Channel to the Swiss frontier were to operate. They discussed with complete amiability the line which the B.E.F. was to hold and on 26th September Gort accepted a sector north and east of Lille, running from Maulde to Halluin with a defensive flank along the River Lys as far as Armentières. The French 51st Division was placed under his direct command and he stationed it to guard the industrial area on the left of his own army. On 3rd October Dill's corps, having covered 250 miles from its assembly area, took its place on the right of the British line, next to the French 1st Army. It consisted of two divisions, the 1st, commanded by Major-General the Hon. Harold Alexander and the 2nd by Major-General H. C. Loyd. On 12th October Brooke's corps was ready for action: its 3rd Division, under Major-General Bernard Montgomery, moved into the line on the left and Major-General D. G. Johnson's 4th Division was held in reserve. Gort established his headquarters west of Arras, spread over an area of outlying villages, a precaution against air attack which had its attendant administrative disadvantages. He himself settled into the Hôtel Univers at Arras for ten days and then, as he wrote to Jacqueline: "I am off to a château with no water, no light and no loo." It was the Château of Habarcq, west of Arras. As the weather became increasingly cold he deliberately lived and worked with all the windows open because, as he put it, "I am in the process of hardening off." A year earlier, at the War Office, he had remonstrated with Haydon, who had casually mentioned that the nights were growing cold and that he had found an extra blanket necessary. We should, Gort had told him, be at war within a year and it was important to get used to privations.

Before the end of October a new division, the 5th, was formed out of three regular infantry brigades which arrived from England and placed under the command of Major-General H. E. Franklyn. There were reports of an impending German attack on 15th October, necessitating a "stand to" all along the line, and there were patrol skirmishes on the Saar front to which a British brigade was in due course sent for battle practice. By the end of October Gort personally believed that no attack would come before the spring. In this he differed profoundly from Gamelin, who believed the Germans would open their offensive in November. Gort wrote to Hore Belisha on 28th October: "For an army which depends for success on tanks and low flying I can imagine no worse combination than Flanders' mud and low cloud." It became clear that General Gamelin, who had at one time spoken of "leaning against" the Siegfried Line, and at another said that he would bombard it violently on 17th September, was in reality determined to do nothing offensive at all. "*Je ne veux pas casser les meilleures Divisions de l'Armée Française,*" he repeated again and again to Major-General Howard Vyse, head of the British mission at his headquarters. Gort was often to be heard quoting Foch – "Attack, always attack," – although there could clearly be no possibility of the B.E.F. so doing for months to come; Gamelin was calmly and confidently relying on the unbreakable superiority of defence.

The problem that obsessed everybody, soldiers and civilians alike, was how to persuade the Dutch and particularly the Belgians that, for them, neutrality spelt destruction. What was to be done if, as seemed increasingly probable, the Belgians stuck their heads deeper and deeper into the sand until the dawn of invasion actually broke and then called urgently on the French and British for protection? They had twenty-two divisions, several strong fortresses and a defensive line along the Albert Canal and the River Meuse. In September, while the Germans were concentrating their army and air force on Poland, it might have been practicable to move French and subsequently British forces eastwards to reinforce the Belgian army and to strengthen the country's natural and artificial barriers of defence. No invitation came and scarcely any military intelligence or information could be extracted from King Leopold or his Government.

Queen Wilhelmina and hers were still more unforthcoming. The two rabbits recognised the fox, but they tried to convince themselves and each other that he was less predatory than so often painted and that the only safe course was to sit absolutely still, however noticeably he was licking his lips and however alarming his grimaces. The fate of Brer Austria, Brer Czechoslovakia and Brer Poland had done nothing to shake this conviction.

The British with so small an army, and having readily accepted French command, were not in a strong position to call any strategic tune. All the same, Gamelin's first proposal, which was to advance to the River Scheldt in the event of a German invasion of Belgium, was disputed by Ironside and was regarded with reservations by the B.E.F. because, even though Ostend and Zeebrugge would thus remain in friendly hands, there were no prepared positions, the ground on the east bank of the river was much higher than on the west and the B.E.F. would have no defence in depth. Moreover, the lines of communication would run parallel with the front at an unacceptably short distance behind it. Gamelin was, however, resolved to move the battle as far as possible from French soil and, in particular, he was anxious that the industrial towns of Lille, Tourcoing and Roubaix should be out of range of the firing line. He was sure that the Germans would come through Belgium. If they attacked south of the B.E.F., it was true that the prepared French defences were weak and that there were none in Belgium, but he had no fears if they came head on against the formidable French 1st Army with its plentiful supply of tanks, tough Somuas and some of the new "Chars B", which were generally agreed to be the most formidable tanks in existence and which Mr. Anthony Eden, who had himself served an attachment to the British Armoured Division, vainly urged His Majesty's Government to buy or build on licence. South of the 1st Army the mountainous Ardennes were, Gamelin believed, impenetrable to tanks, and south again was the still more impenetrable Maginot Line. Ironside ventured to argue that the Ardennes might in fact be the danger spot, and Pownall had similar thoughts; but although on 6th October Gamelin did suggest to Ironside the possibility of an attack through the Ardennes, with the German right based on Valenciennes, and an outflanking of the Maginot Line, he discarded this thought in favour of a firm conviction that the offensive would come through Belgium and the 1914 axis of attack be repeated. Even if the Germans did go through the Ardennes, how could they possibly force their tanks across the fast flowing, steep-banked Meuse where every bridge was mined and ready to explode?

Much ill has been written of Gamelin, and to defend him would indeed require greater skill than he showed in composing his own *Mémoires*; but his conclusion that the Germans would attack through Belgium, as they had in 1914, was no disgrace to his intelligence. Nobody but the Dutch and the Belgians supposed for one moment that Hitler would be more scrupulous about a solemn Treaty of Non-Aggression than the Kaiser had been twenty-five years before: to describe a treaty as a "scrap of paper" was shocking to the 1914 conscience; in 1939 it was, whenever the "Axis Powers" of Germany, Italy and Japan were concerned, standard practice. Gamelin rightly discounted the possibility of the Germans hurling their armies to destruction against the Maginot Line. He thought it evident that armoured forces would shun the rugged hills and defiles of the Ardennes. The obvious path of attack was across the flat plains of Belgium and more particularly the twenty miles or so north of the Meuse, the Gembloux gap as it was called, where there were no rivers or other natural obstacles to impede the advance of an army. He was all but proved right. If, as Hitler intended, the Germans had begun their offensive in

November, 1939, or in January, 1940, they would have advanced precisely as he foresaw. Unfortunately, and partly because their plans inadvertently fell into allied hands when a plane crashed on Belgian territory, they did, after January 1940, review and revise their entire strategy.

On 1st September, 1939, Gamelin had submitted a memorandum to his Government in which he wrote: "If the Belgians called on us only at the moment when they were attacked by the Germans, there is no doubt that they would not have the means, in numbers or in strength, to defend their front effectively before they were submerged; and we should have to run all the risks of a battle of encounter, with the difficulty of supporting armies in retreat – a difficult task with modern motorised forces and aviation." Subsequently on 20th September, he and his Prime Minister, Daladier, met two British Ministers, Lord Hankey and Hore Belisha, and emphasised that there were two cardinal points of strategy to be accepted: there must in no circumstances be "an encounter battle" with the enemy in open country; and it was vital to fight in well-prepared positions. All the same, Gamelin decided that the allied armies must move forward to meet a German onslaught. In addition to the other good reasons for this decision he, and Georges too, held that the consideration which surpassed all others in importance was the avoidance of battle in the fields of France. There had been too much of that between 1914 and 1918: there might be unhappy experiences ahead for the Dutch and the Belgians but France had, after all, suffered more than her share.

On 9th November, while the armies stood to for another alarm on the front, Gamelin held a conference at Vincennes to decide allied strategy. Ironside and Newall were there, and Gort found himself staying in unaccustomed comfort at the *Crillon*. Gamelin put forward a proposal, known as "Plan D", for an advance not merely to the Scheldt but much farther eastwards to the River Dyle, so that the Germans might be halted on a front stretching from Antwerp through Louvain to Namur, and Brussels might be saved from occupation. There was much to recommend it. It was a far shorter line to hold; behind it lay four additional defensive positions, the rivers Senne, Dendre and Scheldt and finally the existing defences on the Belgian frontier; the ports on the Belgian coast, which had been pernicious submarine nests in 1917, and Antwerp itself would be denied to the enemy; the German bombers would have much greater distances to fly, over hostile country, before they could reach Paris or London; the lines of communication would be longer but less vulnerable; the substantial Belgian army could fall back, fighting for hearth and home, into the welcoming arms of allies who would already be shielding some two thirds of the country from occupation; and last, but by no means least, a strongly held allied front from Antwerp to Namur would be a threat to Germany itself. The Germans could not safely mount an attack on the Maginot Line, or through Switzerland or even through Luxembourg, if great armies, stronger month by month as the resources of the British Empire were mobilised, stood poised to attack south-eastwards towards the Ruhr and the north German plains while R.A.F. bombers used Belgian airfields from which to raid the centres of German industry. Gamelin was assured that the Belgians would prepare strong fortifications to be ready and waiting for the incoming Anglo-French forces, although admittedly the Dyle itself was not a wide or fast flowing river and nothing like as formidable an obstacle as the Scheldt. Ironside, Gort and Newall therefore agreed, and after Ironside had convinced the War Cabinet, who had not been previously informed of the project, it was submitted to the Supreme War Council, by which it was awarded supreme approbation on 17th November. It was left to Gamelin to decide which of the alternatives, Plan E for an advance to the Scheldt or Plan D for an advance to the Dyle, might be the more advantageous when the time came. Gort reached agreement with Georges that if Plan D were chosen the British should hold the sector of the line from Wavre to Louvain. For good measure Gamelin revealed his plan to constitute a powerful 7th Army, between the B.E.F. and the sea, which under the command of General Giraud, and well supplied with armour, would advance even beyond Antwerp into Holland and reach Breda and Walcheren before the Germans. According to Churchill, who had close links with Georges, this was Gamelin's personal decision: Georges, with greater prudence, would have preferred to keep Giraud's 7th Army in reserve, just in case there were ever a gap to be plugged.

Both Dill and Alan Brooke regretted the proposal to move forward to the Scheldt, let alone to the Dyle. They were doubtful of the administrative feasibility, uncertain that their men were sufficiently trained to do battle outside a well known and well-fortified line and alarmed at the prospect of being bombed during the forward move. Bridgeman, who was in almost daily contact with Gort, believed him to have serious misgivings himself; but neither he nor the British Government, contributing at that stage a mere five divisions to an Anglo-French army of more than ninety divisions, were in a position to argue. It had been a political decision, and a logical one, that the French should command on land. A suggestion by the commander of the French fleet, Admiral Darlan, that allied naval strategy was at fault would have been greeted with contempt and indignation in London. Britannia indisputably ruled the waves: she just as certainly did not rule the battle fields.

"The question of such an advance," Gort subsequently wrote, "was one of high policy with a political as well as a military aspect; it was therefore not for me to comment on it. My responsibilities were confined to ensuring that the orders issued by the French for the employment of the British Expeditionary Force were capable of being carried out; and, indeed, events proved that the orders issued for this operation were well within the capacity of the Force." No commander-in-chief could fail to see the danger of leaving a line of defences which, after a hard winter's work, had been effectively strengthened and risking the very encounter battle in the open against which both Gamelin and Georges had inveighed so often and so emphatically. The fact remained that it had been universally agreed Gamelin should decide, and Gamelin believed the evident advantages to outweigh the hypothetical risks. He was keenly supported by General Billotte, commander of the 1st Group of French Armies, an officer much respected for his suave manner, martial air and Roman *gravitas*.

The sombre pessimism of Brooke and Dill was in accordance with the realities of the situation. But what purpose could it serve? The B.E.F. was in the line for better or worse, and no amount of anguished lamentation over the wasted years could strengthen the defences or increase the supply of Mark II tanks. None knew better than Gort, who had wrestled with the shortages for two years, what opportunities had been lost. Now, whatever the odds, it was essential to maintain a high morale and he was well aware that defeatism at the top could spread downwards through the army as rapidly as any physical infection. He was a lifelong student of military history. If Leonidas had been a realist he would not have stood with his three hundred Spartans at Thermopylae. Fortunately for England, it was Drake, and not a commander of greater caution, who faced the overwhelming superiority of the Armada. An analyst of chances more professional than Wellington might have declined to give battle at Waterloo. Gort had seen the Ludendorff offensive sweep all before it, breaking the 3rd and 5th Armies in its forward rush; but he had also taken part in Foch's decisive counter-stroke a few months later. One evening, walking back to the Château with Munster, he told him he had heard that the Germans had ten armoured divisions prepared for attack on the western front. "In that case," he said, "we haven't an earthly chance." The sole British armoured division had received no more than half its complement of medium tanks by the beginning of March, 1940, and could not be ready for action with the B.E.F. till the end of May. Yet the only alternative to fighting was a grovelling peace with total dishonour and eventual submission to Hitler's every whim. In the circumstances he, and Pownall and Alexander too, noted with uneasiness the feelings of increasing hopelessness exuded by the two corps commanders. Gort, for his part, expressed his fears on this solitary occasion and to Munster alone. Neither in his letters home, nor in his talks with the endless visitors to G.H.Q., nor in the intimate circle of his personal staff did he allow words of doubt or anxiety to escape him. No; it was pointless to be depressed and it would be treasonable to show it. On the contrary, during a conference held on 10th April at I Corps headquarters he went out of his way, knowing what would be expected of his divisions, to stress "the danger of concrete and the consequent dislike of being in the open". The B.E.F. was in the line: while he led them, they would do their best, however small their numbers and inadequate their armament. Training, in and out of the line, went ahead with unrelenting ardour, but Gort wrote to the Duke of Connaught, colonel of his old regiment, the Grenadier Guards: "I still feel there is a good deal to teach the officers this winter about modern war as too much training in my opinion has been based on the last war, which is a common failing in our Army."

While the training of Territorial divisions, future strategy and present security in the face of a possible German assault engaged his attention and that of his staff Gort, who believed in the traditional concept of a chain of command, held conferences with his corps commanders but did not interfere with the disposition of their units. He was a frequent visitor to all sectors of the B.E.F., but the divisional commanders noted that he paid more attention to matters of detail, such as the defensive positioning of a company or even a platoon, than to the tactical handling of brigades and divisions. It was, they felt, a pity that the commander-in-chief should concern himself with such matters as tear-off igniting paper on rockets, anti-freeze mixture and night-flying pigeons. However, Gort conceived it his duty to command the B.E.F. as a whole and to maintain its efficiency by remarking on the smaller points of discipline and organisation: it was for each individual corps commander to control the units for which he was responsible. Thus he never arranged sand-table exercises so that he and his divisional commanders could rehearse and debate major tactical problems; but whenever possible he conducted an after-dinner staff discussion at which matters large or small could be brought to his notice. Life was made no easier by a steady, by no means always welcome, flow of visitors to G.H.Q. and the necessity both of entertaining them and of conducting the more important on a tour of the front. He also had to travel incessantly and to visit and feed with all the neighbouring French generals. "And so the round of winning the war with a knife and fork proceeds," he wrote after one protracted luncheon on Gamelin's special train.

Nothing was allowed to deflect him from his weekly letter to Jacqueline, now a senior commander in the A.T.S. and working in the War Office. When war broke out, Sandy temporarily shook off his dislike of the army and having, to his father's gratification, joined the Grenadiers, was learning to be an officer at Sandhurst. But it was, as ever, to Jacqueline that he opened his heart and on her that he counted for the fulfilment of commissions at home. Late in October he told her that he had motored 128 miles that day "and had only two sandwiches and some tea from a Thermos. Leaving my H.Q. at 8.45 a.m. it was after 6.0 p.m. when I got back to do my office work, and I then had 15 minutes to get ready for supper, three quarters of an hour eating and then another conference until just after 11.0 p.m. That is an ordinary day." In another letter he asked her to buy him shaving soap, razor blades and writing paper. The B.E.F. were apparently unable to supply his simple requirements. From time to time he thought it expedient to remind himself and her about the censorship regulations. It is difficult to imagine who would have had the temerity to censor the commander-in-chief's private correspondence, but it did not occur to Gort that his letters would be differentiated from those of any private soldier. Just before Christmas Jacqueline was doubtless surprised to read: "Have you got any cash-names, as I have had several pairs of socks given me and I dare not wear them till marked in case they are pinched when washed." Evidently the commander-in-chief was not being over-cosseted, or perhaps even adequately served.

Then there was the problem of the plum puddings. There were forty Other Ranks at G.H.Q. On 9th November, in the midst of the conference with Gamelin on Plan D, and while the opening of the enemy offensive was expected (though not by Gort, who thought the Germans had left it too late in the year), he found time to reflect that Christmas at G.H.Q. without plum puddings for the men would be a dismal affair. So he wrote to ask Jacqueline whether she could persuade Mrs. Mackenzie, his cook at 98 Mount Street, to make the required number, but "not too high class as with rationing coming into force we cannot let the country down by being extravagant". It is pleasant to know that Mrs. Mackenzie, who was probably all too familiar with His Lordship's antipathy to extravagance, sent a large supply of brandy-butter as well. Gort's solicitude for the welfare of the troops did not stop at plum puddings. He was much exercised by the problem of filling their leisure hours during the months of operational inactivity and he corresponded with the B.B.C. to such good purpose that early in the New Year a special "Forces Programme" was instituted. It remained a significant feature of wartime life for the next six years.

Late in November there was an incident known as the "Pill-Box Row", which brought little credit to some of the parties concerned. Its importance lies in the fact that it caused the downfall of Hore Belisha. It was a storm which would have done no more than ripple the tea in the cup of a more popular Secretary of State, but it became the occasion for unleashing the pent-up dislike which most senior soldiers, many civil servants and latterly a number of Ministers felt for Hore Belisha. It involved the King, the Prime Minister, Gamelin, Ironside, important Ministers of the Dominions and almost all the powers behind every throne. It could not have happened while battles were being fought: it was the product of a situation, unique in the history of war, when three powerful nations were theoretically in deadly conflict but in fact waiting nervously, biting their figurative finger-nails, for something to happen.

In October, when the B.E.F. moved to their allocated position in the line, they found awaiting them an anti-tank ditch, a not very formidable array of barbed wire and, at intervals of a thousand yards, a line of large concrete pill-boxes which were constructed so that guns might enfilade the anti-tank ditch.

Alterations were required in order to house the British type of gun. There was no defence in depth and a considerable labour force of men and machinery was necessary both to strengthen and modify the existing line and to provide defensive positions in depth behind it. Hore Belisha thought it would be helpful to recruit experienced British civilian contractors, such as McAlpines and Costains, to provide the skill, the labour force and the earth-moving equipment required. Gort welcomed this initiative and, together with his chief engineer, Major-General R. P. Pakenham-Walsh, studied a number of alternative designs for new concrete pill-boxes. They were rectangular edifices, far less elaborate than the vast underground fortresses built over the years to form the Maginot Line, but nevertheless capable of sheltering from bombardment reasonable numbers of men and weapons. Hore Belisha knew nothing of the technical military requirements, but eager to help the B.E.F. fortify its position to the best possible advantage in the short time likely to be available, he took a keen personal interest in the progress made. He did not deserve the unworthy suspicion of Ironside, Pownall and others that, not content with the publicity he had acquired when Minister of Transport by the introduction of Belisha Beacons at pedestrian road crossings, he was now enthralled at the prospect of a magnificent Belisha Line to rival the Maginot Line.

In November he decided it was time for a personal visit to the British front. Ironside inquired whether he wished to concentrate on seeing the men or the defences and Hore Belisha, proud of his reputation as the private soldier's friend, had no difficulty in making up his mind. Gort was informed that the object of the Secretary of State's visit was to see the men. From an account of the visit given by Major-General John Kennedy, then Director of Plans at the War Office, it seems that Gort gave rein to the school-boy sense of humour which he occasionally found irresistible and took pleasure in subjecting Hore Belisha to every form of climatic and gastronomic discomfort which the Flanders climate and Gort's spartan régime could provide. There were visits in the rain to both corps and to the French division on the left, and there were uncomfortable wet picnics consisting mainly of bully-beef sandwiches. There was also a discussion with Pakenham-Walsh, who showed Hore Belisha the various pill-box designs on which his engineers were working.

He saw little of the defences except in so far as the majority of the men were working on one or another section of them. He did, however, conclude that pill-boxes were not springing up with the mushroom-like speed for which he had hoped, and he was depressed by the variety of designs with which Gort and his staff appeared to be toying. His anxiety was increased when on his way home through Paris he understood Gamelin to say that the French were building pill-boxes in three days. Gamelin subsequently explained that what he had meant was that once a site had been prepared and the materials brought up to it, actual construction took three days. In all, the building of a French pill-box required three weeks. After returning to London, Hore Belisha wrote to Gort, on 22nd November: "The impression that is deepest in my mind is of the great knowledge which you show of every detail. Your interest in the task and in the men is most inspiring. I do not suppose we have ever had a commander who kept in such close touch with men and things. You will emerge from this business having done a good job of work for the country and as a national figure.

"I am seeing the engineers tomorrow. I really think the Pill-Boxes should spring up everywhere. The Dominions representatives and Anthony Eden commented on their absence. I thought you would like to know this.

"Gamelin told me in Paris that they could make them in three days apiece. He also said they were lining and flooring their trenches with cement and that you could have cement works in the area. He hoped you would send down some officers to study their methods."

It was meant to be a tactful, friendly letter hinting that some Ministers from the Dominions, who had visited the front on 13th November, shared Hore Belisha's anxiety about the speed with which the defences were being improved and expanded. The implication that the French were doing better would in any case have caused annoyance at Gort's headquarters, because it was well known that the British were digging and building with far greater enthusiasm than their neighbours on the right and left and, indeed, Gamelin subsequently made a request for British troops to act as a labour force in the French sector. The Dominion Ministers included Crerar from Canada, Casey from Australia and, from South Africa, Deneys Reitz, Gort's old neighbour during the Ludendorff offensive of March, 1918. None of them could pretend to knowledge of the developments in defensive science which had taken place in the twenty-five years between the wars. Perhaps they expected to see lines of carefully revetted trenches and acres of barbed wire, or perhaps, as the adjutant-general maintained, they were making comparisons with the Maginot Line, expensively constructed over many years, which they visited on the same tour. Whatever the grounds on which their superficial impressions were based, they passed them, through the Secretary of State for the Dominions, Anthony Eden, to Hore Belisha, who received them as an endorsement of his own doubts.

He accordingly summoned Pakenham-Walsh, who had returned to London for consultations, together with the Controller of Engineering Services at the War Office, Lieutenant-General D. S. Collins, but he was unimpressed by their technical explanations. On 24th November he informed the War Cabinet of his disquiet. He did so after the C.I.G.S., Ironside, who was only summoned to the Cabinet for the routine report on the military situation, had left the room. Unaware that the new French defences on the left of the British sector had in fact been built by the B.E.F., he made the blunder of comparing them favourably with what he had seen on the British front. Returning to the War Office from No. 10, he summoned a meeting of the Army Council, which the adjutant-general was the only military member able to attend, and he asked Pakenham-Walsh to be present. After stating that the Prime Minister had expressed grave concern, he instructed Pakenham-Walsh, a member of Gort's own staff, to return to France and inform the commander-in-chief that Chamberlain, on hearing the report of the Dominion Ministers, of Eden and of himself wished him to know that the War Cabinet were deeply perturbed by the reported weakness of the British sector. He saw Pakenham-Walsh again the following day and repeated the message.

Gort was furious because he believed the accusations to be unjustified, but still more so because of the tone of the message and the method of its delivery by a member of his own staff. On being apprised of Hore Belisha's allegations, Ironside set out for France to report on the facts of the case and, after talking not only to G.H.Q. but also to Dill, Brooke and the divisional commanders, he returned to England convinced that Hore Belisha's strictures were baseless. The knowledge that they had been made spread throughout the B.E.F. as the result of Ironside's inquiries and universal indignation was aroused. General Montgomery, commanding the 3rd Division, told Ironside that Hore Belisha had actually thanked him for sparing him a tour of the defences on his divisional front. How could he presume to comment on what he had deliberately avoided inspecting? Some resented the aspersions cast on their commander-in-chief; others were incensed that their own conscientious efforts had been denigrated; all were united in finding an outlet for their anger and for their boredom by vituperation against the Secretary of State.

Gort might have been able to pacify his angry officers, but though it would have been contrary to his standards of discipline and behaviour to exacerbate the matter, he did not prevent others from so doing. Sensitive as always to reflexions on his own efficiency, his feelings on this occasion were strengthened by personal dislike and his conviction that Hore Belisha was unsuited to his office. Pownall felt the slight even more strongly than his chief and he had fewer inhibitions. Indeed, he looked upon it as a patriotic duty to be rid of Hore Belisha. Accordingly, when there was an opportunity of going to London early in December, he found occasion to explain the facts of the case as he and others had witnessed them to the King's private secretary, Sir Alexander Hardinge, to Sir P. J. Grigg, to Sir Horace Wilson, and to Lord Hankey. He left them in no doubt of the damage this affair, and in particular the implied slur on Gort's competence, had caused throughout the entire B.E.F.

After Ironside had reported to the King, the Prime Minister and the Cabinet that the B.E.F. were constructing pill-boxes as well and as fast as possible, Hore Belisha decided to let the matter drop. He wrote to Gort, on the 3rd December, blamed Pakenham-Walsh for misquoting him in the offending message and concluded: "We shall have some hard times to go through and we can afford to put the pill-boxes in perspective. The incident is closed." Gort asked Pakenham-Walsh for his comments and learned that the offending message had not only been delivered at the Army Council, but also had been repeated on two other occasions in the presence of witnesses. Gort also learned from the War Office that Hore Belisha had subsequently amended the minutes of the Army Council to record a statement by himself to the effect that he wished to cast no slur on the commander-in-chief. Unfortunately, none of those who had been present remembered his saying any such thing. Finally, Sir P. J. Grigg confirmed that there was nothing in the Cabinet Conclusions, nor in the Confidential Annex to them, to justify the impression Hore Belisha had given that his message was sent on instructions from the Prime Minister or the War Cabinet. Gort sent no answer to Hore Belisha's letter.

The King had received a report from Ironside. He was angered by what he heard and distressed by the offence evidently given to his army in the field. He instructed the C.I.G.S. to inquire what effect the affair had had on Gort personally. Ironside relates that the King spoke gravely to the Prime Minister on the subject. Meanwhile his private secretary, Sir Alexander Hardinge, received reports of resentment not only among the staff, but also among the rank and file, who in adverse weather conditions had spent long days of laborious labour on the defences. Hore Belisha's complaint had undermined the army's confidence in the support they could expect from home and it was being said that there was an enemy behind as well as in front.

The King decided to go and see for himself. He arrived at Gort's headquarters on 4th December and remained in France a week. Comforts were few, as Gort made clear in a letter to Jacqueline: "In our new house where he will stay the *chauffage* works dubiously, the analysis of the water shows 40 per cent sewage and the electric pump to get it from the well has already broken." Nevertheless, the visit was well conducted. The King, who was by nature and training outstandingly observant, was shown the defences as well as the men, and he returned to Buckingham Palace with full personal confirmation of the angry discontent seething in the B.E.F. He spoke to Chamberlain who decided he, too, must visit the British front.

On 12th December Hardinge wrote to Gort saying that he had asked both Kingsley Wood and Anthony Eden about the event. Kingsley Wood, he wrote, "was emphatic that the War Cabinet, with the apparent exception of H.B., has entire confidence in you, and that the form in which the message reached you was a complete misrepresentation of the attitude of the War Cabinet. His language about his colleague was quite violent, and he was much distressed to think that you should feel you were not receiving support from home . . .

"I saw Anthony Eden in the evening, and he was equally distressed, not only for himself but for the Dominion Ministers. They had repeated time after time that, in drawing attention to the obvious contrast between our line and the Maginot Line, they implied no sort of criticism of you and your Staff, for whom they expressed nothing but admiration. They were only trying to be helpful in suggesting that we at home might be giving you greater assistance in the making of your concrete defences . . . The

Maginot Line had made a deep impression upon the Dominion Ministers."

On 15th December the Prime Minister arrived at Gort's head-quarters. Two days previously Sir Horace Wilson and Sir Edward Bridges, Secretary of the Cabinet, had conferred with him in his room at the House of Commons and had made it plain that in their view Hore Belisha's continued tenure of the War Office would give rise to serious discontent in Whitehall.

Chamberlain's visit to France was no more comfortable than the King's. He wrote to his sisters: "I left with my train fairly early on Friday for Heston and flew over in the best plane I have encountered. It was so overheated that I had to take off my parachute in order to remove my top coat lest I should be boiled alive, in spite of which an imaginative journalist declared that I looked 'pale and chilled' when I alighted. I had a fairly long drive to G.H.Q. which is installed in a château, fairly large but sadly lacking in comforts. There is no running hot water for instance so when I wanted a hot bath the corporal had to trail upstairs four times carrying 2 heavy buckets. The C.-in-C. is said to be com-pletely indifferent to cold, dirt or fatigue so he doesn't mind.

"I went over a good part of the line with him and saw the various defence systems of which I understood very little. We finally had a march past on the aerodrome which as usual is completely exposed and the icy wind so froze my face that I could hardly move my jaws afterwards to talk to the airmen."

Gort took this opportunity of giving the Prime Minister a list of the principal deficiencies in equipment and he followed this up with a memorandum to the War Office about the alarming shortage of tanks.

It was clear to Chamberlain that even the mirage of confidence formerly seen as existing between the officers of the B.E.F. and their Secretary of State had dissolved. On returning home he wrote pointedly to Gort: "I was particularly impressed by the great progress that has been made, in so short a time, and despite many difficulties, with the construction of defences." In reply he received a letter from Gort which paid full tribute to Hore Belisha's qualities and "to the many and varied reforms he has brought about in the Army". Gort went on to say that the Prime Minister's visit had dispelled the worries felt in the B.E.F. and that he had every confidence the atmosphere would improve still further. Nevertheless, Chamberlain decided to speak frankly to Hore Belisha and having done so he was distressed to find him neither contrite nor indeed aware that he had caused so much offence at home and abroad. Chamberlain was sorry, because he liked Hore Belisha, valued his drive and shared Gort's genuine admiration of what he had achieved for the army. After careful reflexion he concluded that since Horace Wilson and Bridges saw eye to eye with the generals and with P. J. Grigg, and in view of what he himself had seen and heard in France, Hore Belisha must leave the War Office. The problem, which so often besets Prime Ministers, was where to put him.

By good fortune there was every prospect of a ministerial reshuffle in the offing. The Chancellor of the Exchequer, Sir John Simon, was even a shade less popular than Hore Belisha. Mr. Montagu Norman, the Governor of the Bank of England, who shunned publicity to such an extent that he would never use the front door of 10 Downing Street, arrived one evening at the garden door, dressed in a black cape and soft sombrero such as eminent artists wore in the nineteen-twenties. With his short white beard, he was indistinguishable from Mephistopheles. He had come to suggest to Sir Horace Wilson that Simon should go and that he might usefully be replaced by Lord Stamp, formerly chairman of the London Midland and Scottish Railway Company, and recently ennobled, to whose denoblement the King could be asked to agree as an unprecedented but nevertheless useful act. Chamberlain did not reject the idea, and it was accordingly suggested that Simon be promoted to Lord President of the Council, Stamp be made Chancellor, Oliver Stanley be Secretary of State for War and Hore Belisha display his undoubted talents for public relations in the increasingly important post of Minister of Information. The Foreign Secretary, though by no means anti-semitic, objected that to put a Jew in such a Ministry would be an unwarranted bonus to Dr. Goebbels and since this argument, which had occurred to nobody else, was at once agreed to be indisputable, Hore Belisha was hypothetically allotted the Board of Trade instead. It was thought improper to tell Sir P. J. Grigg, though it was known he would greatly approve, and on the *dies irae*, 4th January, he and Hore Belisha lunched unsuspectingly together.

At 2.45 that afternoon Hore Belisha was due to see the Prime Minister. What, he asked the private secretary on duty, was the object of the summons? The private secretary felt it expedient to be evasive. "I will tell you what," said Hore Belisha, "and this is one of the marvellous things about the P.M., which makes us all love him so. When I get into the Cabinet room, he will say to me in a fatherly way: sit down, Leslie, and tell me whether you have any departmental or personal problems. If there is any way in which I can help, you know that is what I am here for." It was an uncomfortable conversation. At that moment the bell rang from the Cabinet room: Mr. Chamberlain had come down from luncheon. A quarter of an hour later Hore Belisha, who had duly been offered the Board of Trade, emerged with a look of shattered incredulity on his face and, with a few polite remarks about the weather, passed out of public life. In the event it was the only change in the Government because Lord Stamp declined to be Chancellor, so that no denoblement was necessary, and Sir John Simon remained unaware of the plan for his deposition.

That night Hore Belisha telephoned to the First Lord of the Admiralty, who was in Paris. Churchill counselled him to accept the Board of Trade, even though it carried no seat in the War Cabinet. He was ill-advised to disdain this recommendation, for Churchill later asserted that if Hore Belisha had been in office on 10th May, 1940, he would have been included in the new Government. Churchill was displeased that Hore Belisha had dissented from a plan he had recently conceived to deny Swedish iron ore to the Germans, but he shared Chamberlain's view that, while not well placed in the War Office, he was none the less a man of drive, energy and imagination. To go into the wilderness, against Churchill's advice and supported by a campaign in the popular press, was an error of judgment from which he never recovered.

The reactions to his resignation were varied.

On 8th January the King wrote to Queen Mary: ". . . After my conversation with the Prime Minister, and his own visit to the B.E.F. I am sure he was impressed that all was well with the defence works in France. However I am still in the dark as to how it took place, though I shall know tomorrow. I shall be in London for the day to hold a Privy Council, and I shall see both H-B and the P.M. The Press have taken up the attitude they have of championing H-B, because they knew nothing about it before-hand, and this always makes them very angry. Oliver Stanley I am sure will do well at the W.O. though of course he is of a retiring nature."

On the 14th he wrote further: "H-B's resignation came about suddenly, as the P.M. knew it was no use his going on at the War Office, as he was so heartily disliked by soldiers and by civil servants."

P. J. Grigg wrote to his father: ". . . here I am in the process of saying goodbye to one Secretary of State and waiting for another to appear. I knew that trouble was brewing but didn't expect it to happen so soon. In some ways H.B. has only himself to blame, in others he has been badly treated but a situation in which the C-in-C in France and the S. of S. in England didn't trust each other was too dangerous to be allowed to last and I dare say the P.M. was right to change it sooner rather than later." On 6th January, Ironside wrote in his diary: "At 8 p.m. last night when I went to see Belisha's secretary I was told that Belisha had resigned. I had no inkling that it was coming. Changing horses in mid-stream is always a bad thing, but I must say that I had a feeling of intense relief on the whole. The man had failed utterly in war to run his show and we should have had a disaster. He is much better out of it."

Gort wrote nothing, but he was worried. He disliked the thought that Hore Belisha had come to grief over the stumbling block of the B.E.F., the more so that whatever poison his staff and his friends might, as the champions of his cause, have poured into important ears, he himself had been scrupulous in his official restraint. He had never disguised his dislike of Hore Belisha, and he had been deeply affronted by the aspersions which "The Pill-Box Row" had appeared to cast on his competence as commander-in-chief; but, unlike Ironside, P. J. Grigg and Pownall, who were resolved to get rid of their Secretary of State in what they held to be the public interest, Gort was distressed by the suggestion that he, a soldier owing obedience to the Crown and its delegates, should have been instrumental in procuring Hore Belisha's fall from grace and power. Pownall, returning from London on 10th January, found him tired and worried: it was a relief when by the 21st the outbursts in the press and Parliament, and the threat of a German attack in France, had sufficiently subsided for Gort to go home on ten days' leave.

Before leaving for England, he was joined by Ironside in a much publicised ceremony at which Gamelin decorated them both with the Grand Cross of the Légion d'Honneur. This anticipatory reward for services to come was the sequel to the conferment of a G.C.B. on Gamelin and G.B.E. on Georges during the King's December visit to France. The King, with much good sense, had thought the awards would be more appropriately bestowed after victory was won than before anything but a few rifle shots had been fired. However, he was advised that the French were sure to make some early chivalric move and that there would be advantage in the British getting in first. The possible aftermath of receiving a British knighthood is often alarming to foreigners, and Georges was no exception. Gort described the sequel: "General Georges was delighted with his G.B.E. and he was rather sweet as on the drive back he said to Brigadier Jack Swayne, 'Does that make me in England Sir Georges?' He said 'Yes, certainly you are Sir, but you will be Sir – christian name – Georges.' He looked upset at that and said: 'That I can't do as my christian name won't bear showing. You see, my father went to register my birth meaning to call me Albert but forgot and wrote it down as Alphonse. I could not be called anything so dreadful as Sir Alphonse Georges.' Brigadier Swayne said 'Oh well, why not be Sir A. Georges?' whereupon he beamed and was then '*trés content*'."

The year ended with significant personal news. Jacqueline, who had always told her father about the young men with whom she danced, dined or went out, indicated a marked predilection for Captain William Sidney, Grenadier Guards, who had recently been home on leave from the B.E.F.

CHAPTER 12

COUNTDOWN

TOWARDS the end of January, 1940, an exceptionally hard winter descended on Europe. It delayed and dislocated the programme of strengthening the northern sectors of the Allied line and it accelerated the deterioration of morale in the French civil population, thus in turn affecting the French armies as they stood, chilled and bored, in the Maginot Line and along the less well fortified defences to its north. The anti-Nazi zeal of the Communists, who were numerous in France though negligible in Britain, cooled as a result of the Molotov-Ribbentrop Pact; the right wing considered Hitler a less formidable enemy than their own *Front Populaire*. The thought, sedulously cultivated by extremists at either end of the political spectrum, that England was preparing to fight to the last Frenchman began, if not to gain wide acceptance, at least to be aired, even in politically moderate circles. By every month he postponed his offensive Hitler profited from increasing moral disintegration in France.

The plain truth was that the French had no stomach for another war. They had fought consistently, in each succeeding generation, for two hundred and fifty years and the glory they had won was not adequate compensation for the wealth and the youth they had sacrificed. In the eighteenth century war had cost them Canada and India; in the nineteenth, Napoleon's victories and his ultimate defeat had bled the country white. They had invariably startled the world and their late enemies by the speed and thoroughness of their recovery; but recurrent afflictions over a long period had weakened the body politic and lately, in the twentieth century, they had seen their richest industrial area laid waste, large parts of France reduced to rubble or turned into a morass of shell holes and the best part of a generation exterminated. The British, too, had suffered acutely between 1914 and 1918, but not a single invader had stood on their soil and the few bombs which fell had been more exciting than destructive. Their previous wars had been inexpensive in manpower and had increased rather than drained their wealth and influence. They did not want war, but

Visit to G.H.Q. Arras by Winston Churchill,
First Lord of the Admiralty, April 1940

A tour of the British Line, November 1939
(left to right: Voruz, Gort, Alan Brooke, Dill, Duke of Gloucester,
Pownall)

The Commander-in-Chief with his troops

With Munster in his bare office at G.H.Q. Arras

once driven to it they would have been untrue to their nature if they had even considered withdrawal, or questioned the justice of their cause, until they were victorious. The French found it hard to see any logical reason why victory should be won: so did the more thoughtful among the British, but they preferred faith to logic. Neither of them was the least moved by nationalist, and only to a limited degree by patriotic, considerations: that was the prerogative of the Germans and the Italians, young countries which had only existed as nations since 1870 and which were smarting, in the case of the Italians from the sanctions sponsored by the Western Powers, and in that of the Germans from the belief that they were the victims of an indefensible peace settlement at Versailles and an insulting "guilt clause".

The efficiency of the French High Command was lowered by Gamelin's dislike for Georges, which was heartily returned. It was symptomatic of a deadly *malaise* from which the whole French army was suffering. The Duke of Windsor had been appointed to the Howard-Vyse mission attached to Gamelin's headquarters at Vincennes and since his duties took him to most of the French army corps and divisional headquarters, as well as to the Maginot Line, he was well placed to form an opinion. He wrote a pungent memorandum in which he expressed the view that the generals were more actively hostile to each other than to the Germans. The French soldiers were, the Duke discovered, dedicated to political feuds. The Roman Catholics looked with horror and suspicion at the Freemasons, for all the world as if the clock had been stopped fifty years previously. The Duke was not alone, but he was among the first to decide that Gamelin was, as he put it, "a weak sister". Gort did not dispute the diagnosis.

The quarrel between Gamelin and Georges, apart from its pernicious effect on their own officers and men, came near to including a dispute over the control of the B.E.F. In February, 1940, Gamelin showed signs of asserting that the B.E.F. was directly subordinate to him rather than to Georges. Gort bluntly gave his opinion that his army would "be better looked after" under Georges. When the War Cabinet had debated the matter, and Ironside had flown out to France for discussions at Gamelin's headquarters, it was finally conceded that since the French armies on either side of the B.E.F. were under Georges, direct control of the British by Gamelin would lead to confusion. Gamelin had to be content with attaching to himself a number of Intelligence and Operations Sections of French headquarters, which had formerly been subordinated to Georges, and thus destroying the hitherto sound working relationship between the staffs of the two generals. A primary reason for Gamelin's anxiety to assert himself and solidify his position was his dependence on the maintenance of power by his champion, Daladier. As Chamberlain recognised in January, when speaking privately about the deterioration of French morale, Daladier was "very rocky". On 20th March, unable to hold on any longer, he made way for Paul Reynaud as Prime Minister, and yet he could still count on sufficient political support to be included as Minister of War in the new Government and Gamelin therefore won a reprieve. Georges had no political champion but he was regarded by most Englishmen and many of his compatriots as the embodiment of the finest French military skills and traditions.

Meanwhile General Weygand had paid a flying visit to France from his command in the Middle East and Gort met him at Georges' headquarters. This active man of 74 owed his reputation partly to an impressive manner and personality, partly to the fact that he had been the shadow of Marshal Foch, whose Chief of Staff he was at the height of his fame and success, and partly to the mystery of his birth. Some said he was the son of the Emperor Maximilian of Mexico; others that his father was the egregious King Leopold II of the Belgians; and there was yet a third school which held that he was the illegitimate child of a Jewish businessman in Bruges with a gardener called Weygand, whose name he thought suitable for his son. Whatever the truth of these irrelevant theories, they made Weygand a figure of still greater interest to his compatriots. He was well known for his monarchist and ultramontane views and it was generally believed that Foch had said: "When France is in danger, send for Weygand." He had for the French an allure roughly comparable to Drake's Drum for the British.

His visit on this occasion was brief and it synchronised with one to London by Wavell, British commander-in-chief in Cairo. They both came to impress on their Governments the importance of reinforcing the Middle East with a view to diversionary operations in the Balkans. Ironside sympathised with the argument that the Middle East must be strengthened, but Gort did not. He thought it would be folly to divert from the slow build-up of his force on the Belgian frontier men and munitions which were vital if he was to stand a chance of resisting a German offensive. It was bad enough that the War Office had decided, in response to Wavell's plea, to send the Turks a hundred 25 millimetre French anti-tank guns out of a limited number promised to a B.E.F. acutely short of these weapons. The prospect of detaching trained soldiers for some Balkan adventure was still more deplorable. Gort wrote to Ironside: "It's odd how just the same old problems are cropping up now as they did last time. We are lucky in having that previous experience to draw from – the knowledge that small detachments almost invariably grow into large scale operations by big armies . . . and also the knowledge of the overriding importance of shipping tonnage . . . As we learned then, we have of course to be entirely sure, before we embark on any overseas adventures entailing long voyages, that we have the tonnage to get the troops there and the certainty of maintaining them whatever may befall . . ."

This was only one of the raids on the strength of the B.E.F. made during the winter. In November the Russians, wishing to extend their defensive belt, had attacked Finland without so much as an attempt to justify the deed. The Finns fought valiantly and for over four months they withstood the superior forces of the aggressor. Frenchmen and Britons of almost all political persuasions, already disgusted by the cold-blooded rape of Poland, choked with indignation and actively contemplated war against Russia. Darlan, the influential and politically conscious head of the French navy, agreed with Gamelin in thinking that such a war might serve the allied cause since it would provide an excuse to bomb the oil wells at Baku, a potentially dangerous source of supply to Germany in view of the new Russo-German entente. The least that could be done for the Finns was to send arms, but the only arms available were those being used to train new divisions at home or emerging in slowly increasing amounts from the factories for the supply of the armies in France. Since September Churchill had been contemplating methods of denying the Germans access to Swedish iron ore supplies, and early in the New Year he put forward a daring scheme which might serve the double purpose of helping the Finns in their struggle for survival and closing both Lulea in the Gulf of Bothnia and Narvik on the coast of Norway to German ships. Plans were made for the mining of Norwegian territorial waters and for military expeditions to Norway and even to Petsamo in Finland. This meant withholding troops who had been destined for the B.E.F., but the plan was welcomed by the French Government, and by Daladier and Gamelin in particular, because they were sure that military activity was the sole antidote to the canker eating so fast into their home front.

The third Corps of the B.E.F., to be commanded by Adam, who had at last succeeded in escaping from the War Office, and consisting of the 42nd, 44th and 51st Territorial Divisions, was due to start embarking for France in February. The 51st Division duly arrived, but the other two were withheld for Scandinavian purposes, as were a number of anti-aircraft, administrative and labour units. However, General Martel's 50th (Motor) Division escaped the net and was allotted to Brooke's II Corps. The remainder of III Corps were finally allowed to sail at the end of March, but the German invasion of Norway and Denmark early in April again changed the scene and a brigade of the 5th Division was withdrawn from France. The rest of the 5th Division was taken out of the line and placed in "War Office Reserve" from which Gort only succeeded in withdrawing it on 10th May. During February and March the despatch of arms and ammunition to the B.E.F. fell away to a mere trickle as the eyes and ears of the British Government were strained, week by week more eagerly, across the North Sea.

During this epidemic of midwinter madness Gort and the army he commanded were bereft of information as well as war material. While on leave at the end of January he was neither briefed about the plans for Finland and Scandinavia nor given an estimate of the repercussions on his own command likely to result from decisions taken by the Supreme War Council. The War Office omitted to inform even Gamelin that the 5th Division was to be withdrawn from France, although this, combined with the withholding of two of the three divisions in III Corps, meant that the B.E.F., intended to contain ten divisions by April and a fourth corps by June, would now be reduced to seven divisions. It would not have been asking overmuch that telegrams, explaining what was afoot and having a direct bearing on the hopes and expectations of the B.E.F., should be repeated to G.H.Q.; but neither telegrams, nor memoranda nor the conclusions of the Chiefs of Staff meetings were made available. The Chiefs of Staff Committee went so far as to cancel and then reopen leave arrangements for the B.E.F. without seeking the approval of the commander-in-chief.

All this led to friction between Ironside and Gort, but both of them were wise enough to restrict their exasperation to a discreet and narrow circle. Ironside, who was years senior to Gort, tended to look upon him as a mere boy, unsuited to large responsibilities and subject to tuition from an older, experienced general. Gort, conscious that as commander-in-chief he was directly responsible to the War Cabinet and not to the Chiefs of Staff or the Army Council, resented Ironside's sometimes impetuous decisions, frequent omissions to consult or inform him and tendency, in the mistaken belief that the B.E.F. was subject to his authority, to interfere in matters which were properly the concern of the commander-in-chief. "He is surely Belli's greatest delayed action magnetic mine," Gort wrote in a moment of exasperation. Yet in spite of the criticisms which each made privately of the other, they worked loyally together on the main essentials; Ironside stood up well against Gamelin and used his best endeavours to expedite supplies for the B.E.F.; but Gort did have good reason to complain of Ironside's excessive zeal for, and concentration on, Scandinavian excursions planned at the expense of the only front on which a decisive battle could be fought. Ironside wrote to Gort on 20th February to apologise for his failure to keep him duly informed and matters improved temporarily in the middle of March when, as a result of Finland's final capitulation after one of the most gallant episodes in the whole of the Second World War, it was decided that the 5th Division should after all remain in France and the build-up of III Corps be resumed.

There was a long-standing divergence of view between the soldiers and the airmen, in which successive Cabinets tended to back the airmen, about the use of the R.A.F. in support of land battles. It sprang from Lord Trenchard's successful campaign to establish the concept of "War in the Air" as a distinct form of military operation. During his first months as C.I.G.S. Gort told Liddell Hart that he believed an army air force essential in modern war. The air marshals, who secretly resented the continued existence of an independent Fleet Air Arm, had no sympathy for such a demand. It was agreed that the projected small Field Force should have its own Air Component, subject to the operational orders of the commander-in-chief, and there was also to be an Advanced Air Striking Force, established in France but controlled from Britain and comparable in size to the Air Component. At a meeting of the Chiefs of Staff in April, 1939, Gort had obtained a grudging acknowledgement that if the main enemy attack came through the Low Countries, the squadrons of Bomber Command might have to be "concentrated in the greatest possible force" on the task of repelling it. This was conceded because at the Anglo-French staff conversations the French had strongly demanded that all British bombers be assigned to help delay a German advance; but the Air Ministry insisted on adding, as a rider: "It is important to be quite clear that the Advanced Air Striking Force is not located in France in order to enable it to collaborate with the French and British armies. There will no doubt be periods when it will be so employed . . .". In the following month Gort, convinced that an army air force must be dedicated to no other task than working with and for the army, raised with his fellow Chiefs of Staff the question of the Air Component, which was to be under the orders of the commander-in-chief. "The time has now come," he wrote, "when, if it is not to be at a serious disadvantage in war against a first class Power, the Army requires further air support than that provided by the aircraft at present allotted to the R.A.F. component of the Field Force . . .". The size of the Air Component was eventually increased to contain four fighter squadrons (two equipped with Hurricanes and two with obsolescent Gladiators), two bomber reconnaissance squadrons, two squadrons of medium bombers and five army co-operation squadrons.

The brief campaign in Poland had provided evidence of the success with which the Germans used their air force, and in particular their Stuka dive-bombers, as an adjunct to their army. The Luftwaffe, like the Panzer divisions, was a new and highly effective component of the land war machine. Gort looked despairingly at the allied side of the coin: he had to take account of four separate air commands with no common authority and only in the case of one of them any direct control on his part. The Air Component was indeed his to command, but there were in addition the Advanced Air Striking Force, the French bombing force and, most unapproachable of all, British Bomber Command. The truth was that the allies had neither dive bombers nor sufficient light bombers to co-operate with the army, because the eyes of the designers had been fixed either on distant horizons or on immediate home defence. The Wellington, Hampden and Whitley bombers of the R.A.F. were not to be squandered in broad daylight on attacking advancing German columns: their role was to soar through the night skies and destroy that source of German strength, the Ruhr.

On 25th October, 1939, Gort wrote to Ironside arguing strongly against the Ruhr strategy: tactical bombing was, he maintained, of much greater importance. He was indignant that the new C.I.G.S. should have accepted a resolution of the Chiefs of Staff in favour of concentrating on the Ruhr. In November Pownall went to London to argue the case for placing the bomber squadrons of the A.A.S.F. immediately under Gort, but his arguments were unavailing against the power of the Air Ministry and the indifference of the Admiralty. Eventually, on 15th January, 1940, Air Marshal A. S. Barratt was sent out to assume command of all the British squadrons in France although the Air Component was still left to Gort for operational purposes.

In the middle of April, 1940, there was a short interlude of hope when the Military Co-ordination Committee in London recommended to the Cabinet that a force of heavy bombers be allocated to attack any German columns which advanced through Holland and Belgium. The Air Ministry at once launched a successful counter-offensive. On 11th April Gort had written to Oliver Stanley, Hore Belisha's successor, stressing that the squadrons stationed in France were insufficient and that "the whole weight of our Metropolitan Air Forces will be needed to help" in stopping the German onslaught. On 20th April he wrote again: "I hear rumours that there are still advocates of the Ruhr as an objective. However valuable the Ruhr may be as a lucrative target, the results can only be a long term policy: they will have no effect on the danger immediately threatening." Sensing that the Air Ministry were in the ascendant, he followed this up with another letter on 24th April in which he said that the Ruhr was obviously "a target which can have no immediate effect on the danger threatening the Allied Armies in the field. The Germans in Norway have shown the importance of concentrating their bombers on the forces in the field with immediate results on our military effort." In spite of these pleas, in spite of Poland, in spite of Norway, the Air Ministry and Bomber Command carried the day. Gort's last word on the subject was written to Stanley on 8th May. He expressed his forebodings of failure to apply the full weight of British bombing capacity at the right place and at the right moment. "Time lost," he said, "can never be regained in war."

On 29th March Jacqueline had telephoned from London to tell her father she was engaged to William Sidney. Gort was overjoyed. Diligent inquiries had produced nothing but favourable accounts of his prospective son-in-law and Jacqueline's happiness counted for more than anything else in his life. He was a little short on the telephone because, as he characteristically explained in a subsequent letter, "they listen in to cut off if they think a private conversation is in progress." Happiness came, too, from reports that Sandy, who had kept himself increasingly aloof from his father since his marriage, had turned into a keen and energetic soldier. It was unbelievable, but it did indeed seem to be true and when, shortly before the fighting began, his son and future son-in-law, each serving under his ultimate command in the 7th Guards Brigade, presented themselves at G.H.Q., he wrote to Jacqueline: "You would never believe it was the same Sandy – fit in appearance, walks like a drill sergeant and obviously enjoying every moment of his time." Thus, as the time for action approached, the commander-in-chief was personally content. He knew that the climax of his life and career was approaching. In a letter written on 11th April, he said: "The war has now hotted up and it looks like becoming hotter still. I look like being very busy and thoughtful in the near future. I trust all will go well and that I shall feel on the top of my form." Gort was a man of simple religious faith, and though his powers of self-expression did not rival Sir Jacob Astley, nor was it his practice to invoke the Deity publicly, this letter to Jacqueline was perhaps as near as he could go to Astley's famous prayer on the morning of the Battle of Edgehill: "O Lord! Thou knowest how busy I must be this day. If I forget Thee, do not Thou forget me."

If all was well with the commander-in-chief the same was not true, in all respects, of the British Expeditionary Force. There was a long list of entries on the debit side of the balance sheet. Tanks were few and mostly of poor quality. Since it took three or four years to design and produce a new tank, nothing but a decision in 1936 or earlier to equip an armoured force for war on the Continent would have assured the provision of tanks fit in quantity and quality to match the Germans. The one armoured division in existence would not, as Ironside informed Gort, be fully equipped with medium tanks or ancillary services till the end of May. In writing to Ironside, on 11th February, Gort had strongly recommended that it be divided into two brigades, for one brigade in good time was to be preferred to a whole division too late. As far as aerial co-operation was concerned, the Air Ministry had won the contest, so that inadequate bomber and fighter cover would be provided, to the detriment of the B.E.F. although, in the long run, to the salvation of the country. There were also, as Gort informed Stanley on 23rd March, many deficiencies in detail: tank tracks and sprockets were in short supply; there were 279 vehicles awaiting spare parts from England; there were no armour-piercing shells for field guns; in March, because of the Scandinavian diversion, the B.E.F. had received only 5,562 tons of ammunition as against 10,836 tons in February. No less alarming was the inadequate training of half the force, and the threat, renewed in April, of still further withdrawals in order to support the faltering Norwegian expedition. Dill, anxious as ever, complained to Gort in March that the resources of his I Corps were inadequate to meet a German attack. Regular units had, he said, been replaced by others with a low level of training. He had lost seventy-four senior officers, who had been posted elsewhere, and 240 of his best non-commissioned officers. He bewailed his shortage of light anti-aircraft guns, anti-tank mines, plastic explosives and reserves of motor transport. If his corps were ordered to advance, many units would be unable to take their full equipment with them.

More serious still was the inexperience of the officers and men arriving from England. In the last war a short period of training at home, followed by the bitter ordeal of being thrown into the trenches among battle-hardened troops, had quickly transformed a civilian into a soldier. Now it was totally different. "I am doubtful," Gort wrote to Stanley on 11th April, "whether the standard is as high as in 1914, owing in great part to the greater complexity of modern warfare ... The standard of training of the Territorial divisions which have arrived in France is low and in my opinion they are, as yet, fit only for static warfare." One of them, the 51st Highland Division, was to be sent to the Saar to take its place in the line with the French, because Gort felt he could not afford to send one of his regular divisions as he had originally promised. As soon as IV Corps arrived in France, the B.E.F. was to be divided into two separate armies, one commanded by Dill and the other by Finlayson, so that Gort could abandon his dual role of commander-in-chief and army commander. At the end of April, however, it was made clear that the advent of this new corps must be delayed owing to a shortage of signals equipment and operators. Finally, Gort was horrified to discover that three territorial divisions, the 12th, 23rd and 46th, which arrived in April, under-equipped and scarcely armed, to undertake labour duties and to pursue their training in France, had not so much as been taught section drill at home: they had been wholly employed in guard duties. Then there was the 42nd (Lancashire) Division: "I never believed it would be possible to see such a sight in the British Army. The men had no knives or forks and apparently lacked mugs. They were eating their meat with their fingers and placing it on the corrugated iron table tops." It all showed, as he wrote to Ironside, "a lamentably low standard in elementary administration."

Gort was never self-important, but some element of respect and recognition was due to his office. One of the territorial divisions excited his half-amused indignation: "I have just been blowing up, as I saw some of General Bulgy Thorne's division this afternoon when I was out. I came across and spoke to a captain and sub-altern at random, whom I met near a dump. I said to the captain, who obviously did not know who I was – 'How do you recognise the C-in-C's car?' He did not know, and having expressed some surprise I then said – 'By the way, who is the C-in-C?' – and he said he did not know. After that I went away and the captain said to Boy Munster: 'Who is that major?'."

On the credit side of the B.E.F. balance sheet the entry was shorter, but it was gratifying. By the end of April there were almost four hundred thousand British soldiers in France and of these nearly a quarter of a million stood ready for combat. In spite of all the Norwegian alarums and excursions the promised ten divisions had arrived. The alternative plans for movement to the Scheldt or the Dyle were prepared to the last detail as far as the advance itself was concerned, although it was disconcerting to discover at the last moment that the anti-tank obstacle covering the Dyle front, on which the Belgians were reported to have been working so assiduously, was constructed on the wrong side of the river and contained serious gaps. The army, short though it might be of tanks, was in other respects mechanised to a far greater extent than either the French or the Germans: for the B.E.F. the old wearisome foot-slogging was largely a thing of the past and units could be moved with a rapidity unknown in the previous war. Serious though the shortages might be in some divisions, the regular divisions had more anti-tank and machine guns to a battalion than either their allies or their enemies.

What above all gave grounds for satisfaction was the excellent health and high morale of the force. All but the new arrivals had undergone the rigorous training in which Gort fervently believed when he commanded a battalion and which he had latterly applied so successfully to an entire army that when spring came it was incomparably better prepared for action than in the previous autumn. Months of idleness and a basic lack of enthusiasm for the war in the neighbouring French armies had led to a demoralisation which was to be painfully demonstrated in the weeks ahead. The British were allowed no opportunity to become listless and the hard labour they endured induced standards of physical fitness which many of them had never before known. Whatever the anxieties expressed from time to time by the two corps commanders, the commander-in-chief, for all his private reservations, never failed to display confidence and his apparent optimism communicated itself to the B.E.F. as a whole. When the test came, Gort's army went into battle without glancing over their shoulders, with no worries about their home front, confident in their leaders and never for a moment doubting the justice of their country's cause nor their own ability to uphold it. Whether they won now or later, they were quite sure they were going to win in the end.

The April full-moon, when Gort expected the German attack to begin, passed uneventfully. Visitors continued to come and go with embarrassing frequency. On 5th April he ruefully informed Stanley that he had entertained forty-two people in the previous ten days. "They are mostly interesting, but one naturally longs occasionally for one free evening." Field-marshals came in droves: Chetwode and Milne first, and then Birdwood, Jacob and Montgomery-Massingberd. Ironside and Gort agreed that the appropriate collective noun for these lion-hearted heroes of the previous war was a Pride. On the other hand, Sir Roger Keyes and Sir Lancelot Oliphant, coming from Brussels, were important sources of information about the coy Belgians and Winston Churchill arrived like a gust of the freshest air, brimming over with ideas, information and encouragement, and looking, Gort said, years younger than he had a few months before.

During the winter some people at home had thought the engagement in Norway might cause Hitler to postpone an attack on France. Gort was convinced to the contrary and he noticed one significant pointer. He mentioned it on 14th April in a letter to the King: "Events seem to be moving towards a crisis . . . As no [German] high commanders of note are being employed in Norway and Denmark, it is possible that the operations now in progress in those waters are designed as a curtain-raiser to precede the great fight for a decision on the Western Front." Nevertheless, the Cabinet withdrew a further infantry brigade from the B.E.F. on 16th April and, two days later, Dill was recalled to the War Office to be Vice Chief of the Imperial General Staff.

He was replaced in command of I Corps by Lieutenant-General

Michael Barker, who, whatever other qualities he may have possessed, was neither liked nor respected by the officers who served under him. In Field-Marshal Montgomery's opinion Gort should have resisted his appointment and demanded a new corps commander of his own choice. It was true that Dill had not radiated confidence in the future although Pownall, at any rate, found him less depressingly pessimistic than Brooke. On all other grounds Gort missed Dill. To Jacqueline he wrote: "I think he was sorry to leave France . . . at the War Office I am sure he will do it all wonderfully"; and to Stanley: "He is a delightful person to work with." He was indeed, and there was never a better liked soldier. His days of greatness were yet to come when, as representative of the British Chiefs of Staff in Washington, he was to perform services for Anglo-American relations second only to those of Churchill himself. Meanwhile he derived little satisfaction from his promotion. He wrote to Gort from London on 24th April: "The War Office is, as far as I can see, in complete chaos and the situation in Norway as bad as I expected . . . If I was to do any good here I feel that I have come too late. I'm not sure that Winston isn't the greatest menace. No one seems able to control him. He is full of ideas, many brilliant but most of them impracticable. He has such drive and personality that no one seems able to stand up to him . . . Our S. of S. is quite charming and has really good judgment but has never been given a chance . . .". Dill must have been gravely discontented because, on 4th May, Gort said in his letter to Lady Marjorie: "Dill asked me if I would have him back again as things presumably are none too easy."

On 9th April the Supreme War Council sought the Belgian Government's agreement to enter their country and were refused unless they were prepared to order their armies to advance the whole way to the Albert Canal. This would have been strategic folly, and so on 22nd April they decided, without consulting the Belgians further, that if the Low Countries were invaded the allies should march across the frontiers without further ado and should also bomb the Ruhr. All was now prepared, the whole way down the chain of command from Gamelin to the smallest units, and there was nothing for the B.E.F. to do but wait until the operative signals were received from General Georges, under whose leadership and co-ordination the armies would advance.

Whether the decision were to move to the Scheldt or the Dyle, the details of the advance had been worked out with meticulous care, but it was distressing that the Belgians, for fear of offending the Germans, would still allow practically no reconnaissance of the territory which their friends and deliverers would be invited to occupy. Such information as could be obtained came from Colonel Blake, the military attaché at the British Embassy in Brussels, but close inspections were denied even to him. On 9th November, when a German attack was thought imminent, Gamelin had told Gort there was a new system of fortifications covering Brussels, although there was a gap between Wavre and Namur. On the same day a telegram from Brussels stated: "Military Attaché considers that no defences have yet been constructed on the Namur–Wavre line. He has motored across it. The absence of defences may be the reason for the Belgian hesitation to allow him to see it." Nevertheless, as the Germans did not attack, the Belgians were given time to repair their omissions and until the end of April, 1940, it was reported and believed that they had built the latest type of anti-tank defence, known as a *de cointet* obstacle, along the Dyle and southwards to cover the riverless gap between Wavre and Namur. It was therefore a shock to learn, early in May, that they had done nothing of the sort: they had indeed built part of a *de cointet* obstacle but it was in the wrong place, on land sloping the wrong way, and so far east of the Dyle as to be useless in conjunction with the defence of the river barrier itself. Moreover, it still had a number of large gaps in it. On 8th May Gort summoned Colonel Blake to his headquarters at Arras and required him to find out precisely where this Belgian artificial defence line had been sited, and at what points it was incomplete; but by the time Blake had addressed these urgent inquiries to the Belgian Government it was already too late. Gort decided, and so informed Georges, that if the order should be to advance to the Dyle, to the Dyle alone he would go. There, at least, was a river, however narrow and however low, to oblige advancing tanks to hesitate.

As April turned into May it was the increasingly dismal news from Norway that occupied men's thoughts. There was to be a debate on the subject in the House of Commons on 7th and 8th May. When it opened Captain David Margesson, the chief whip, was confident that nothing could shake the Conservative Government's large majority; but the personal attack which was mounted against Chamberlain, not only by Lloyd George and the Labour leaders but also by some of the most stalwart Conservatives, found so many supporters that in the afternoon of 8th May

Margesson and the whips were feeling and looking worried. Lloyd George begged Churchill across the floor of the House not to allow Chamberlain to use him as an air-raid shelter: Churchill, who was personally implicated in the Norwegian fiasco and would never in any case have betrayed his leader, used every endeavour to prove himself a highly effective air-raid shelter; but it was in vain that he made the most eloquent defence of which he was capable, because the Government majority fell to eighty, a figure which was unacceptably low on account of the abstentions it revealed among Chamberlain's former supporters. The victory in the lobbies was unmistakably a defeat.

During and after the debate rumours of moves by the enemy began to be received. Late on the 7th a report of an imminent attack on Holland reached the Foreign Office. In the early hours of the 9th the American Ambassador, Mr. Joseph P. Kennedy, disturbed a sleeping 10 Downing Street with a telephone call to say that President Roosevelt had been on the line to inform him of a German ultimatum presented to the Dutch Government on the previous afternoon. No. 10 were rightly sceptical of the Nazis being so polite as to present an ultimatum. On the same day the Parliamentary Under Secretary for Foreign Affairs, Mr. R. A. Butler, was bemused by the receipt of a report that the coming attack was aimed at Hungary rather than Holland. His Majesty's Government, the Members of Parliament, all Britons, most Frenchmen and millions elsewhere refused to have their attention diverted from the drama at Westminster and the absorbing questions whether the King would send for Halifax or Churchill and whether the Labour and Liberal Parties might agree to join a Coalition Government. By the time night fell on 9th May General Georges had seen no reason to reimpose the *alerte* from which all the northern armies had been released once the period of the April full-moon was over.

Part 3

Three Weeks

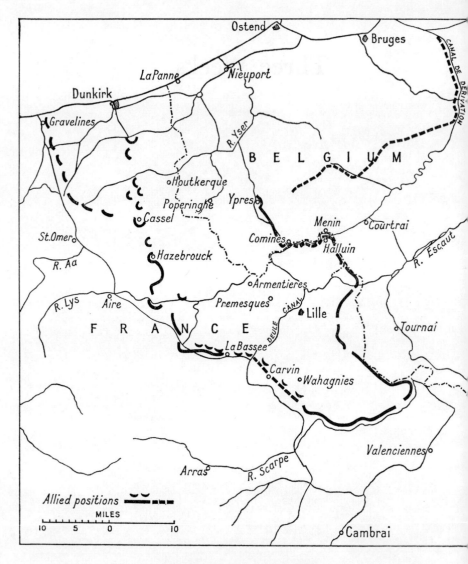

THE RETREAT TO DUNKIRK

APPROXIMATE POSITION 26TH MAY 1940

CHAPTER 13

ADVANCE

If by nightfall on 9th May the British were about to resolve a
political crisis, the French had just entered on theirs. During the
nineteen-thirties they often seemed, by unhappy chance, to be
without a Government at times of particular stress. It was so in
1936, when the Germans marched into the Rhineland, and it was
so when Hitler seized Austria. Since, under the Third Republic,
Governments were seldom of long duration, and sometimes only
lasted weeks or even days, this was not entirely surprising. Now,
on 9th May, the dislike which Reynaud and Daladier felt for one
another, more venomous because more articulate than the mutual
antipathy of Gamelin and Georges, erupted at a Cabinet Meeting.
Reynaud's wish to dispense with Gamelin, whose competence he
doubted, was the long gestating *casus belli* and, as in the British
House of Commons, the failures in Norway, for which Reynaud
blamed Gamelin and Daladier blamed the British, were the
subject at issue. In the early afternoon Reynaud submitted his
Government's resignation to the President of the Republic. On
the following morning the President had good reason to decide
that it was not a day to reshuffle Governments: Reynaud must
stay and so must Daladier. So, of course, must Gamelin.

Thus when 10th May came, a bright and cloudless summer's
day, Neville Chamberlain was about to step down from his office
and Reynaud to be confirmed in his. The Germans had no such
preoccupations. They greeted the dawn by invading Holland,
Belgium and Luxembourg while their airmen competently
prepared the paths for the advance of the armies, and their well
trained parachutists set forth to seize strongpoints of tactical
importance. At 4.30 a.m. the opening fanfare was sounded at
G.H.Q., Arras, by the distant explosion of some bombs and a few
bursts of anti-aircraft fire. An hour later Brigadier Swayne, head
of Gort's mission at Georges' headquarters, was instructed to
transmit to the B.E.F. "*Alertes 1, 2 and 3*"; and at 6.15 Gort
received orders to put Plan D into effect. Nobody had expected
it to be Plan E, which would have meant but a short leap forward

to the Scheldt, but a few days previously, in order to make quite sure there was no risk of failure in any circumstances, General Pownall had instructed one of his senior intelligence staff, Lieutenant-Colonel Whitefoord, to assess all the possibilities affecting an advance to the Dyle assuming the worst conditions that were conceivable. Whitefoord had therefore taken a grim view of collapsing Belgian resistance, roads choked with refugees and enemy saboteurs lurking by every bridge; and he had gone so far as to suggest that the Belgian fortress of Eban Emael on the Albert Canal, more strongly and extravagantly built than anything in the Maginot Line itself, might fall on the second day. He concluded, as the result of this exercise, that even in such improbable circumstances Gort could count on his troops establishing themselves on the Dyle before the leading German formations appeared.

The order to advance went simultaneously to all the armies under Georges' command. From the Maginot Line to the North Sea four out of five armies, totalling some eight hundred thousand men, prepared to swing forward into Belgium in order to hold the banks of the River Meuse as far as Namur and thence a line stretching northwards through Wavre, Louvain and Malines to Antwerp. Far to the south the French 2nd Army under General Huntziger had but a few kilometres to move. The pivot of the swing was to be at Mézières-Charleville, a few miles from Sedan. From there northwards General Corap's 9th Army, consisting of reservists and troops of inferior quality, whom Gamelin believed safe from attack through the impenetrable Ardennes, were to advance to the steep banks of the Meuse. It is interesting to speculate what might have happened if, as Gamelin at one stage contemplated, this sector had been allotted to the B.E.F. Next in the line, north of the River Sambre, was General Blanchard, commanding some of France's best troops in the 1st Army. His force of eight infantry divisions and two light armoured divisions would in all probability bear the brunt of the German armoured attack across the flat, well-drained country between Wavre and Namur where there was no prepared line of defence and no river barrier. It was for this reason that it included the strong French Cavalry Corps, under General Prioux, and was thus provided with a force of some four hundred tanks.

North of the 1st Army came the B.E.F., and between them and the sea was General Giraud with his 7th Army, a force as highly trained and regarded as the 1st Army. Keen and confident of success, they were away up the coast even before the appointed hour. The B.E.F. was thus flanked by the best troops that France possessed and it was intended to share with them the honour of receiving the full shock of the assault. Georges' wish to hold the six infantry divisions of the 7th Army in reserve, ready to strengthen any sector of the northern front which might buckle before the German onslaught, had been finally overborne. It was true that the Germans could freely choose their main point of attack and none could do more than guess where it might be. However, Gamelin had refused to be deterred from his favourite project, which was to add to the 7th Army a fast armoured division, one of the best equipped in the French army and capable of moving into Holland well ahead of the main allied advance, so as to save and occupy Breda and the Dutch islands at the mouth of the Scheldt. Of the strategic reserve behind all these armies little was known to the British and French Governments or to Lord Gort. It was not a subject which Gamelin or Georges had seen fit to discuss with them in recent months. Neither the Howard-Vyse mission with Gamelin nor the Swayne mission with Georges had discovered that the French strategic reserve existed mainly on paper. Such reserves as there were had been concentrated behind the Maginot Line.

As there had been no previous *alerte* and thus the B.E.F. was not on a footing of immediate readiness, Gort decided that the move into Belgium should wait till 1.0 p.m., the hour when his advance guard, the armoured cars of the 12th Lancers, would be ready to cross the frontier and motor straight to the Dyle. There was therefore plenty of time for the staff to take stock of the situation and to remark to each other, with monotonous un- animity, how tragic it was that the human race should choose such a singularly beautiful summer's morning to plunge into total war. Lieutenant-Colonel Gerald Templer, General Staff Officer, Grade I (Intelligence), found some verses awaiting him on the breakfast table. They read as follows:

> "Whether my life be long or short
> Largely depends on Viscount Gort
> Or on the steadiness of hand
> Of some benighted Allemand."

The warrior poet little knew how prophetic the first two lines of his quatrain were to be.

There was naturally a certain feeling of elation that the weary, soul-destroying months of waiting were over, and Gort had succeeded in imbuing the B.E.F. with an element of his own cheerfulness. It is difficult in retrospect to understand why anybody should have felt cheerful at all. The Germans were known to be better armed, better trained and more numerous, with ten armoured divisions and an air force which co-operated closely with the army and had learned the lessons of active war in Spain, Poland and Norway. Allied confidence had been shaken by the Norwegian Campaign and at the meeting of the Supreme War Council late in April there had, for the first time, been some signs of apprehension.

However, all this was hidden from the rank and file and even most of those who were better informed had a faith in the French army almost as firm as their inherited faith in the Royal Navy or the pound sterling. As late as 3rd May Dill said at 10 Downing Street that he did not think the German army was in good fighting shape. Their soldiers were, he believed, young and enthusiastic, but not steady. Since the allies had no plans for marching to Berlin, nor even crossing the German frontier, expectations of victory were based on the belief that Germany could only win a short contest and that this aim would be thwarted by the lethal power of defence in modern war. Thereafter, the effects of the allied blockade and the bombing of Germany's war industries would induce the armed forces and the people to realise they had been misled and to rise against the small clique of ruthless charlatans whose dupes they had been. The new Prime Minister, Mr. Churchill, who kissed hands on his appointment that evening, did not share this complacent optimism; nor did Lord Gort, who had been constant in his assertions that wars could only be won by attack and had been derided by some for his unshakable addiction to the aggressive military philosophy of Marshal Foch, an addiction he shared with Mr. Churchill.

During the morning Gort sat for the last time at the trestle table that served as his desk in the bare cellar of the bishop's palace in Arras which he used as an office. He found time to write a farewell letter to Lady Marjorie:

"Hitler has good weather for his venture and the start he gets from going to total war with no warning at all. Anyhow, we are now approaching the real test and on that the fate of democracy and our Empire depends. We shall get through as we have done in the past, but it will be a tough struggle for a while. I have never ceased to warn them at home that this would happen, but nobody

seemed to be particularly interested in it. Now they will realise
that the third and principal act of the great and impassioned
drama will be performed by the armies of France and the B.E.F.
May we have the strength, the skill and the staying power to see
it through to the finish without faltering. I am sorry for the luck-
less Low Countries who have no quarrel with anyone but who are
condemned as usual to be the cockpit of Europe."

The British line on the Dyle, including the city of Louvain
and the smaller town of Wavre, was seventeen miles long. Gort
had nine divisions with which to hold it because his tenth, the
51st (Highland) Division, had recently left to gain battle experience in the Maginot Line and to convince the French soldiers
that there really was a British army in France. Its return had been
promised as soon as the German offensive opened, but it must be
some time before it could be back with the B.E.F. There were also
the three incomplete and ill-equipped territorial divisions, digging
and training behind the line, but it would be weeks before they
were fit for action. Mindful of his experiences in the last war, Gort
believed that ideally a division should not be expected to hold
more than two and a half to three miles of the line, and he had
expressed surprise at the beginning of the war when he found that
Gamelin and Georges were thinking in terms of greater distances.
However, he decided that since defence in depth and carefully
placed reserves were the basic tenets of his own strategic thinking,
he would hold the Dyle line with three divisions only, two from
I Corps and one from II Corps, each on a front of ten thousand
yards. Two of the remainder were to be in close support behind,
two he would hold himself in G.H.Q. reserve, ready to strengthen
the line wherever the main stroke might fall, and III Corps
would be left, at least temporarily, to prepare or improve whatever
defensive positions might be found on the Scheldt.

The advance to the Dyle would be made by day as well as by
night, even though Blanchard's 1st Army, on the right of the
B.E.F., was proposing to move by night alone. The 7th Army, on
the left, had motor transport for two of its six infantry divisions
and they, like the B.E.F., had no need to tarry. On the other hand,
much of the 1st Army's transport was horse-drawn and many of
the infantry must march on foot, so that the progress of its main
body would be slow. However, its corps of tanks could, like the
12th Lancers, race ahead to the ultimate goal and delay any
Germans who might unexpectedly cross the Albert Canal in
advance of the time schedule allotted to them by the Anglo-

French planners. Gort preferred to reach his destination as quickly as possible, whatever risks he might run from the attentions of the Luftwaffe. It was better to have plenty of time to find and fortify the new positions than to take cover during sixteen hours of daylight in order to keep level with the 1st Army; and the faster he went, the less time there would be for saboteurs, who were wrongly believed to abound in Belgium, to blow up the bridges over rivers and canals.

Once the 12th Lancers had crossed the frontier Gort set off with a body of pre-selected officers and drove through Lens to a Command Post prepared for him at Wahagnies, a village ten miles south of Lille. He left behind, in the cramped quarters of the bishop's palace at Arras, some two hundred and fifty officers, clerks and orderlies, including all but a few of his Intelligence and Operations staffs. For the next fortnight the burden of running the main G.H.Q. fell principally on Lieutenant-Colonels Lord Bridgeman and P. G. Whitefoord, because Gort took forward with him his Chief of Staff, Pownall, as well as the majority of the other senior officers at Arras.

By this carefully premeditated move Gort separated himself for the major part of the campaign from his main G.H.Q. It was an administrative disaster because as the days went by an already imperfect system of communications deteriorated to such an extent that the link between Gort and the nucleus of his staff was all but severed. Thus the special Operations Intelligence Section at Arras to which, by long prearrangement, all reports of German movements were sent was often unable to pass the information to the Command Post. This section was connected by specially laid cable to Gort's Air Component and to the Advanced Air Striking Force; but in order to speak to Gort himself, they must rely on an inefficient civilian telephone exchange from which, during air raids, the operators frequently fled.

Yet he had little choice. He was commander-in-chief, presiding over an elaborate headquarters, but he was the army commander as well, responsible not only for the three corps of the B.E.F., but also for infantry, tanks, reconnaissance units, engineers and artillery under his direct command in G.H.Q. reserve; and it was he who must fight the battle. The arrival of a fourth corps in France had been postponed until June, mainly because of a lack of signals equipment (which was one of the more serious deficiencies in the B.E.F. itself). Had this corps arrived earlier, two separate armies, each with its own commander, would by now

have been ready to take the field and it would have been Gort's
lot to confine his energies to the sufficiently onerous duties of
commander-in-chief, operating from new headquarters which
were being prepared at Doullens.

He had no doubt that it was his duty to go forward towards the
battle zone, for he was a fighting soldier by temperament no less
than by training. Perhaps in his position Dill, with greater
wisdom but with far less dash, would have stayed to conduct
the battle from Arras; to Gort such an alternative was unthinkable, nor did he take into account the possibility that he and
his Command Post might have to retire on their communications.
Field-Marshal Montgomery was never one of Gort's leading
admirers as a soldier, although he has paid high tribute to him as
a man. He has written, however, that in combining the roles of
commander-in-chief and army commander Gort was asked to do
the impossible.

At Wahagnies Gort learned that the 12th Lancers were across
the Scheldt and the Dendre. Shortly after dark they reached the
Dyle and immediately behind them came the "cavalry", four
armoured reconnaissance units, still proudly calling themselves
Hussars and Dragoons, which Gort had allocated to I and II
Corps from his G.H.Q. reserve. The infantry, too, had started on
the sixty-mile drive to their destination and overhead the Air
Component flew 160 sorties to guard against enemy bombers. The
Luftwaffe was notably absent from the scene. Pownall remarked
that the enemy could not bomb everywhere all the time and
presumably the Luftwaffe was fully occupied in Holland and
on the Albert Canal. It occurred to nobody that the Germans
might not wish to deter the allied armies from their eastward
progress.

Whitefoord's estimate of what might befall in the worst possible
circumstances had in one respect been insufficiently pessimistic.
German gliders landed troops on Eban Emael, the jewel of the
Belgian defence system, even before the main attack began and
within twenty-four hours it was captured. The Germans had
established bridgeheads over the Albert Canal before the 12th
Lancers sighted the Dyle. However, neither this information nor
the first faint uneasiness that accompanied it had reached the
French and British High Commands by the night of the 10th of
May. There was nothing to disturb a good night's sleep in
preparation for the activities of the morrow and in ignorance of
the fact that, while all believed the main impetus of the attack to

be directed against Holland and Belgium, German armoured divisions, with the flower of the infantry behind them, were stealthily advancing through the impenetrable forest of the Ardennes towards the impassable barrier of the Meuse.

CHAPTER 14

RETREAT

I n London it was generally thought, and in particular by Ironside and Newall, that the main German objective might be to seize Holland and use the Dutch coast and airfields to mount an assault against the United Kingdom. On land the front would perhaps be stabilised in Belgium, hopefully east of Brussels, which had been declared an open city. Gort avoided speculation and devoted his entire attention to the punctual fulfilment of his task, which was to establish the B.E.F. in its allotted position and await orders from General Georges.

Such problems as arose during the next four days were caused neither by the Germans nor by the French, but by the Belgians; "our hosts," as Gort called them with courteous exasperation. When General Montgomery's 3rd Division reached its sector of the line, a Belgian corps was found in occupation. Then efforts were made to prevent the B.E.F. from advancing through the suburbs east and west of Brussels although no alternative roads were available. Gort, always conscious of the menace refugee traffic might become in the rear of his army, asked on the 10th that the movement of civilian cars might be restricted and petrol be rationed, but no attention was paid to his request. Finally, as the Belgian army, which in October, 1939, Gamelin had deemed capable of holding the Albert Canal for at least two days and Georges for seven, immediately recoiled in headlong retreat, King Leopold and the Belgian High Command gave way to panic and consumed much of Gort's time with urgent representations about illusory dangers.

Wahagnies was overcrowded since so many officers from G.H.Q. had been selected to accompany Gort to his Command Post. Moreover, as the main body of the B.E.F. advanced eastwards, it was further from the front than he found convenient. Thus on 12th May he was far away, visiting the corps and divisional commanders, when a message arrived that Daladier, Gamelin and Georges were motoring to the Château de Casteau, near

Mons, for a meeting with King Leopold, Gort and the commander of the First Group of Armies, General Billotte. He could not immediately be found because although several years previously the British had invented Very High Frequency wireless and were second to none in the development of communications devices, the B.E.F. was so singularly ill-equipped in signals. The Chief of Staff, Pownall, therefore took his place at the conference table and accepted on Gort's behalf a proposal that since Georges could not, from his distant headquarters, personally control the movements of the Belgians, the B.E.F. and the 1st and 7th French armies, Billotte should be designated "co-ordinator". On the following day Gort endorsed Pownall's action by sending General Eastwood to Billotte with a message that even if Billotte were officially only the co-ordinator, Gort would always be glad to receive orders from him if he thought fit to issue them.

On 13th May Gort and his command post left Wahagnies for Renaix, a small town on the road from Courtrai to Brussels. There he received a valediction from the outgoing Secretary of State for War, Oliver Stanley, whom he had personally liked and respected. Stanley's letter ended: "There was so much to do, and so little time," a conscious or unconscious indictment of the Governments in which he himself had served since 1931. There was no time now for reflexions on the past, for the battle was joined that day as the German advance guard clashed with British units east of the Dyle and a threat began to develop against Louvain at the northern end of the line. On the 14th, anxious to ensure that all was going according to plan, Gort was away from his command post for eight hours, including in his tour a visit to the Belgian King, who was still worried that British troops might enter Brussels and thus compromise his capital's chances of remaining a bomb-free open city.

King Leopold was sitting in his office at Willbroek Fort, deeply depressed. He could scarcely fail to be so, for as Gort arrived there was streaming westwards an apparently endless line of Belgian soldiers, some in boots and some in carpet slippers, a few, but very few, still clutching their rifles, practically none wounded and not an officer to be seen. It was the penalty for trusting in neutrality and for the refusal of even clandestine staff conversations. There were still brave and determined Belgian units, as the next ten days were to prove, but by their King and commander-in-chief they could only be seen as a rabble in retreat. In the whitewashed waiting-room outside the King's office General

Giraud inveighed against the Belgians, who had blown the bridges before his own retreating troops could cross them. Gort did his best, by assuming an air of confidence which he may even still have felt, to cheer the doleful monarch up and it seems that, for a time at least, his efforts were successful; but he left Willbroek with grave doubts about the Belgian armies on his left flank.

On the 15th, the commander-in-chief and a skeleton staff advanced still farther forward to the village of Lennik St. Quentin, twelve miles west of Brussels. It was, as Gort and Pownall saw, impossible to fight the battle as army commander, in constant touch with the corps commanders, and yet perform the functions of commander-in-chief. Gort chose the role of army commander and moved himself physically closer to the scene of action.

This day, 15th May, was the high tide of the British advance. Meanwhile, to the south, disasters had occurred of which only rumours reached the British command. On the 14th Gort was informed that the Germans had crossed the Meuse at Sedan. It was disturbing, but the full extent of the catastrophe, including the rout and approaching dissolution of the French 9th Army, was as yet unknown at Lennik St. Quentin and communications with Arras had already become difficult and intermittent. In Paris, however, and at Billotte's 1st Army Group Headquarters, it was a different matter. The British liaison officer with Billotte, one of the so-called "Twelve Apostles" whom Gort had attached to neighbouring French units, was Major O. A. Archdale. After a winter at Billotte's headquarters, where the staff were allowed neither recreation nor exercise, and could only with difficulty obtain permission to visit the individual French armies to whose destinies their work was related, Archdale had for some time noticed a staleness, a nerve strain and an absence of personal liaison with the armies of the group, all of which boded ill for efficiency in time of crisis. Now, as soon as news of the German break-through on the Meuse reached group headquarters, there was consternation coupled with an entire absence of decision. At the very time that Billotte was selected to co-ordinate the activities of all the allies, his own bewildered attention was concentrated on events to the south and as the news grew worse many of his staff, to Archdale's Anglo-Saxon horror, broke down and wept.

Conditions were, if possible, worse at the headquarters of the 1st Army, where Blanchard was every day losing the respect of his officers. Nor, with one or two exceptions, did they deserve his. Captain Miles Reid, the member of the "Twelve Apostles" attached to Blanchard, was driven to desperation by the administrative chaos prevailing. There was no planned division of duties among the staff officers, who fell asleep at their desks from unnecessary overwork; no proper maps were available; inadequate arrangements were made to feed the staff; there was no provision of accommodation or rations for the Other Ranks as the headquarters moved from place to place; the only protection against raids or parachutists was one Bren gun provided by the British; and at an early stage in the fighting the operations section ceased to function as a whole and its entire duties were taken over by two senior officers who had no facilities for recording incoming and outgoing messages. Incredible though it might be, the professional staff of one of Europe's most professional armies was totally unorganised for war.

Plans were made, on the 15th, to move Giraud's 7th Army southwards, across the B.E.F.'s lines of communication, in order to reinforce the shattered French 9th Army; but the efforts of Georges to transfer northwards the reserve divisions, lacking motorised transport and so ill-advisedly stationed by Gamelin behind the Maginot Line, were thwarted by shrewd German bombing of the vital French railway lines and rolling stock. Billotte's staff began to suspect that there was in fact no strategic reserve. Archdale, as was his duty, retailed his impressions of Billotte's headquarters to Gort who, late in the afternoon of 15th May, also received the news that the Germans had made a 5,000 yards breach in the front of the 1st Army on his right. This was due to the temporary failure of a highly rated North African division in General de la Laurencie's III Corps. Gort later told Thorne that it was then he began to have serious misgivings about the French army's fighting qualities. He immediately offered a brigade of British troops to help fill the gap but learned that the French had decided to withdraw to a new line. He was therefore obliged to swing back the right of I Corps in order to conform. He had no detailed or accurate knowledge of the rapidly deteriorating situation to the south and was only an intermittent beneficiary of the reports which Bridgeman and Whitefoord relayed from Arras. Bridgeman was obliged to prepare the defence of the town against the approaching Panzers without waiting to consult advanced headquarters.

Gort was, however, disturbed by the absence of orders. Therefore, in the early hours of 16th May he sent General Eastwood and Major Ulick Verney to see Billotte, instructing them to point out that the withdrawal of the 1st Army would oblige the B.E.F. to defend an untenable salient at Louvain and that this in turn must have grave implications for the Belgian armies. The "co-ordinator" must co-ordinate. Billotte thereupon issued orders that the whole allied line was to move back, first, on that same Thursday night, to the River Senne, then on the Friday night to the River Dendre and, finally, on the night of Saturday, 17th May, to the Scheldt where all the armies would stand and fight. Gort held a corps conference to arrange for the new dispositions and then, after one solitary night at Lennik St. Quentin, he returned to Renaix while his army began its withdrawal to the Senne.

Meanwhile in London Churchill had been awakened on the morning of the 15th by a telephone call from Reynaud to say that the Germans had broken through and the battle was lost. The Prime Minister wisely decided to fly to Paris and assess the situation himself. General Ismay, now appointed head of the office of the Minister of Defence and Churchill's trusted agent in all military affairs, remarked that the French were a volatile race and that "it may take some time to get them into a warlike mood". At least until that afternoon Gort, remembering the great days of 1918, had entertained equally comforting thoughts.

The Dutch army, overwhelmed by the German *blitzkrieg*, surrendered on the 15th after the Luftwaffe had shown at Rotterdam the same mastery of the art of reducing undefended cities to a heap of rubble as it had exhibited at Warsaw in the previous September. The British War Cabinet, to the delight of the air marshals, thereupon decided to bomb the Ruhr and, on the night following the Dutch surrender, the heavy bombers which, however unsuitable for military co-operation in daylight might nevertheless have been used to bomb the German communications by night, set off on their first, not very damaging raid. On the 15th Dill wrote to Gort: "The War Cabinet decided to bomb the Ruhr tonight . . . When one thinks what bombing has done to make the German's advance difficult and costly, I cannot see how anyone could suggest taking any available bombers off targets on his communications and installations. I feel I have let you down in this matter . . .".

The Hurricanes of Gort's Air Component fought heroically to shield the B.E.F., but after two days' fighting serviceable aircraft had been reduced to fifty. Gort had sent a personal message to Anthony Eden, the new Secretary of State for War, asking for further squadrons and three had been despatched with commendable promptitude. Even as they arrived their loan to the French was requested and granted, while Churchill, aghast to discover in Paris that the French had indeed no army reserves, sought the War Cabinet's agreement to the provision of a further ten fighter squadrons so that, as he put it, "the armies can fight under a clean sky". The B.E.F., unlike the 7th Army to their north and all the armies to their south, had not as yet felt the full horror of attack by concentrations of German "stuka" dive-bombers. When, a few days later, their turn did come they withstood the shock with remarkable equanimity, for whereas the training of French soldiers had been related to static defence in prepared positions, the British had been taught to seek refuge in the open by digging slit-trenches. They were also encouraged to fire at attacking aircraft with whatever weapons they had, an exercise highly beneficial to morale.

By the afternoon of 17th May the withdrawal of the B.E.F. behind the River Senne was complete. There was an unfortunate incident when the 1st Army Tank Brigade, about to embark its heavy machines for withdrawal by train, had to be diverted to resist an incursion of German tanks and motor cycle troops into the front of the French 1st Army. Intervention proved unnecessary, because the North African division on the immediate right of the B.E.F. counter-attacked with energy and success. However, by the time the British tanks returned to the railhead the engine drivers, alarmed by their proximity to an advancing enemy, had decamped. Thus the tanks were obliged to retire on their own tracks, with consequential wear and tear which much affected their later employment.

While this diversion occupied part of his attention, Gort at last learned enough about the rapidity of the German advance, and became sufficiently doubtful of the 1st Army's powers of resistance, to decide that he must by one means or another take steps to defend his rear and his southern flank. He had, in addition to his nine fighting divisions, the three scarcely trained, under-strength territorial divisions which had been sent out to France to help perform labour duties and to continue their training behind the lines. The German Panzers, already across the Oise, were said to be approaching St. Quentin and the Canal du Nord, where Gort had won his V.C. Early on the 17th Georges sent orders to G.H.Q., Arras, to despatch a brigade from one of these inadequately armed divisions, the 23rd, to hold fifteen miles of the Canal du Nord. Georges promised that French troops would hold the remainder of the canal line, but there were no signs of them when the unfortunate 23rd arrived nor, indeed, subsequently. Gort ordered plans to be made for G.H.Q. to move from Arras, first to Wahagnies and then to Hazebrouck, and all "useless mouths" were despatched to Boulogne. He then set about providing an impromptu defence for his south-western flank and established the first of many independent forces which were to figure prominently in the events of the next few days.

The failure of the British to plan and prepare has throughout history been matched by their ability to improvise, just as the social and military accidents to which the French are prone are compensated by their extraordinary powers of recovery. It was now Gort's lot to prove himself, as necessity demanded, a master of improvisation. He began at 4.0 p.m. on the 17th by the creation of Macforce, a scratch collection of fighting units commanded by his Director of Military Intelligence, Mason-Macfarlane, with Templer as his chief staff officer. This force added to its strength by collecting smaller units, which had been lost or had strayed, and a number of individual stragglers. Its instructions were to protect the right flank of the B.E.F.

In Field-Marshal Sir Gerald Templer's words: "Macforce, over the period of its existence, performed this task satisfactorily. It reconnoitred, it carried out considerable demolition programmes over canal and river lines (and indeed occasionally blew bridges too early on wrong information), it was an organised force, it directed stragglers, it kept its finger to the best of its ability on the pulse of the French formations on its right, it did what it could to direct the terrible refugee traffic, it shot down a considerable number of German dive bombers, it fought some small actions, it fed itself without worrying superior authority, it controlled looting." As events turned out, Macforce initially had a lesser part to play than the other independent forces subsequently organised, because the French 1st Army, battered and bombed in these early days far more severely than the B.E.F., held together and protected Gort's right flank. Its creation was nevertheless a wise precaution, even though the removal from Gort's advanced headquarters of two able intelligence officers added to the already grave administrative and communication difficulties caused by the partitioning of a G.H.Q. in retreat.

Back at Renaix there were air-raids. There was a large bomb hole in front of the door of the old command post and new accommodation had been found on the ground floor of a heavily sandbagged factory. During one of the raids Captain R. P. Tong, G.S.O. 3, took refuge under a heavy table with the telephone and, as he puts it, "bitterly chided a pair of field boots which suddenly appeared from a chair and placed themselves firmly in the middle of my back. I was brought to my senses by hearing the Chief's voice say: 'I always find it less inconvenient to telephone in a sitting or standing position'."

Meanwhile Billotte changed his mind about the withdrawal to the Dendre. The B.E.F. should, he thought, in deference to Belgian susceptibilities, stay a further night on the Senne and protect Brussels. Georges, from a great distance, sent quite contrary orders. Gort, for the first time, decided he must disregard his French superiors because he believed the safety of the B.E.F. to be at stake. It was now the 18th and Gort, according to his Chief of Staff, "is splendid, not at all rattled, rather enjoying himself, with a fine grasp of the situation as a whole". The more difficult the situation was, the more apparent it became that he was commander in fact as well as in name.

Billotte, however, was in a totally different frame of mind, changing his intentions as contradictory appeals from Blanchard reached him, at one moment begging Billotte to delay the withdrawal because the troops were exhausted, at the next imploring him to hurry it on because he believed he could no longer resist the pressure on the 1st Army front. Late in the day Billotte decided to withdraw not to the Dendre, but to the Scheldt and Gort was obliged to inform him that such an impetuous change of plan was impossible for the B.E.F. He sent a message asking that the 1st Army should hold a line south of Ath, so as to remain in alignment with the B.E.F.; but, as he put it, Billotte "refused to accede to this request". Let the French go, he decided; he would, with Macforce, look after his own southern flank. In the event the 1st Army, still suffering much harder blows than the B.E.F., stood its ground until 8.0 p.m. when it was ordered to retire in alignment with the B.E.F.

As the day wore on Gort moved back from Renaix to Wahagnies where he found time to write two letters. The first was to Dill:

"Our Great Co-ordinator vacillates instead of sticking to what has been arranged in the times of greater tranquillity and therefore of cooler judgment.

"Bombing the Ruhr certainly did nothing to aid the war . . .

"The operations so far have shown what we in the Army have always known and that is that air forces co-operating with armies in the field must be under the operational control of the man responsible for the conduct of the operations . . .

"How we miss not having an armoured division! Put shortly I should say the opening battle has started badly owing to:

1. Lack of prepared defences in Belgium. There was no depth, as we knew, on the Albert Canal position. When the bridges at Maastricht were captured the Belgian troops in front disintegrated, I believe. No pill-box line on the Dyle position. No A.T. ditch on the Namur-Wavre sector and only a de Cointet obstacle, with gaps, too far in advance of the general line.

> Nothing on the Senne line!
> Nothing on the Dendre line!
> Nothing on the Scheldt line!

2. Blanchard had too few formations on his sector. Prioux covered him but later had to go, and First Army then only had 6 divisions with virtually no reserve out of the line. The troops had walked up for the most part and were not unnaturally exhausted later on in the fighting. When anything pushed at all hard they had to give but the D.I.N.A. [North African Divisions] on our right were good and tough.

   Actually, had we stayed out on the Senne after last night, I might easily have found today an open flank of 20 miles with armoured troops attempting to work round it. My right yesterday south of Hal was held by *groupes de reconnaissance* only and the bridges had not all been blown.

3. Brussels being declared an open town did not make matters any easier. To have to defend a large city and yet to have to circumnavigate it imposes a considerable handicap on the defence! Our Sappers prepared all the bridges most successfully for demolition and had they been blown as successfully elsewhere a very considerable delay would occur."

In the second letter, to Lady Marjorie, he wrote scathingly: "Fortunately our hosts, having evacuated their forward positions on the Albert Canal all too hurriedly, were not attacked: had they been, I have no doubt that I should have had two flanks in the air. The speed with which allies suddenly evaporate without warning is one of the great harassments. At one moment, for about 12 hours, I was afraid the Huns would push a large hole round my right and then attempt to turn me northwards which, in the words you use, would be 'just too much' . . . but the French have a wonderful aptitude for pulling themselves together and rallying as they did at the Marne and again after the Chemin des Dames disaster in 1918. The Germans prancing about in the gap must be

undoubtedly very tired . . . The troops in the B.E.F. are tired
but otherwise in good fettle and having had the retreat with which
all British campaigns start, let us hope it will now improve." In a
postscript, headed Sunday morning (19th), he added: "I am afraid
I am not feeling at all optimistic today, but no time for more."

The decline in optimism was due to a visit he received from
Billotte in the early hours of Sunday morning. Archdale was
determined that Gort should not remain ignorant of the "malig-
nant inaction" at 1st Army Group Headquarters. He had seen
that all Billotte could do was to stand in front of a map which
showed the positions of the ten German Panzer divisions, count
them up one by one and say: "*contre ceux-là je ne peux rien faire*".
Archdale decided that the best tonic would be a visit to Gort at
Wahagnies and thither he conducted Billotte, who repeated again
and again in the car: "*Je suis crevé de fatigue – et contre ces Panzers je
ne peux rien faire*." On arrival he gave an account of the catas-
trophes to the south and told Gort he had no plan, no reserves and
little hope.

In these circumstances there was no doubt that Gort's preferred
role of army commander had to be exchanged for that of commander-in-chief. Henceforward his attention must be mainly
concentrated on organising defence on two or even three fronts,
bolstering the morale of shattered allies and planning the future
movement of his divisions without the slightest attempt by his
nominal superiors to issue orders or offer guidance. He was
fortunate that the detailed defence of danger points was in the
hands of officers who deserved and received his confidence: they
included his trusted friends Adam and Thorne and three of the
greatest names in the British army during the Second World
War, Alexander, Montgomery and Alan Brooke, as well as others
whose discipline, commonsense and capacity for leadership
brought their men safely through the dangers that beset them and
maintained their morale in retreat. Gort's belief in the importance
of a chain of command, and the unquestioning acceptance of
responsibility at every link in the chain, was vindicated by the
response of almost all the officers serving under his command.

On the 19th the Germans surrounded Cambrai, crossed the
Canal du Nord and even established a bridgehead south of the
Somme. By some strange administrative muddle Georges had
decreed new zones for the various armies which excluded from the
B.E.F. sector Arras, where its G.H.Q. was still established. Gort
paid no attention: he continued to hold Arras and he established

a second independent force, "Petreforce," to defend the town and
the banks of the River Scarpe to the east of it. The 50th Division
was moved to the line Carvin–La Bassée, west of his own command
post at Wahagnies, so as to be ready to support the Arras garrison
or reinforce the southern flank. He was now fully conscious of the
threat to his line of communication westwards across the Somme
as well as to his own undefended rear, since the Panzers were
evidently advancing not on Paris but northwards towards the sea.
The B.E.F., the French 1st Army, the Belgians and what was left
of the 7th Army were in grave peril of being cut off; and since
writing his comforting words to Lady Marjorie on the previous
day, he had been given reason to doubt the fortitude of the
French generals and the capacity of their troops to rally.

There were, as he subsequently wrote, three possible courses to
adopt. The gap between the northern armies and the allied
forces south of the Somme might be closed by counter-attack so
that the Scheldt could be held, or at the very least the frontier
defences prepared during the winter, and the line continued
south-west along the Canal du Nord to the Somme. If this were
impracticable, the northern armies might fall back on their lines
of communications and join their comrades south of the Somme.
This would mean leaving the Belgians to hold a perimeter on their
own coast or else prevailing on King Leopold to sweep his already
demoralised armies westwards, far beyond their national frontiers.
It was almost certainly too late for such a manœuvre. Thirdly, it
might still be possible to withdraw to the Channel ports and, at
the expense of abandoning all their precious equipment, for the
B.E.F. and such of their allies as would accompany them to sail
away from this north-eastern corner of France and fight another
day. Temperamentally Gort was attracted to the first of these
courses, closing the gap; but even at this stage he doubted the
ability of the French command to execute it and suspected there
were insufficient troops for the purpose. He therefore took the
realistic precaution of instructing Pownall to telephone to the
War Office and inform the Director of Military Operations that
in the end the only course open to the B.E.F. might well be to
evacuate from Dunkirk. Pownall carried out these instructions at
11.30 a.m. on the 19th.

In London the War Cabinet were wrestling with urgent and
incessant demands from Paris for all the fighters the R.A.F.
possessed. If, said Reynaud, the battle in France was lost, then the
war was lost. So why hold back the fighters? Churchill had

initially been swayed by this argument, but partly because Dowding, the commander-in-chief, Fighter Command, put up a notable resistance and partly because Churchill himself had been so shocked by the attitude of hopeless defeatism he had found in Paris, his attitude changed. Already on 17th May he was saying that the French were crumpling up as completely as the Poles in their unequal struggle eight months previously; but then he would comfort himself by the thought that the Panzers, far ahead of their supporting infantry, must stop to feed and refuel and that determined men might slaughter them while they did so. "The tortoise," he averred, "is thrusting his head far beyond his carapace." He drafted a message to Reynaud: "It would be shortsighted to squander bit by bit and day by day the fighter squadrons which are in effect our Maginot Line . . . we have recently sent additional fighter squadrons to France over and above the numbers agreed before the war and our fighter strength in this country has now been reduced to a minimum."

This vital decision once taken, to the lasting credit both of Dowding and of Churchill, the Prime Minister, after a gruelling week, retired to Chartwell on the morning of Trinity Sunday for a few hours' sunshine and sought distraction by feeding his surviving black swan (the remainder had been eaten by foxes) and his greatly cherished goldfish. Almost before the last ant's egg had been offered, the telephone rang to inform him, quite erroneously as it turned out, that the French 1st Army had melted away entirely and had left a vast gap on the right of the B.E.F. With the police car's bell ringing incessantly and a total disregard of red traffic lights or Belisha beacons, the Prime Minister returned posthaste to Downing Street, only to be informed that the report was exaggerated but that Pownall had telephoned to say Gort was contemplating a retreat to the sea. Churchill had himself, two days previously, given instructions that plans for such an eventuality should be made, and Ironside had made similar provisions in consultation with the Admiralty; but both of them had considered this a mere precaution against disastrous necessities which still seemed far away.

Churchill summoned the Cabinet at 4.30 p.m. and after its members had listened to Ironside, who advocated an energetic effort to close the gap, instructions to Gort were drafted, ordering him to march the B.E.F. southwards to Amiens. Churchill decided to go to Gort's headquarters and discuss the situation personally with him, taking General Ismay and the author of this book, who was standing expectantly on the doorstep, clutching a small suitcase, when he learned that the Prime Minister had with difficulty been dissuaded from going and Ironside chosen as the bearer of the War Cabinet's instructions. Churchill, remaining in London, broadcast to the public a fighting speech which he began to dictate at 6.0 p.m. and delivered at 9.0 p.m., and in which he said that "mastery can only be regained by furious and unrelenting assault".

That same day Reynaud told Churchill that on the following morning Weygand would succeed Gamelin as supreme commander of all the allied forces. Ever since 10th May Gamelin had remained in the background, considering that while he was still the fount of all strategy, it was the business of Georges to conduct the battle. Churchill's judgment of Gamelin was that he was occupied in saving not France but his own position. Now that occupation, too, was lost, just when he had at last, on 19th May, drawn up an order for French divisions south of the Somme to attack northwards and join hands with divisions of the B.E.F. and the 1st Army which were to advance through Arras and Cambrai towards Albert and Péronne. Weygand's first act on arriving from the Middle East and assuming command was to cancel Gamelin's order. Before anything was done he must himself go and examine the problem on the spot. He had yet to realise that not only days but even hours counted in the struggle for the survival of the allied armies.

CHAPTER 15

DECISION

WITH Amiens in German hands, "the picture was," Gort wrote, "no longer that of a line bent or temporarily broken, but of a besieged fortress. To raise such a siege, a relieving force must be sent from the south and to meet this force a sortie on the part of the defenders was indicated." However, at 6.15 in the morning of 20th May, Ironside arrived with the order from the War Cabinet for the B.E.F. to march south to Amiens, attacking all enemy forces encountered on the way, and to take its station on the left of the French army. The War Cabinet were under the impression that there were a few German armoured units roving to the south and that the B.E.F., with its 250,000 men, could sweep them like flies off a window-pane as it retired behind the barrier of the Somme. Ironside personally believed that the B.E.F. would have time to insert itself between the over-eager Panzers and the supporting German infantry still marching to join them from the Meuse.

Gort viewed the situation quite differently. Seven of his nine divisions were holding the line of the Scheldt, where a full-scale German attack was imminent. How was he, with neither ammunition nor food in plentiful supply, to disengage on his front and, while fighting a rearguard action against the strong German forces which would pursue him across the Scheldt, do battle with the armoured divisions blocking his retreat? And what of the French and Belgian armies on his flanks, neither of them, he already felt sure, in a position to make a fighting get-away? It was, he told Ironside, an order that as commander-in-chief he found it impracticable to obey; but he had already planned a limited offensive to avert the seizure of Arras and would strike southwards on the 21st with his two reserve divisions, the 5th and the 50th, while General René Altmayer's V Corps of two divisions from the 1st French army would at the same time advance on Cambrai. This was the most he could do, especially as he must now take steps to defend his own rear, along the line of the canals that run from La Bassée through St. Omer to the sea at Gravelines.

Far away, and out of touch with the realities, it was easy to demand that pincers be snapped together from north and south so as to wrench off the armoured head of the tortoise; but the Germans themselves were rapidly consummating an ambitious plan which had every chance of success. Their Army Group B, under Colonel General von Bock was an anvil, spread across the Belgian plains, against which the allied northern armies were to be smashed by a hammer wielded by the still more powerful Army Group A of Colonel General von Rundstedt. The intended victims could, as Gort again and again insisted, make a limited sortie southwards, but it was only by counter-attack from south of the Somme that the stroke of the hammer could be arrested. Meanwhile a Panzer division was attacking Arras, another was approaching Abbeville and others were securing Doullens and Albert. No orders had come from Billotte who, in his turn, had received none from Georges.

After Gort had made his intentions clear, Pownall accompanied Ironside on a visit to Billotte and Blanchard into whom the powerful, resolute C.I.G.S. did his best to instil an element of initiative. While they were talking, Weygand telephoned to urge Billotte on to greater activity and said that he would himself arrive on the following day; but Pownall left without any indication where or when Gort might be expected to meet him. Nor did Gort hear any more of the new Supreme Commander's plans apart from a statement that "Weygand is coming your way *tomorrow*" in a telegram from Churchill dictated on the 20th but unfortunately despatched in the early hours of the morning and thus dated 21st May.

When Ironside had gone, Gort proceeded with his plan for an attack beyond Arras and the River Scarpe with his two available divisions. They were to be reinforced by the Tank Brigade, in spite of tracks worn beyond the safety limit by the long drive back from the Dyle, and also by the ubiquitous 12th Lancers. The advance of the Panzers was being heroically delayed by units of the 12th and 23rd Divisions, which, scarcely trained and inadequately armed, stood their ground until they were overwhelmed; but, with Boulogne and Calais threatened, it was essential to provide a rear defence of the canal line. Gort therefore established "Polforce", to hold forty miles of the canals from Carvin to Aire, and in the next two days "Usherforce" and "Woodforce" carried the line northwards. These, like "Macforce" and "Petreforce" before them, were recruited from units in the back areas, strengthened whenever possible by some more fully trained battalion or battery which could be spared. They were the fruits of a rapid, remarkable and in the event successful improvisation. Soldiers whose normal duties would seldom have brought them near the firing line joined with engineers, men returning from leave, medical orderlies, P.T. instructors, the R.A.S.C., chemical warfare units and every able bodied man who could fire a rifle. A mobile bath unit fought with gallantry; and at one point, according to Pownall, "a posse of Padres" took to the sword and gallantly defended the bridge at Bergues. The resistance of these egregious bodies lasted long enough to enable Gort to man his threatened rear with divisions which a new disposition of forces permitted him to disengage from the main front.

Gort had an interview with Blanchard, who was accompanied by Reid, to impress on him that the armies could not remain where they were: the British attack south of Arras must succeed and the French must recapture Cambrai. Otherwise their flank would be turned and they would be isolated. Pointing to Cambrai on the map, he said in that lamentable French accent distinctive of an English public school education: "*Il faut tuer les boches, et il faut les tuer ici.*" Blanchard was stimulated, as he always was by Gort's determination, and when they were leaving Reid heard him say to his Chief of Staff: "*Tiens; ce Lord Gort a raison: il faut tuer les boches.*" Whatever the immediate effect of this tonic on Blanchard, Reid felt obliged to warn Gort that in his view no reliance could be placed on further resistance by the 1st Army. A fortnight later, Reid, safely home and walking with his wife in St. James's Park, met Gort, temporarily in mufti, his bowler hat pulled well down over his eyes. Gort referred to Reid's warning: "I didn't want to believe you," he said, "but I had a feeling you were right."

In the early hours of the 21st, General Altmayer decided that his corps was too exhausted to attack towards Cambrai. The venture must be postponed till the morning of the 23rd. Blanchard did not inform Gort of this change of plan till 12.30 p.m. on the 21st, one and a half hours before the British half of the attacking force, under the command of General Franklyn, was due to start. The French Cavalry Corps under Prioux, a general unwilling to admit defeat, were not deterred by the weariness of their compatriot infantry: weakened though they were by days of hard fighting, they honoured their pledge to participate.

Franklyn's attack from Arras was led by the tank expert, Major-General Martel. There were but few of the British tanks of

quality, the highly effective Mark II; indeed Martel only had
sixteen of them and some sixty of the lightly armed Mark I.
Moreover, the infantry divisions had each had one brigade
detached for service elsewhere. Yet tanks and infantry fought with
perseverance and captured four hundred prisoners. Though the
British had miscalculated the size of the forces opposing them,
the Germans, under General Rommel, were so impressed by the
vigour of the assault that they believed themselves confronted by
an imposing army of five divisions. The stalwart persistence of
Franklyn's scanty troops was matched by that of the Arras
garrison and it was the more remarkable in that Gort's Air
Component had retired to English bases, the Advanced Air
Striking Force had vanished from the scene and for the next few
days the R.A.F. were small, ineffective participants in the events.
The dive-bombing Stukas, which had contributed so much to the
disintegration of French and Belgian resolve, were thus left free
to experiment on the nerves of the more phlegmatic British.

While Franklyn's men fought their way forward, Gort awaited
a summons to meet Weygand. No summons came and in the
afternoon he left Wahagnies to preside at a corps conference
relating to the defence of the Scheldt. The German attack there
had started and it was necessary to consider how long the B.E.F.
could hold their forty miles with no supporting obstacles apart
from the river itself, now much reduced in depth because the
French had closed the sluices at Valenciennes in the hope of
flooding the area they were trying to defend. It would soon be
essential to fall back to the frontier defences.

Weygand duly arrived, at an airport where he was not expected,
and met King Leopold and Billotte at Ypres. By the time Gort
had been found and transported to Ypres, Weygand was on his
way back to Paris. However, King Leopold and Billotte were still
there, ruminating on Weygand's proposal that the Belgians should
fall back to the River Yser, the line they had held throughout the
First World War, and that the rest of the northern armies should
strike out boldly for the Somme. The trouble, as Billotte explained,
was that the French 1st Army was in no position to strike out
anywhere: it was, he said, barely capable of defending itself.
As for the Belgians, their General Staff felt that yet another night
retreat, abandoning ever more of their territory to the enemy,
would finally destroy the morale of the troops, and the King
warned Sir Roger Keyes, Churchill's personal representative,
that a southward march by the B.E.F. must eventually lead to

Belgian capitulation. All present concluded that the B.E.F., less attacked and less war-weary than the other armies, was alone capable of making a sustained effort to carry out Weygand's orders. It was therefore agreed that, on the following night, Gort should withdraw to the frontier defences, bring three of his seven divisions out of the line in preparation for a southward attack on the 26th and be relieved of a part of his frontal responsibilities by one Belgian division on his left and two French divisions on his right. Had Colonel-General von Bock himself been asked his tactical advice, he could scarcely have improved on the plan; for he was proposing to aim his main blow at the point where the northern end of the B.E.F. adjoined the unhappy Belgian army.

Gort left Ypres, not for Wahagnies but for a new command post farther north at Premesques, between Lille and Armentières, where a small empty château of two stories had been found for him and where the resourceful local butcher contrived to provide some steaks and a few bottles of wine for his staff. Here the main body of G.H.Q., separated from their Commander-in-Chief since 15th May, rejoined Gort and his Command Post. Billotte left for Douai and on the dark, encumbered road he was mortally injured in a collision with a lorry. There was now not even a nominal co-ordinator.

At Admiralty House, where Churchill still lived, he telephoned that evening to Ironside who said he expected to be able to hold Boulogne, invested though it was by two Panzer divisions. Churchill gave instructions that preparations should nevertheless go ahead for the evacuation of the B.E.F. in case of necessity. There was a general feeling of exasperation at Admiralty House because communications had evidently broken down and the Prime Minister, who liked to be kept fully and constantly informed, was fretting at the absence of news. He tried to telephone to Reynaud, exclaiming, as he waited vainly for the call: "In all the history of war I have never seen such mismanagement." Finally, against the advice of the Chiefs of Staff and the many friends and colleagues assembled in the ground floor rooms, he decided to fly to Paris on the morrow and impress on Reynaud and Weygand that it was useless to concentrate on the destruction of German machines which had penetrated into France: the allies must themselves attack the main body of the advancing Germans. As he went at last to bed the news came of Billotte's fatal motor smash. There were those who thought, callously enough, that Churchill would be relieved; but all he said was:

"Poor man, poor man; I am indeed sorry." It was not for him to suggest a replacement. He assumed Weygand would do so.

Churchill and Ismay duly flew to Paris on the 22nd and were met by Dill. They were well impressed by Weygand who seemed alert and resolved on action. He was modest too: when Churchill asked him privately whether he believed he could induce the French Army to fight, he only replied: "I will try." The same evening, before returning home, Churchill sent Gort a telegram demanding that he and Blanchard should attack south-westwards on the following day with about eight divisions and with the Belgian cavalry corps covering the right flank. Gort's actions should accord exactly with the general instructions he had received from the War Office. When the telegram reached Premesques the problem was seen to be that there were no eight divisions available, there was no extant Belgian cavalry corps and no general instructions had been received from the War Office. Moreover, ammunition supplies were inadequate for a large scale offensive. After Churchill's departure, Weygand issued a general order for closing the gap almost identical to that which Gamelin had prepared on the 19th and Weygand himself had cancelled. In the intervening three days the gap had become far more difficult to close and Weygand apparently discounted all he had been told at Ypres about the state of the 1st Army and the Belgians. He also demonstrated his misunderstanding of the situation by proposing that "the British Army should be moved in its entirety to the right".

At Premesques there was intense activity in providing stop-gap defences for the canal line to the west and preparing the move back from the Scheldt to the frontier defences. Gort was beginning to be worried and he told Archdale that he believed the time was approaching when his responsibility for the safety of the B.E.F. was going to outweigh his obligations to the French High Command. Blanchard, still commanding the 1st Army and not yet appointed to succeed Billotte, went to see him at 7.30 on the morning of the 23rd. Gort, well remembering what Billotte had said about the state of the 1st Army, again emphasised that the weight of attack in closing the gap must come from the south: the beleaguered garrison could do no more than make a sortie. The three British divisions to be withdrawn from the Scheldt by the agreement reached at Ypres were urgently required to replace the scratch "forces" holding the canal line. Gort would provide two divisions for the southward move and they would be ready by the

26th. Blanchard initially offered one infantry division and Prioux's greatly reduced cavalry corps. Meanwhile Weygand, who had told Churchill that he was collecting eighteen to twenty fresh divisions along the Somme, was none the less counting on the strength of the punch emanating from the north, while his new divisions would attempt to form a bridgehead or two across the Somme from which to hold out a hand to the northern armies as they neared their objective. There was no meeting of minds; there was no attempt to issue orders except in general terms and exasperatingly rhetorical language; there was a lack of intelligent communication between the northern armies and Paris; and there was a total failure by Weygand and Georges to interpret the realities of the situation. No wonder Archdale thought that Gort looked strained.

The Arras garrison, Petreforce, and Franklyn's two divisions supporting it were hard pressed. As the afternoon of the 23rd drew on it was evident that they must retire or be surrounded, and so at 7.0 p.m. Gort ordered them to withdraw during the night through the narrow escape corridor still open to them. It was now a question of defending the long canal line from La Bassée to the sea while the French held the southern flank and four divisions of the B.E.F., together with the Belgians, rejected the increasingly ardent advances of von Bock on the eastern front. It was regrettable that Arras, the most important road junction for the Germans in their northward march, should have to be abandoned, but its resistance had delayed the Panzers for nearly four days and the vigour of its defenders had alarmed them. Von Rundstedt, with Hitler's consent, ordered the Panzers to stop. Their losses had been severe, the remaining tanks were in urgent need of servicing, much of the country east of the canals was boggy, wet and uninviting to mechanised vehicles, the attack from Arras might herald an even more serious offensive from both flanks; and it would be folly to waste on a beleaguered garrison, short of food and ammunition, energies which would soon be required to defeat the main French armies and to occupy Paris. Von Rundstedt's infantry must maintain a steady pressure against the canal line while von Bock's less weary armies, aided by the Luftwaffe, went in for the kill. Since the R.A.F., concentrating its efforts in support of the garrison at Boulogne, was still absent from the scene, it seemed reasonable to expect that the Stukas would have every kind of opportunity.

The same afternoon Churchill and the Chiefs of Staff learned that the Germans were in Boulogne, that the attack at Arras had made no progress and that Gort had put the B.E.F. on half rations. Churchill concluded that the only course open to Gort was to retire to the sea and embark. He telephoned to Reynaud to discuss this distasteful necessity, but before he had even broached the subject, Weygand came on the line with the totally false information that a re-formed French 7th Army under General Frère had started its northward assault and had already re-captured Amiens, Albert and Péronne. There was no reason to doubt Weygand's report and gloom gave way to elation. The Germans must have shot their bolt; perhaps the Miracle of the Marne, that historical parallel of which everybody had been daydreaming, was really going to be repeated.

On the 24th, while the Panzers stood restively immobile, Gort ordered the 2nd and 44th Divisions to reinforce the canal line and General Thorne's 48th Division was sent to relieve Macforce, fighting hard at Cassel. He put Adam, Commander of III Corps, in charge of the British element detailed for the breakthrough on the 26th. At a corps conference held that morning news was received that the Germans were over the canal line and were advancing on Hazebrouck, to which G.H.Q. had retired from Arras; but the 5th Division was fighting a rearguard action to hold the Germans away from Vimy Ridge. However, the main consideration was that all the northern armies were enclosed in a pocket seventy miles in depth from the sea and some fifteen to twenty-five miles across. Gort gave instructions that his staff should again examine the arrangements for a withdrawal to the coast which he had first considered a wise precaution five days previously. Bridgeman had been instructed to draft the first provisional plan in detail on the 21st. The fact that von Bock was assembling four divisions for an attack at Courtrai, where the best elements in the Belgian army later fought well against superior arms and odds, made the prospects still darker; but, as in London, spirits were suddenly raised by the receipt of a telegram from Weygand informing Gort that the attack from the Somme had started and "was in very good shape". Two minutes later an intercepted German wireless message was brought in. It contained the order Rundstedt had given for his armour to halt.

Gort received an embarrassing request that day. One of the Twelve Apostles, Captain Guy Westmacott, was attached to the best unit in the French 1st Army, III Corps, commanded by General de la Laurencie, who shared with Prioux, de Gaulle and the defender of Lille, Molinié, what little credit French generals earned during these weeks of disaster. La Laurencie told Westmacott he had received no orders for several days and he believed Blanchard incapable of formulating a plan. There was, he said, chaos in the French High Command. He wished "to have the honour" of placing his corps directly under Gort's command, because Gort was a fighter. La Laurencie had made the same request through Mason-Macfarlane on 22nd May and some of the staff of the 1st Group of Armies had been making similar representations to Archdale and Reid since the 20th. Gort, however, was trying to fight on three fronts: it was a hard enough task without assuming command of other armies, and in any case his acceptance would have been the signal for apoplexy in Paris, although, surprisingly enough, two days later in Paris Archdale was asked by Marshal Pétain whether Gort might not assume command of all the northern armies. This was certainly just a thought which passed through Pétain's mind during the conversation. It cannot have represented a possibility seriously considered by the French Government. In any case Gort sent Westmacott back to La Laurencie with a polite but firm refusal.

By the morning of the 25th von Bock's offensive against the Belgians was becoming dangerous. Courtrai still held out; but the enemy were across the River Lys and there was a dangerous gap developing north of Brooke's II Corps through which the Germans might soon be pouring to cut off the allies from Dunkirk and from their sole remaining line of supply, communications and possible retreat. Gort sent his last reserves, one brigade and one machine-gun company, to Brooke's aid. This was scarcely accomplished when Dill arrived from London to discuss the forthcoming sortie to the Somme. Disconcerted by the evident incomprehension in London, and the paucity of information he had received, Gort had invited Dill to assess the facts on the spot. Pownall thought that Gort needed cheering up, because although the years of hardening exercise and deliberate privation were now paying off, in that his physical stamina was totally unimpaired, his ability to exercise cool judgment in large matters was not matched by a capacity to rise above the smaller worries. In addition, the constant need to patch, make and mend was uncongenial to him. To advance, to fight and, where necessary, to stand defiant in defence: it was for this that he was temperamentally suited. To cope with the problems of the Belgians and the

French, and never to be master of his own destiny, he found intolerable.

Far from cheering him up, Dill – for once lacking in tact – hinted that the B.E.F. was being criticised in London for in-activity; and as if all this were not enough, Gort received a copy of a querulous telegram from Reynaud to Churchill, complaining that the withdrawal of the 5th and 50th Divisions from Arras had jeopardised the operation to close the gap. It stated that Weygand had heard from Blanchard of a British withdrawal forty kilometres from Arras, in the direction of the ports, just when the recapturers of Amiens and Péronne were making excellent progress, and that in consequence Weygand was obliged to give up his plan to continue the northward advance. It was immediately clear that Blanchard knew nothing of his own alleged complaint. No doubt Weygand, discovering that the southern échelon had made no progress at all, and was not even across the Somme or in a position to advance a kilometre, was hoping to use the British as scapegoats and the story of Gort's perfidious withdrawal con-tinued to be quoted in Paris as an excuse for the allied disaster.

All the same, the planning for the southward move went ahead. Blanchard, at last appointed co-ordinator in Billotte's stead, no longer spoke of one French division and the cavalry corps, but told Dill he could provide two or three divisions and 200 tanks. Unfortunately, Adam quickly discovered that Blanchard's estimate of the strength he could muster was a mirage, for he spent the morning with General René Altmayer, who was to be the supreme commander of the sortie, and found that the 1st Army could spare no more than one division. Moreover, the German motorised infantry were already across the canal on Altmayer's left. Adam at once telephoned to Gort while Dill, believing that a five- or six-divisional attack was in prospect, returned to London. Two days later he was appointed to succeed Ironside as C.I.G.S.

During the afternoon of 25th May distress signals arrived from Brooke. On receiving a report from III Corps Artillery, Adam sent independent confirmation that Belgian units had vanished from the scene in a vital area. It seemed doubtful whether Brooke or the Belgians could fill a void left north-west of Menin or hold the im-portant road from Comines to Ypres. The moment had come to make a crucial decision. The Panzers to the west would soon be on the move again; the possibility, for which Gort had hoped against hope, that at least part of the British armoured division might arrive to reinforce him, had finally vanished; all his reserves were allocated, and if he was to answer Brooke's increasingly urgent appeals for reinforcement, there were available only the 5th and 50th Divisions, earmarked for the great adventure southwards. That would mean unilaterally calling off the attack, letting down Blanchard and Altmayer and giving apparent justification to Reynaud's hurtful innuendoes. He alone could decide.

Lieutenant-Colonel Templer had been sent by Mason-Macfarlane to tell Pownall about the position at Cassell. This is his account of what he saw at Premesques:

"It was a difficult drive to say the least of it. Having found the small villa in which the C-in-C and his Chief of Staff were working, I asked at the door to see the latter. I was told the only way into his office was through the C-in-C's room, and was advised to go through it quietly as Lord Gort was busy. I then walked in, to see Gort standing in a very typical attitude – with his legs apart and his hands behind his back. He was staring – quite alone – at a series of maps of Northern France and the Channel ports, pinned together and covering most of the wall of his small room. I tiptoed across the room behind him to get into Henry Pownall's office through the other door. Gort turned round and said 'Hullo, Gerald, what do you want?' I said 'Nothing, Sir – but I have to report to General Pownall.' Having done so, I asked Pownall (who had taught me at the Staff College in 1928 and 1929) how I could get out again. He said the only way was the one I had come. I imagine my reply was 'not ruddy likely' or words to that effect, and I left by climbing out of a window into the garden.

"Such had been the effect on me of seeing a man, of the stature of Lord Gort, wrestling with his God and his duty at a moment of destiny. It was only later that I realised that he was, at that precise point of time, taking the decision as to whether to bring the remains of the B.E.F. out through Dunkirk, or whether to continue with the plan of retreating south. Though I had no precise idea of the problem which was then facing him, all my heart went out to him in his loneliness and tribulation."

Shortly afterwards Archdale arrived, because Gort in despair had decided to send him to Paris to explain orally to Georges what neither Weygand nor Georges seemed to have learned from Blanchard or their own staff officers. At 5.30 p.m. Archdale entered Gort's office at Premesques:

"The C-in-C was sitting at his table very silent, and looking rather bewildered and bitter. I felt most strongly that he was wishing that he could take an active physical part in this battle: that it was irking him terribly to be forced to sit there with nothing but weary Allies all round him: weary in body but oh! so terribly weary in mind.

"He said that he had had a raw deal from the Allies; not only had their Army continually pleaded that it was too tired to fight, and their staff work broken down, but from start to finish there had been no direction or information from the High Command. 'Why' – he asked – 'did they retreat to the Scheldt when they knew of the great gap in the middle – why not retreat south and preserve a front and lines of communication?' "

Hardly had Archdale left when Adam rang up with the news that Altmayer could only provide one division for the attack. Gort also heard that the Moroccan troops, who had hitherto fought courageously and well, had bolted at Carvin and that two battalions of the 50th Division had been rushed to the scene to save the day. It was increasingly clear that if he went south, he would in all probability, as at Arras, have to go without the French. Martel's tank force had dwindled away and there were only two Mark II and fifteen Mark I tanks left. He would therefore be sending infantry divisions, almost unprotected by armour, to do battle with the Panzers. Further ominous news came from Brooke, and Montgomery's 3rd Division captured some enemy plans which showed the strength of the assault von Bock was about to launch between Ypres and Comines. The colonel of the 12th Lancers arrived to report that, from his observations, the Belgians had no fighting spirit left.

Gort decided. At 6.30 p.m., on Thursday 25th May, without wasting the hours which finding and consulting Blanchard would entail, he cancelled the British offensive planned for the next day and despatched the 5th Division with all speed to hold the line north of Brooke's embattled corps. As soon as the units which had been detached from the 50th Division when the Moroccans fled were reunited to the main force, that division, too, was sent to the Ypres front. He asked nobody's advice. He did not stop to take account of what the War Cabinet or Weygand or Georges might require. He merely sent word to Altmayer that the attack was off. Thus at Britain's gravest hour, it fell to Gort, deprived of all instructions from higher authority, outnumbered and outgunned but not outwitted, to take a prompt and solitary decision which thwarted von Bock and saved the whole British Expeditionary Force from death or captivity.

CHAPTER 16

SALVATION

━━━

IT was 9.30 p.m. on the 25th before the cancellation of the British offensive could be made known to Blanchard, who was away on a visit to King Leopold. When Reid gave him the message he was distressed and his two principal staff officers were outspokenly critical. Overnight, however, Blanchard became reconciled to the decision and when Gort went to his headquarters at Attiches early on the 26th, he gladly co-operated in drawing up the lines of withdrawal to the north. Gort did not mention the delicate matter of eventual embarkation since he was expressly ordered not to do so. He had telegraphed to Anthony Eden the reasons for his decision to cancel the offensive and Eden, who had meanwhile learned that the exciting French advance from the Somme was a myth, replied that all beaches and ports east of Gravelines were to be used for embarkation. The Prime Minister would tell Reynaud, but "in the meantime it is obvious you should not discuss the possibility of the move with the French or Belgians". That evening "Operation Dynamo", the evacuation of the armies from Dunkirk, was set in motion though only non-combatants were embarked.

The French generals of 1940 were more adept in the use of their language than of their troops. Hardly had Blanchard and Gort decided to retire northwards when a flowery message arrived from Weygand. Referring to "the battle on which the fate of our country depends", he exhorted all concerned to be "animated by a savage desire to fight where they stand until they die". He concluded with the words: *"Activité, Solidarité, Résolution!"* Prioux, now commanding the 1st Army in Blanchard's place, obediently passed the message on to all corps commanders, adding that in conformity with this imperative call the battle would be waged without any thought of retreat. It was, to say the least, an ill-timed pronouncement when the decision to retreat northwards had already been made, and imitations of the First World War declarations of Foch or Pétain, themselves patterned on the clarion calls of the French Revolution and Napoleon, were as flat and unappetising in 1940 as an overcooked soufflé.

The B.E.F. began the withdrawal to the coast, fighting by day and retiring by night, while Gort instructed Adam to hand over the command of III Corps and organise the defence of a perimeter round Dunkirk. The French 1st Army, fighting under Prioux's inspired leadership better than it had ever fought, withstood an assault in the south. The flanks were valiantly held. To the west, the southern end of the canal line was defended by the 2nd Division till only a remnant survived, and later on the 145th Brigade of Thorne's 48th Division stood at Cassel with equal fortitude and equally heavy casualties. To the east, while the Belgians sent messages demanding a counter-attack by the B.E.F. between the Lys and the Yser, Brooke, left as he had to be to his own devices but reinforced with every remaining man who could be found, conducted the defence north and south of Ypres with brilliant military skill against greatly superior forces. The 5th Division, which Franklyn had brought post-haste from its area of concentration for the southern offensive, and which was short of an entire infantry brigade, fought so well against three German divisions between Ypres and Comines that Brooke saluted it as the saviour of II Corps and the B.E.F. There were indeed many contributions to the salvation of the B.E.F.: the stand of the untrained labour divisions, delaying the Panzers in their north-ward sweep while the defence of the canal line was being organ-ised; the resistance first of Boulogne and then of Calais; the decision of Rundstedt to halt for nearly two days the advance of the Panzers and German fears of an Anglo-French flank attack; the promptness with which, at all levels, orders were given and obeyed in the B.E.F.; the initiative of individual commanders when, as so often happened, communications failed; and by no means least, the self-sacrifice of the divisions and independent units directed to hold the two flanks while the main body retired to the sea.

On the 27th Gort moved his headquarters to Houtkerque, travelling on roads congested with refugees and French horse-drawn transport, for although Blanchard and he had carefully specified the separate roads reserved for the British and French armies, French staff work had completely disintegrated and an order did not guarantee a response. An Anglo-French Staff Conference at Cassel drew up plans for the joint defence of the Dunkirk perimeter. No orders about withdrawal had been sent to Blanchard, but at the Cassel conference he received another stirring message from Weygand, this time requiring all concerned to attack the Germans and recapture Calais, which had fallen on the 26th and was separated from the allies by several Panzer divisions and large bodies of German infantry. Next day Weygand sent a personal message to Gort beseeching him to take an active part in all counter-attacks. Gort rightly concluded that from now on he should reserve his attention for orders received from his own Government, although late on the 26th Churchill had still been under the impression that the B.E.F. might despatch a column to relieve Calais. Indeed, Churchill continued to maintain that Gort missed an opportunity in not making a lightning move to the relief of Calais with one of his divisions, although it is difficult to conceive whence he supposed that division was to come.

The refugee problem, which had been building up day by day since the allied withdrawal from the Dyle, was magnified by the decision of the French authorities to close their frontier with Belgium, so that the hapless stream of humanity making its pedestrian way westwards was forced to change direction north. As the stream became a flood, the movement of the armies was seriously hampered, but it was the misery of the victims which imprinted itself on the memory of all ranks of the B.E.F. Gort, speaking on a wireless programme two months later, recalled his own feelings:

"Never shall I forget the savagery of the total war which heralded the arrival in Western Europe of the new and revised version of the German doctrine that 'Might is Right': the pitiable terror of men and women in Belgium and Northern France running, many of them for the second time in their lives, homeless and penniless, before the invader."

In London the War Cabinet, already foreseeing that France might collapse entirely, took stock of Great Britain's ability to carry on the war alone. A telegram arrived from Lord Lothian, British Ambassador in Washington, saying that President Roosevelt believed America would enter the war if Britain were *in extremis* and suggesting that the British war effort might be continued from Canada. He added the quaint suggestion that the new seat of the British Government should be in Bermuda rather than at Ottawa, because public opinion in the United States would be sensitive about a monarchy functioning on North American soil. Churchill said, but did not reply, that neither the monarchy nor the Government should consider functioning anywhere but in London.

At 10.0 p.m. on the 27th the Cabinet met to discuss a decision by King Leopold, taken against the advice of his Government, which was now established on English soil, to ask the Germans for an armistice. It was a decision of which Gort as yet knew nothing, because he had set off with Pownall in search of Blanchard, with whom it was urgently necessary to co-ordinate the more rapid withdrawal of the armies and explain about embarkation. Blanchard could not be found and Gort was in pursuit of him until 3.0 a.m. Since Houtkerque was not on the main line of buried cable, wireless communication was ineffective and Gort at G.H.Q., no less than Brooke conducting his vital engagement at Ypres, depended on personal visits or messages by the hand of liaison officers. In the course of this unavailing hunt Gort reached Dunkirk and there, at 11.0 p.m., he heard that the Belgians would lay down their arms at midnight. Premonitory messages sent by the King and by Keyes had failed to reach him. The news was less of a shock to Gort, who told Munster that he had been expecting it, than to the British and French Governments; but Belgian surrender must leave an undefended gap of twenty miles between the left of Brooke's divisions and the sea. The Belgians had in any case chosen to withdraw north-eastwards, towards Antwerp rather than the line of the Yser, so that even without the armistice a gap would have developed; but the event added still greater urgency to a withdrawal within the Dunkirk perimeter before the Germans could themselves cross the Yser and attack along the coast.

In the morning of the 28th the elusive Blanchard arrived at Houtkerque where Gort told him he had orders from the War Cabinet to embark the B.E.F. for England. Blanchard, having received nothing from his own High Command apart from exhortations to perform the impossible, was aghast. Captain Reid had observed that since the opening of the campaign the only definite views ever expressed by Blanchard were those he had received from Gort. Now, however, he could no longer be an echo: the British were about to sail away while his understanding had been that the allied armies would form a semi-circular redoubt to be supplied and reinforced by sea and that, as he had put it after the Attiches meeting on 26th May, "the bridgehead will be held with no thought of retreat".

He was still suffering from the shock of this disclosure when Gort said that owing to the Belgian surrender, and the con-centrated pressure of German attacks at Ypres, the armies must that very night move back to the line Ypres–Poperinghe–Cassel. Blanchard considered the proposal and on hearing from Prioux that his men were tired and could not move back for another twenty-four hours demanded a postponement. Gort judged that delay would be fatal: von Bock's divisions, advancing from the east, would seize the coastal town of Nieuport and occupy the perimeter before the allies could reach it. He therefore told Blanchard that he would go back without him and he moved his own headquarters to a seaside villa at La Panne, which had been used by King Albert of the Belgians in the First World War. There he was able to re-establish direct telephonic communications with London. Later in the day Prioux relented to some extent and though one corps of the 1st Army stayed in the south, fighting resolutely until it was obliged to surrender (and was allowed by the admiring Germans "full battle honours" in so doing), La Laurencie's III Corps was sent to the bridgehead to join the B.E.F. and the remnants of the old French 7th Army. On this day, too, von Rundstedt's tank commanders, whose assault against the encircled armies had recommenced after the fall of Calais, called off the attack. They had lost half their fighting strength, the marshy country west of Dunkirk was still less inviting to tanks after a sudden spell of heavy rain and it was necessary to regroup for the coming attack across the Somme. It was officially decided that the *coup de grâce* should be administered to the B.E.F. and the French 1st Army by von Bock and the Luftwaffe.

The R.A.F. were fully back in the fray. The closer the B.E.F. came to the sea, the more they were in range of fighter cover. As Gort arrived at La Panne, there was a violent thunderstorm and a temporary lull in aerial activity. Dunkirk harbour had already been bombed to rubble and ashes but for the next few days, with the safety of the British army hanging in the balance, Dowding and the Air Ministry discarded all their inhibitions and every Spitfire and Hurricane in the south of England did battle against the over-confident Luftwaffe. It was a dress rehearsal for the Battle of Britain, fought too high for the troops on the beaches to know what feats were being performed on their behalf, and the German losses in planes and pilots were out of all proportion to those of the R.A.F. Against the other designated administrator of the *coup de grâce*, von Bock, the B.E.F. could only fend for themselves.

They did so admirably, withdrawing unit by unit within the perimeter and driving out German infiltrators with unvarying success. The French held four miles of coast west of Dunkirk and the British an enclave seventeen miles long, stretching from Dunkirk to Nieuport. The French at the western end distinguished themselves in the fighting. They did not, however, distinguish themselves in other ways, for they ignored instructions to destroy their transport before entering the perimeter defences and they disregarded the orders for road and beach discipline. Blanchard and his headquarters moved into the bridgehead, where Admiral Abrial, in charge of the port and the garrison, was in command; but until the 29th neither he nor Blanchard received any orders about embarkation. Churchill was insisting that the British and French should depart in equal numbers, but Gort was obliged to telephone to Dill at the War Office and inform him that Abrial was showing signs of obstructing the departure of all fighting troops. He demanded that pressure be brought on the French Government, advised of British intentions by Churchill as long ago as 26th May, to issue the necessary instructions to the authorities at Dunkirk. This, at long last, they did, and French ships joined the British rescue armada. Gort had originally supposed he would be lucky if 30 per cent. of the B.E.F. were saved, but now, in spite of the appalling difficulties in the port and on the beaches, the rescue operation was being so well conducted that much greater optimism was already justified. Moreover, when Weygand's orders to Abrial and Blanchard were finally received, equal numbers of British and French soldiers were taken off the beaches.

Some French officers created problems for the British naval and military authorities who were endeavouring, under constant bombardment, to make orderly arrangements for embarkation. One recalcitrant French colonel refused to go to the allotted beach. His arrest was ordered, but he resisted to such an extent that Reid and another British officer felt obliged to draw their revolvers in order to emphasise that orders given at this time of emergency could not be flouted. The angry colonel thereupon sent a personal telegram to Weygand which read: "*Urgent. Des officiers anglais nous menacent au point du révolver. Situation très pénible.*" Reynaud was informed and complained to General Spears, elevating the aggrieved colonel to the rank of general in the flow of his indignant expostulation. There were more important matters demanding the attention of the senior officers at Dunkirk, but the French Government was becoming daily more sensitive to slights, real or imaginary, from their allies.

In the early days of the evacuation non-combatant troops had been the principal beneficiaries. Gort was conscious that he had under his command almost all the best trained officers and men in the army and that, even though the equipment of the B.E.F. must be lost, on these men depended the reconstitution of a fighting force. They were, as Churchill put it, "the whole root and core and brain of the British Army". Gort therefore decided to send away a number of key men, of all ranks and all units, at an early stage. Amongst them Pownall was shipped home on the 29th and Brooke, protesting strongly, went with Adam on the 30th. Montgomery was selected to command II Corps in the final stages but he, too, was to sail on the 31st. On the 29th Churchill had telephoned to say that when Gort judged further resistance useless, he was authorised to surrender, but Gort told Reid that he would stay to the end. Meanwhile, from his royal villa he conferred with Abrial and Blanchard, directed the evacuation, supervised the deliberate shrinking of the perimeter as unit leap-frogged unit, and inspired his staff by his cool disregard of bombs and machine-gunning air raids, even though from time to time he found it irresistible to seize a rifle and have a shot at low-flying raiders. There was no doubt of his popularity with the men. He walked on to the beaches, among the crowds of soldiers patiently awaiting their turn to embark; a regimental sergeant-major recognised him and was loudly supported when he called for three cheers for Lord Gort.

In resolving to stay Gort had counted without Churchill, nor could he know that immediately on their return to London Pownall and Munster had both raised the question of ordering the commander-in-chief home. On the 30th he received from the War Office a telegram which Churchill had drafted personally. It instructed him to leave when his fighting force was reduced to the equivalent of three divisions and it included the words: "This is in accordance with correct military procedure and no personal discretion is left to you in the matter. On political grounds it would be a needless triumph to the enemy to capture you when only a small force remained under your orders." Gort was distressed, because it was an order he could not disobey, although he tried hard to have it rescinded, and he felt like a captain compelled against his will to leave the bridge of his sinking ship.

On 31st May, his last day at La Panne, where the beaches were now under shell fire as well as bombardment from the air, Gort had an amiable conference with Admiral Abrial and the French commanders. He was able to arrange for the embarkation of men of the French Cavalry Corps and some of those commanded by La Laurencie, who had once again, as soon as he entered the perimeter, sent Westmacott to ask Gort to assume command of his troops in preference to Blanchard. Gort had once again refused and now La Laurencie wrote thanking him for an offer to accompany him to England: "I do not feel entitled to leave before assuring the safe departure of my men: my Flag will remain planted on the Dunes until the last of my men have embarked. . . . We have fought in closest co-operation of heart and of mind, and I am sorry not to have the honour of returning to France under the British flag." For they all, Gort included, expected and intended to return to France. Churchill, indeed, was already working on plans to create a second B.E.F. based on St. Nazaire and to build up its strength behind twentieth-century "Lines of Torres Vedras" securing the Brittany Peninsula.

II Corps completed its evacuation on the 31st, and by nightfall nearly two hundred thousand troops had left. Gort handed over command of the remainder of the B.E.F., some forty thousand men, to Alexander and early on 1st June, in the bitterness of defeat, he was carried to Dover by fast motor-boat across waters which had remained obligingly calm throughout a week in which rough seas would have been still more deadly enemies than von Bock and the Luftwaffe.

At home there was praise for the conduct of the retreat and thanksgiving for the safety, against all expectations, of beleaguered armies which had seemed doomed to destruction. The Secretary of the Cabinet, Sir Edward Bridges, did indeed remark, with cynical disapproval of the general ecstasy, "evacuation is becoming our greatest national industry"; but there was, in the first flush of enthusiasm, a renewal of faith among the British people in their eventual capacity to win the war and unstinted admiration of the gallantry with which the B.E.F. had fought its way out of one of the tightest corners in which a British army had ever been trapped.

Its success in so doing had been made possible by the critical decisions taken by its commander-in-chief who, however much he might fuss over details and worry himself and his close collaborators about things that were of comparatively little consequence, had exercised a clear, unvacillating judgment on every occasion that an issue of vital importance was at stake. He had declined to stay an extra night on the River Senne when Billotte proposed that he should do so. He had refused point blank to obey the order from the War Cabinet brought to him by Ironside on 20th May. He had attacked south of Arras without waiting for the French. He had, in the nick of time, withdrawn his two divisions defending Arras from the German counter-attack. He had, by his own solitary exercise of judgment, cancelled the projected advance towards Amiens and transferred to Brooke the forces engaged on it in time to stave off disaster at Ypres. He had, on 28th May, turned a deaf ear to Blanchard and Prioux, whose proposal to wait a further twenty-four hours before continuing the retreat to Dunkirk spelt irretrievable disaster.

It may be that each of these six decisions, individually as well as collectively, saved the B.E.F. One of them, the cancellation of the southwards offensive, certainly did. Gort took it alone. It was his moment of destiny, to which his whole previous career was the prologue. It was also a moment of destiny for Britain, ranking in history with the defeat of the Armada and the victory of Trafalgar.

Part 4

Proconsul

CHAPTER 17

UNEMPLOYED

NEVILLE CHAMBERLAIN, now Lord President of the Council and for the few remaining months of his life a colleague whose advice and loyalty were of gratefully acknowledged value to Churchill, wrote to his sister on 1st June, 1940:

"Gort got back this morning and gave us a thrilling account of the whole operation. There seems to have been hardly any mistake that the French did not make and they invariably started retiring about 6 hours before the time they had arranged with us so that they constantly uncovered our flank. Their generals were beneath contempt and with some notable exceptions the soldiers would not fight and would not even march. The Belgians were better but not steady and in short as usual the brunt of all the hard fighting and the hard work fell upon the British. In view of the repeated assertions by the Herald and again by Garvin this morning that the glorious B.E.F. was flung into the inferno 'unarmoured' owing to the lethargy of the late Government I particularly asked Gort how his equipment stood up. 'On the whole it stood up to it extraordinarily well' he answered. In particular the anti-tank gun and the Bofors gun were extremely good, so were our armoured vehicles. The accusation in fact is groundless and is only part of the political and personal campaign against me. Gort did not think very highly of the German soldier but said the German junior officers outclassed ours in initiative and leadership. I think this is what one would expect from their training which has been specialised to give them these qualities whereas ours, at any rate the Territorials, have been mainly engaged in peace avocations. Gort said the Terriers had done extremely well."

Anthony Eden, Secretary of State for War, was equally impressed by the lucid account Gort gave to the War Cabinet.

In the official despatches which Gort, assisted by Bridgeman and initially by Pownall, lost no time in composing, he was less enthusiastic about the equipment with which his troops had been provided, but it was of the quantity rather than the quality that he complained. As he wrote to Cis Hamilton on 6th June: "A large part of the material we have lost would anyhow have been lost or wasted through wear and tear . . . To replace men takes 20 years, the equipment quite a short time once the factories go full out."

He had been given an office in Buckingham Palace Road and there he awaited developments while on 4th June Churchill informed the House of Commons that "we have to reconstitute and build up the B.E.F. under its gallant Commander, Lord Gort." This was the first and the last public tribute he received after his return, though the King, on the very morning of Gort's arrival, had sent for him, invested him as a Knight Grand Cross of the Bath and shortly afterwards appointed him, together with Dill, Aide-de-Camp General. Sandy and Jacqueline's fiancé, William Sidney, had both fought in the campaign, had acquitted themselves well and had returned safely from the Dunkirk beaches, being among the last to leave. Now, in the respite before the Grenadiers must sail again, a respite expected to be brief, there was time for Jacqueline to be married and Gort gave his daughter away at the wedding in the Guards Chapel on 8th June.

While Gort stood waiting in the wings for his return to the French stage, Brooke was sent to assume temporary command of the hundred and forty thousand British soldiers still in France. He arrived at Cherbourg on 12th June in time to supervise the departure of most of them, but too late to save the 51st Highland Division, which had been unable to rejoin the main body of the B.E.F. in Flanders and had come from the Maginot Line to take its place, west of the Somme, under French command. Weygand issued yet another order bearing no relation to the circumstances actually prevailing and in consequence the 51st Division was trapped at St. Valery. If Gort or Brooke had been there to countermand Weygand's order, the Highlanders might perhaps have been saved. Weygand had proved no better than Gamelin. Unable to control the armies, stem the retreat or shore up the collapsing walls of the French fortress, he now fell into what Sir Ronald Campbell, British Ambassador in Paris, called a "mystic mood". France having erred must atone by suffering. As for the British, that was none of his affair; but they would, he prophesied a few weeks later, shortly have their necks wrung like a chicken.

When the French, on the eve of the 125th anniversary of the Battle of Waterloo, acknowledged by their formal surrender a national disaster far greater than the defeat of Napoleon, it was clear that it would be a long time before a new B.E.F. could land on the Continent. Britain, rising to the challenge, cast aside all thought of defeat and Churchill exemplified the spirit of the people. In the intimacy of his own circle he had already made clear his intentions in his reply to a suggestion from his private office that the pictures in the National Gallery should be shipped to Canada: "No. Bury them in caves and cellars. None must go. We are going to beat them."

Defence against invasion was now the paramount duty of the Government. With the B.E.F. safe and sound at home, forty million rifles being transported across the Atlantic, Lord Beaverbrook already working miracles in fighter production and a new Home Guard, recruited from young and old and armed with sporting rifles, shotguns, home-made grenades, swords and scythes, the islanders became daily more confident. On 19th July, Ironside relinquished the command of Home Forces to Brooke, but no active command was available for Gort. He was therefore given the all but meaningless post of Inspector of Training and the Home Guard.

In the interval he had been sent on one short wild-goose chase. On 25th June the War Cabinet, learning that a number of former French Ministers, including the brilliant, uncompromising Mandel, had reached North Africa, and desperately anxious to establish an emigrant French Government to rally the colonies and the fleet, sent Gort to Rabat with Duff Cooper, now Minister of Information, and his private secretary, Lord Hood. They landed by flying boat on a narrow waterway in the middle of the town, were received with embarrassment by the French authorities, found that their quarry, the Ministers, were under surveillance at Casablanca and were refused permission to communicate with them. Gort was arrested by the gendarmerie, but was released with personal apologies from the French Resident, and the party flew disconsolately home to announce that their mission had been a failure.

On the evening of Sunday, 4th August, Gort was invited to give the address during a service broadcast by the B.B.C. to commemorate the outbreak of the First World War. Although not a man of devotional habits, he had never wavered from a firm and simple religious faith and, when circumstances allowed, had always been a regular attendant at Matins on Sunday mornings. Indeed, he cornered Mr. James Stuart, the deputy chief whip, during luncheon at White's Club, and spoke vehemently on the theme that a religious revival was vital to the salvation of the country. Now, addressing a wireless audience swollen by the gravity of the times, he lamented the growth of materialism at the expense of spiritual values between the wars. "Neglecting our religious obligations, and in the pursuit of leisure, we filled the roads, but we deserted the churches. The neglect of a Sunday tribute to God, which had meant so much to our forefathers, disturbed our conscience and undermined our faith. Do we not all too gladly accept the material benefits which come our way without pausing to remember that everything worth having in this world demands *some* sacrifice in return?" He spoke from his heart words which were the basis of his own sometimes austere, but always severely practical creed. "Are we not shy of speaking about religion? British people always are . . . But it is a plain fact that unless a country bases its life on a religious faith, it cannot endure." As for the Nazi brand of religion, dedicated to Führer-worship, it was "ruthless in conception and sets no store on human life . . . It achieves temporary advantages; but it kills the soul of the people, of the very soldiers on whom victory ultimately depends. Were the Nazi creed to triumph, the four characteristics of the soul of Britain: our religious faith, our love of freedom, our sense of tolerance and our respect for individual rights, would all perish."

It has been recorded that Lord Halifax asked his friend and adviser, Charles Peake, to suggest a suitable hymn for this service. Peake proposed: "O Gort, Our Help in Ages Past"; but Halifax replied that the second line of the hymn might be taken amiss by the Prime Minister.

As long ago as June, 1938, the Executive Committee of the Other Club, whose names were, by the rules of the Club, wrapped in impenetrable mystery, had elected Gort to membership. This political dining Club, founded by Winston Churchill and Sir F. E. Smith in 1911, after they had been blackballed for another company of diners called "The Club", was Churchill's own preserve. He admitted none but those with whom he found it agreeable to dine. The names of those with whom he did not find it agreeable to dine were almost as distinguished as those with whom he did. No members of the pre-war Cabal were members, nor was Hore Belisha, nor were any of the Army Council. Few whom Churchill wanted to join ever refused, with the exception of Anthony Eden who found dining clubs uncongenial. It is noteworthy that Gort should have been elected at a time when the Sandys case obsessed the House of Commons and Churchill was in direct parliamentary conflict with the War Office.

As August and September, 1940, wore on, the threat of invasion and the Battle of Britain were the urgent considerations. The War Office had conveniently consigned Gort to oblivion. The Other Club, supposed to dine at the Savoy Hotel on alternate Thursdays when Parliament was in session, had not met since May, but on the 5th September it did so and since, with the Prime Minister in the Chair, there was not a member who would voluntarily miss the uninhibited conversation to be expected, the company was a large one. Gort was there, seated between his old Grenadier comrade, Sir Edward Grigg, and Churchill's associate of "Black and Tan" days, Lord Greenwood.

Churchill was stimulated by this meeting at the Other Club to ask Gort to stay at Chequers. There, during the weekend of 21st September he met Dowding, another commander whose resistance to a Government proposal had contributed to saving the country. Gort was unreasonably resentful that Churchill should have prevented his remaining on the beaches at Dunkirk until the last of his men had gone, nor did he ever quite forgive this interference with his personal decision. He believed that he was being widely criticised for deserting his post and that it was the Prime Minister's fault. Nevertheless, he could not fail to admire Churchill's spirit of resolution and defiance and the offensive energy with which he was already planning to attack the enemy in North Africa and elsewhere. Moreover, they had one characteristic in common: a single-minded determination to win the war, at whatever cost, public or personal. My diary for the weekend reads:

"Saturday, September 21st.

Lord Gort and Sir Hugh Dowding came to dinner. Conversation turned at first on the German use of landmines in their air-raids. As these cannot be aimed, and mean indiscriminate slaughter, the P.M., though averse to such action on principle, is bent on retaliation. He proposes that one should be dropped on an open German town for each dropped in this country. 'It is the only language they understand', said Lord Gort.

Sir H. Dowding said the Poles in our Fighter Squadrons were very dashing, but totally undisciplined. It was generally agreed they were magnificent fighters. 'When we have abolished Germany', said the P.M., 'we will certainly establish Poland – and make them a permanent thing in Europe'. He suggested that one Pole was worth three Frenchmen. Gort and Dowding said nearer ten!

It becomes daily more apparent how well prepared the enemy is for invasion. The P.M. thinks that from the North Foreland to Dungeness is the real danger point and that the most dangerous condition will be fog. Ismay is sceptical about the Germans being able to keep contact in fog. Gort says he would guarantee to land on that coast in a fog and he points out that once landed the Germans will push straight ahead. He is afraid of the mentality of the British army which, based on Lady Butler's picture of 'The Thin Red Line', is always to fall back in order to keep the line intact. This is what ruined the French: against rapid penetration by small forces the only thing to do is to stand firm and let isolated detachments get through. The P.M., Dowding and Gort think that the first wave of invaders would be storm troops – all picked men – lightly armed and conveyed in fast motor boats. The second would be tanks, landed from craft with specially constructed bows. The third would be heavy artillery and the mass of the infantry. The first two should be able to effect a landing before darkness, or the fog, lifted. But, of course, meanwhile our bombers would be throwing their full weight against the ports of embarkation.

Sunday, September 22nd.
A telegram from Roosevelt who has heard from 'a most reliable source' in Berlin that the invasion will be put in train at 3.0 p.m. today. The P.M., though slightly sceptical (as who would not be after so many false alarms throughout the summer) kept himself busy telephoning to people about it all morning. I aroused Lord Gort (whose flat was bombed last night for the second time in succession) and he said that frankly he did not think invasion very likely . . .

Sir F. Pile, C-in-C Anti-Aircraft, and General Loch of the War Office came to luncheon. . . . We talked of France, the P.M. expressing surprise at the speed with which we had been able to re-orientate ourselves to the collapse of an ally upon whose support so much seemed to be staked. He said that a fortnight before the débâcle, when the possibility first began to dawn on him, he had thought to himself that the position would be little worse than if Germany had right at the beginning masked France and thrown the full weight of her airforce against us.

After lunch the troop of Generals and the P.M., together with Professor Lindemann, retired to the Hawtrey Room to discuss the Egyptian battle which now seems to be opening. The P.M. is full of confidence and says that we have enough good troops out there to do what is necessary 'unless, of course, our men fight like skunks and the Italians like heroes'. But he feels the opposite is more likely to be the case . . .

Motored up from Chequers after tea. The P.M. drove with Gort whom he seems to like. I shall not be surprised to find him back in high military office before long. On the way up we stopped at Lord Gort's twice bombed flat, which is indeed a mess of charred wood and water. The P.M. was most compassionate, but Lord G. seemed unmoved by the havoc."

The Prime Minister did not forget Gort, nor did he ever speak ill of him or denigrate his achievements; but there was no command available and events were moving too fast for much time or thought at 10 Downing Street to be devoted to the worries of an unemployed general. "How wonderful it would be," Churchill had written on 3rd June, "if the Germans could be made to wonder where they were going to be struck next, instead of forcing us to try to wall in the Island and roof it over. An effort must be made to shake off the mental and moral frustration to the will and initiative of the enemy from which we suffer." The enemy themselves obliged, first by the threat of invasion and secondly, in September, by inaugurating the systematic bombing of London and other cities so that the people of Britain became more united and less inclined to bicker among themselves than ever before or since.

However, nothing could entirely dispel backbiting in high military and political circles. There was a sense of inadequacy stemming from a series of crushing defeats, and an indignation fed by the fear that past incompetences and misjudgments might be repeated by those relics of the old establishment whom Churchill had retained in office. The search for guilty men began, a search which their most eminent victim, Churchill himself, was in his magnanimity the first to deprecate. Already in July Sir Edward Bridges had declaimed to a group standing outside the Cabinet Room about the danger of "looking over our shoulder" and attacking in the press or Parliament men such as Chamberlain and Ironside, and institutions such as the Civil Service or the Chiefs of Staff organisation; for such attacks were comforting to none but the enemy. Being on the defensive brought many dangers and disadvantages.

Gort was among those who suffered, though not in the eyes of the ordinary soldiers he had brought back from Dunkirk. Senior officers made hurtful insinuations. Mason-Macfarlane spoke of his leadership with contempt; Brooke, who had been irritated in France by Gort's constant preoccupation with matters of small detail, annoyed Thorne by referring to his former chief as "a lance-corporal"; others began to whisper their denigrations in the clubs and the corridors. It was reported that Lord Leicester, aged 93, had said of Gort: "He's quite a good fellow, but he's not a patch on Arthur Wellesley." But other fabrications, less agreeable than this apocryphal story, were circulated. Dennis Wheatley wrote a book about Dunkirk which put blame on Gort; and surprising military experts emerged. Bernard Shaw confined himself to writing to Churchill: "Why not declare war on France and capture her fleet (which would gladly strike its colors to us) before A.H. recovers his breath? Surely that is the logic of the situation. Tactically yours, G.B.S." However, H. G. Wells, a no greater military genius, went further. He wrote articles in the *Sunday Despatch* which were as ill-natured as they were ill-informed. In one of them he asserted that Gort's leadership had been as thoroughly incompetent and out-of-date as that of the French High Command.

The War Office made no attempt to contradict or defend; and they obdurately refused to allow Gort the only self-justification open to him, the publication of the full story in his despatches. At first it was maintained that publication would hurt the feelings of the French and that no gratuitous offence must be given to the Pétain-Weygand régime at Vichy. Next, they argued that paper was in too short supply for publication to be warranted. Then they employed a public relations officer to write a bowdlerised edition of the despatches without referring the matter to Gort. "It was all most tendentious," he wrote to Cis Hamilton, "and hinted that I might be 'shaky' by a remark that it was not cowardice but candour that prompted me to send home a warning that a large proportion of the men and equipment might be lost." Not surprisingly Gort concluded that the real reason for delay was that "they" found his remarks about lack of equipment unpalatable.

In his new, superfluous appointment Gort had nothing constructive to do. He visited Iceland, where the sea reminded him of the Solent in April "when there is a complete calm and reflections appear all over the water"; he inspected isolated detachments in the Orkneys and Shetland; he was again invited to Chequers for the weekend before Christmas; but there was little to distract him from fretting about the publication of the despatches, and he could not fail to be aware that his friends and acquaintances were beginning to pity him. He was lonely, too. On Christmas night, the only one during the winter when both the R.A.F. and the Luftwaffe deliberately refrained from raids, and London could celebrate and sleep in peace, Gort had nowhere to go except White's Club. Only two other diners had groped their way through the blackout, Nicholas Lawford, who was one of the private secretaries at the Foreign Office, and myself. The conversation at dinner gradually turned to the events of the previous May and in particular to the order Gort had received to march south to Amiens. Recording what Gort had said, I wrote that night: "The Cabinet and Chiefs of Staff seemed to think that he could march his nine infantry divisions southwards against eight German Armoured divisions in the Gap and a reserve of motorised divisions behind. The order which he received took no account of the reality of the situation, scouted the tactical impossibility of facing an army about while it was engaged with the enemy on the other side and did not consider the position of the Belgian army on Gort's left. History would have much to say on this order. Had he tried to obey it, he would have lost the whole B.E.F. and the war.

He talked very modestly throughout, never vaunting himself nor complaining of his treatment; but he obviously has a certain grievance against those in authority and feels the injustice of holding up the publication of his despatches."

A few weeks later Lawford wrote in his diary: "I recently told Gort that he ought to go and visit the Dutch troops, who are not very popular with the local people where they are stationed; and he has asked me, since, whether the Foreign Office would approve of his doing so. I have said yes: so now the poor dear has something to do for a few days. And he will go and see the Belgians as well."

In another excerpt, Lawford recorded lunching with Gort's former A.D.C., Captain J. Crawshay, "who told me of all sorts of intrigues against Gort". Most hurting of all was the indifference of his two corps commanders, Dill and Brooke. Perhaps there was jealousy: Gort who was less intellectually gifted than either of them had been promoted over their heads – in the case of Dill twice. Perhaps, on the other hand, they genuinely felt that Gort was now too senior to occupy the sort of command for which his qualities of leadership in the field fitted him. Perhaps, too, it seemed to them, as in his gloomier moments it seemed to Gort himself, that the commander of a defeated army, however innocent of blame, could never command again, even though, if offered the chance, Gort would gladly have accepted any appointment, however junior, which took him back near the firing line.

In 1941, at the end of a cold, wet February, when present

frustration was matched by a growing hopelessness of future employment, there came a tragedy which called for all his reserves of moral courage. His son Sandy, an unwilling soldier who had temporarily forced himself to take a pride in his uniform, crashed on a motor bicycle, was severely concussed and a day or two later blew his brains out. Gort had never been close to Sandy: temperamentally they were poles apart and it was disconcerting to a man for whom soldiering was a hobby as well as a profession, and physical hardness an obsession, to have a son to whom all things military were abhorrent and a soft life, with agreeable artistic overtones, the ideal. All the same, Sandy was his only surviving son and Jacqueline, who could do no wrong in her father's eyes, adored him. Remorse, most deadly of human afflictions, and a puzzled self-examination whether and how he could have made things different, were added to the burden of his unhappiness. He was saved by his iron control and his limited imagination: the country was at war, others were losing their sons and the call of duty came before all else. He wrote to Captain Arthur Fitzgerald: "The victory of Britain in this war is all that really matters and one can't allow one's personal sorrows to get the better of one, however hard they may be to bear." There was unhappy, unforeseen irony in words he had used in his broadcast on 4th August: "We, the older soldiers, the veterans of the last war, stand proudly in the ranks with these sons of ours: for on their shoulders will fall a large part of the responsibility for rebuilding a better and a happier world."

In April employment was found for him, unexpected and unsolicited. Churchill, in consultation with Lord Moyne, the new Colonial Secretary, and Captain Margesson, who had succeeded Eden at the War Office, offered Gort the governorship of Gibraltar. None could say whether General Franco, who in October, 1940, had courageously denied Hitler access through Spain to Gibraltar, might not by some twist of policy reverse his decision. If there were another siege of Gibraltar, such as that of 1782 which the 1st Lord Gort made a midshipman's contribution to raising, his descendant would be the ideal man to inspire the garrison and hold the Rock.

On 24th April the King said he was glad Margesson had made it clear to Gort that this appointment did not bear the usual significance of the end of his military career, but was attributable to the possibility of future developments in the area. Margesson evidently failed to make this as clear as he thought he had, or else he was simply not believed; for Gort was far from being gratified. If, as a beaten general, he was in disgrace and the army had no further use for his services, he wished they would say so openly. A colonial governorship, with a direct command of only three battalions, was the last thing he wanted. It seemed to him a face-saving way of pensioning him off; "but," he wrote, "when one is an inconvenience to politicians and colleagues alike, one does not stand much chance of survival". Such sentiments were, however, reserved for his intimate friends. He would do what he was told; and he would do it well. To Cis Hamilton he wrote: "The great thing is to do one's best in whatever plane one may be called to do so in war time, and so one has no grouse beyond a little pique that one is to end the war without ever having a chance to get one's own back at the Hun." There was some compensation: on the last day of April Churchill agreed in principle to the publication of the despatches, although there were in the event further delays and they were held up until October. At least, and at last, the world would be able to read Gort's own account of the Dunkirk story.

CHAPTER 18

GIBRALTAR

THERE were normally over twenty thousand residents of the three square miles under the jurisdiction of the Governor of Gibraltar. Now, many of them had been temporarily evacuated to Britain and some who found such an ordeal unbearable had sought refuge in Tangier or Lisbon. Every day six thousand Spanish workers, including a handful in the pay of German Intelligence, came to work in the dockyard; but the main concentration of Nazi agents was across the bay at Algeciras. Three battalions of British troops guarded the Rock and its naval base, which was of primary importance to the safety of the Atlantic trade routes and to British sea power in the Mediterranean. There was a small airstrip built on adjoining land which the Spaniards had originally leased to the British so that the garrison and the Royal Navy might have the amenity of a race course. Lastly, there were the Barbary Apes, whose presence was traditionally deemed essential to the maintenance of British rule and whose declining numbers had, on direct orders from Churchill, recently been reinforced by Mauretanian recruits.

Gort arrived on 7th May. His predecessor, General Sir Clive Liddell, had for a time been adjutant-general when Gort was C.I.G.S. He resented being superseded and blamed Dill, who was, he wrote to Lord Munster, jealous of Gort and determined to send him abroad. This was doubtless an exaggeration, though Gort had noticed or imagined a coolness on Dill's part since Dunkirk. Liddell was particularly aggrieved because he had done his utmost to strengthen the landward defences of Gibraltar. When Gort surveyed them, he decided they were capable of still further improvement, and he threw his energies into making the Rock impregnable. In particular he turned his mind to the inadequacy of the airstrip. He was sure that sooner or later an attack would be mounted against the Axis Powers through the Mediterranean. In that event no mere airstrip, but a landing ground capable of receiving fleets of heavy bombers and transports would be almost as important as the naval base itself.

With Guy Russell at 'The Convent', Gibraltar

Awaiting the King at Malta, June 1943, Sir Keith Park,
Lord Tedder and Gort

The King hands Gort his Field Marshal's baton, Malta, 20th June 1943

There was a Canadian tunnelling company engaged in adding miles of additional tunnels to those burrowed into the Rock during the famous siege of 1780. The excavated spoil was ideal material for a new aerodrome, but the British Government did not share Gort's enthusiasm. The Foreign Office thought it would tip the delicate Spanish balance in favour of the pro-German Falangist faction, and the Colonial Office for once agreed with the Foreign Office. The Air Ministry saw no need for the project, even though the existing aerodrome could hold so few aircraft at a time. The War Office said they had neither men nor materials to spare and in any case the Admiralty could not have shipped them. Oppositions of this kind stimulated Gort. He set the garrison and the tunnellers to work and he completed the new airfield, projecting a new runway on to land he reclaimed from the sea. Months later, after he had left Gibraltar and intensive operations in the Mediterranean were planned, the War Cabinet had the grace to thank him for his foresight.

He was determined to create a closer working relationship between the armed services stationed at Gibraltar. It was not easy because they had little in common apart from a conviction that their affairs were none of the Governor's business. Three weeks after his arrival, he wrote to Munster: "I have myself to co-ordinate the military, civil, naval and air viewpoints, as well as compete with the Governor of Algeciras and local notabilities in Spain." He found his military staff inadequately trained, suspicious of all foreigners and "resolved that the Governor should be an amiable figurehead". He persuaded the First Sea Lord, Sir Dudley Pound, to provide a sailor as his Chief of Staff and was fortunate in the choice of Captain the Hon. Guy Russell. The task of encouraging the three services to work together was not facilitated by the secretiveness of the admiral commanding the base, who was such a devotee of security that he disliked discussing naval affairs even with the Governor; nor by the existence of many separate intelligence services, British and allied, each with its own communications and esoteric methods and all as anxious to score off each other as to outwit the enemy. The sergeant pigeonier, who maintained a flock of carrier pigeons in a dovecote hewn out of the rock, furnished one weapon in their armoury and was a greater source of amusement to the Governor than most of their other activities. Their combined or conflicting efforts did not suffice to discover that an Italian tanker, interned at Algeciras, was the base for limpet mine attacks on ships in Gibraltar bay.

Relations with the Legislative Council and the Civil Service
were difficult at first, but Gort patiently set about trying "to get
everything on to a more harmonious footing". He found a close
ally in Admiral Sir James Somerville, commanding the independent naval "Force H" based at Gibraltar. He gratified Gort's taste
for the other elements by taking him to sea in *Ark Royal* and
allowing him to fly in her aircraft. Somerville was an expert on
radar and signals and his advice on these, as well as a happy
relationship with Gort, did much to strengthen the garrison.

The Convent, as the Governor's residence at Gibraltar is
called, is an unpretentious house with a spacious garden. By
comparison with blacked-out, rationed Britain, life was comfortable indeed. "Were you here," Gort wrote to Munster shortly
after his arrival, "you could live on langouste and fresh curried
prawns! And more than one helping." They were not, however,
frequently on the menu, because Gort held frugality to be an
essential element of patriotism. The admiral resided at The Mount,
where Gort dined on the first Sunday of each month. The Chief
of Staff, Captain Geoffrey Hawkins, solicitous for the Governor's
own staff and hoping Gort would take the hint, ensured that the
food was excellent and that a fire was lit after dinner, so that
Gort's staff looked forward to what they called "roughing it at
The Mount". Even in the chilliest evenings fires seldom burned
at the Convent and the physique of the staff was tested by the
Governor's distaste for sitting down. Thus, after walking for miles,
inspecting tunnels and defences, and climbing at a rapid pace up
and down a rock 1,500 feet high, Gort's weary visitors and
entourage would have to remain on their feet while the King's
representative stood with his back to an empty fireplace discussing
the work on the defences or the new airfield.

There were visitors of all kinds; civilians like Sir Stafford Cripps
(whose austerity almost rivalled Gort's), soldiers bound for India
and the east, sailors limping into Gibraltar, their ships often
disabled by enemy action. Gort was eager for the news they
brought, because mails from home took more than a month to
arrive. He interviewed every escaped prisoner of war reaching
Gibraltar and reported home that almost without exception they
had been helped ungrudgingly, and usually at severe risk to their
hosts, during the journey through occupied France, whereas once
they reached the comparative safety of the Vichy zone their
reception was unhelpful and even hostile.

He quickly established excellent relations with the Spaniards, on whom Gibraltar was partly dependent for its well-being and whose heavy artillery was trained on the Rock. Shortly after his arrival, the Governor of Algeciras, Munoz Grande, a captain-general of Spain and a hero of the Civil War, paid an official call. Gort took pains that his garrison should appear more lavishly equipped than it in fact was. The route was lined by men armed with the new and rare Tommy-gun. The pipers of the Black Watch, wearing kilts borrowed from their officers for the occasion, played in the garden of the Convent and by a lucky chance Munoz Grande took this as a personal compliment, since he was a native of the Asturias where the bag-pipes are as cherished as in Scotland. The visit was a resounding success and the two generals delighted in each other's company. Munoz Grande gave Gort a personally signed pass, authorising him to travel freely throughout Spain, and Gort wrote home to Munster: "Spaniards are far superior to Frogs." His old admiration of the French army had vanished: not only the three weeks which led to Dunkirk, but also his experiences of the Vichy Government and its servants, both before and after he went to Gibraltar, had destroyed his esteem for France.

The Spaniards were quite a different matter. He cared nothing for the rights or wrongs of the Civil War. That was over and, as far as Gort was concerned, the victors, favourable though some of their leaders might be to the Axis powers, were proving helpful. On 11th June he wrote to the King: "Although we are not supposed to use the aerodrome for operational purposes, the friendliness of the Spanish authorities has, so far, prevented any representations being made about the increasing bomber and fighter aircraft landings which take place. For instance 26 aircraft are due to arrive here today." Spanish generals became increasingly frequent visitors and since Gort's frankness, friendly attitude and famous record of courage strongly appealed to them, relations across the frontier improved still further with every visit although, as he told the King, "obviously the attitude of the local Spaniards is no gauge of the feeling elsewhere in Spain". He would put on plain clothes and take Captain Russell to luncheon on Sundays at the "Reina Christina" Hotel in Algeciras. On one occasion he heard that Admiral Canaris, Head of German Intelligence, was paying a visit and he arranged to book the adjoining table. To his disappointment the admiral failed to appear and he saw nothing more sinister than some German children playing with toy Messerschmitts.

For years the inhabitants of Gibraltar, in contravention of the Treaty of Utrecht by which Gibraltar was ceded to Britain, had happily earned much of their livelihood by smuggling duty-free goods into Spain. Now that most of them had been evacuated, the Spaniards, suffering in the aftermath of their harrowing Civil War, were painfully short of luxuries from Gibraltar. The Spanish dockyard workers did their best, but the day came when one of their number inconsiderately planted a bomb in an anti-submarine vessel. Security measures on the frontier were immediately tightened and all Spaniards entering Gibraltar were searched. As ill-luck would have it, Gort's favourite Spaniard, a member of the influential Larios family and widow of a Spanish naval and ducal officer who had been killed in the Civil War, was due to lunch at the Convent a few days after the bomb incident. Her name was Talia Povar, she was known to be pro-British and she was strikingly beautiful. The other guests for luncheon were assembled as punctually as the Governor invariably required, but there was no Talia. At last she arrived, three quarters of an hour late, her lovely face ablaze with fury and her tongue vituperatively unleashed. There had been an incident at the frontier. Customs Officers had attempted to search her. Used, as she was, to come and go freely between Spain and Gibraltar, she had considered the proposal an outrage. Rather than submit, she had announced that she would return to Spain. No doubt equally impressed by her beauty and the fact that she was a guest of the Governor, the officials had finally given way and allowed her to cross the frontier unsearched. None the less, she was still seething with fury when she arrived at the Convent, and there were all the makings of an unpleasant incident which, in view of her connections, might well have damaged the Anglo-Spanish friendship which Gort had been so sedulously fostering. He saved the situation and disarmed the indignant lady by meeting her angry outburst with, "Talia, you are using up your adrenalin very prodigally!" The incident was closed.

Captain Russell and Captain Hawkins noted, with varying degrees of disapproval, Gort's obsession with detail, a virtue or defect on which comments had been made throughout his career. At Gibraltar, no longer faced with the high decisions required of a C.I.G.S. or a commander-in-chief, he displayed this characteristic more markedly than ever. "Close attention to detail," he constantly repeated to Russell, "makes the difference between

Victory and Defeat in war." He loved to surprise sentries. He always carried a notebook in which irregularities, however trivial, were inscribed. Perhaps he overdid it, but if so, he erred in good company. Napoleon and Wellington attached significance to the smallest matters, and Sir John Kennedy recalled that in the early nineteen-thirties he attended an exercise conducted by Montgomery, whose chances of high command were generally held to have been ruined by undue emphasis on matters of detail. The Gibraltar apes should have sympathised: they owed their survival as a race to a similar addiction by Churchill.

By March, 1942, the British army in North Africa, which had found the Italians ideal opponents, was confused and delayed by the brilliant tactics of General Rommel, who had brought his Afrika Corps to reinforce Mussolini's shattered legions. Churchill was disenchanted with the British generals and displeased that Auchinleck had failed to sweep Rommel from the desert scene. He had never forgotten Gort and he thought of sending him to North Africa. Brooke, now C.I.G.S. and a more powerful one than Dill, considered the proposal ludicrous. He managed to dissuade Churchill. Was Brooke right? Field-Marshal Alexander, whose lesser brilliance than Brooke as a staff officer was matched by his far greater experience in battle, believed he was wrong. Gort, said Alexander, was the ideal commander of an independent force. He was the British Rommel, with the same dash and the same resourcefulness, but with a thorough staff training which Rommel lacked. The "ifs" of history are tantalising and un-satisfactory; but a few days before he died Alexander told me that he believed Gort might well have defeated Rommel in the summer of 1942. It was, he added, well to remember that by the end of that year he and Montgomery had superior weapons, veteran soldiers and indisputable air superiority. With the equip-ment and allies available to the B.E.F. in 1940, nobody, in his opinion, could have done better than Gort; it was conceivable that in 1942, given his particular qualities, Gort might have done as well or better than anybody else, and done it perhaps a few months earlier.

Gort knew nothing of the Prime Minister's proposal. He persisted in believing that Churchill, like everybody else, had discarded the defeated general. With restless activity he therefore continued doing his best to keep himself and the Gibraltar garrison occupied so that, as he proudly wrote to Munster, "the Rock now reverberates with gunfire and it is good for the Gestapo agents in Algeciras to hear it". He contrived to be busy from 8.0 a.m. till bedtime and to keep himself fit by outmarching everybody else on tours of the tunnels and the defences. He performed feats unusual for a Governor approaching his 56th birthday: "I got round our storm-troop course in the allotted time," he wrote on 16th February, 1942, "up and down the Rock, climbing rope ladders, etc., and at the end charging and clambering over a 7′6″ concrete wall."

It was, however, all contrivance, because the aerodrome was built and the defences were as impregnable as they ever could be. Great events had taken place while he struggled with Gibraltar's local problems: first Russia and then America had been attacked by the Axis and their Governments, the one unwillingly, the other with inward relief, had been forced to join Britain in her solitary fight for freedom. It was stifling to be marooned in a rocky fortress and the future seemed to be offering little chance of greater activity when early in May Mr. Richard Casey, on his way to assume the duties of Minister Resident in Cairo, brought a letter from Churchill. Malta, bombed and besieged, was in imminent danger. Her brave Governor, Lieutenant-General Sir William Dobbie, fighting like Gordon with his sword in one hand and his Bible in the other, was said to be worn out by his exertions. A successor was required to invigorate the defenders and sustain the courage of the population. The British Government had decided that Gort was the man. On 7th May, 1942, a year to the day from his arrival in Gibraltar, Gort left by flying boat for Valetta to meet what he and many others supposed must be death or captivity. Casey, indeed, had told him that Malta could scarcely be expected to hold out for more than six weeks. It was, perhaps, amends for the order to leave the Dunkirk beaches.

CHAPTER 19

MALTA

In July, 1939, Lord Chatfield prophesied to the Committee of Imperial Defence that by 1942 their successors might regret a sufficiently long view of Malta's needs had not been taken three years previously. Considering the general shortage of equipment, Malta did in fact receive a generous allocation of anti-aircraft guns by the time her ordeal came, and Hore Belisha had taken steps to improve the local defence forces; but in a prolonged siege, by no means the first in Maltese history, only replenishment by sea could enable the three hundred thousand islanders to survive.

When Gort emerged from a Sunderland Flying Boat, in the middle of an air-raid, the island was reeling from the effect of two months' concentrated, unceasing bombardment. The docks were pounded to rubble, the harbour blocked by sunken ships, electricity supplies cut off, the fighter strength reduced to six serviceable aircraft and, as no ships had arrived since March, supplies of all kinds had dwindled below the danger level. An invasion was expected from Sicily, only sixty miles to the northwards. It was vital to hold the island, since there was no other base from which to attack the enemy convoys sailing across the Mediterranean with supplies for Rommel, and failure to interrupt them would tilt the North African balance in favour of the Axis. On Malta the fate of Egypt, the Middle East and perhaps even India might depend. It was, moreover, the staging post for aerial traffic through Gibraltar to Egypt and the Far East.

Two days after Gort's arrival sixty new Spitfires were due to fly in. Previous consignments had been destroyed on the ground immediately they landed to refuel. Gort realised that the new arrivals must be saved at all cost. He placed the whole resources of the army at the disposal of the R.A.F., examined the proposed time-table for refuelling and take-off, declared it unacceptable and insisted that it be drastically reduced. In the event some of the Spitfires were ready to take off within six minutes of landing and they made seventy-four sorties that very day. Shortly after-

wards, the gallant *Welshman*, a ship which made a number of
unescorted voyages to Malta, entered the Grand Harbour. She
was attacked by twenty-one Stukas. They were all shot down by
the defences which Gort had personally arranged to concentrate
for the purpose, and *Welshman* unloaded an unscathed cargo.
Reinforcements of fighters followed at regular intervals during
the next three months and few were lost on the ground.

In the island, seventeen miles long and nine wide, Gort found a
British garrison of thirty thousand soldiers and airmen. While
Dobbie ruled they, and the sailors in the naval base, had been
subjected to their own commanders-in-chief in the Mediterranean.
Now, with invasion threatening, Churchill arranged for the new
Governor to be appointed "Supreme Commander of the Fighting
Services and of the Civil Administration". The Service Chiefs in
Malta were displeased and Gort received less co-operation from
some of them than he had the right to expect. A few days after his
own arrival, Guy Russell joined him as Chief of Staff. He was,
Gort later wrote to Sir Alexander Hardinge, "a tower of strength
during the difficult times here". Lord Munster came too, more
successfully lured by the prospect of siege and deprivation in
Malta than by langouste and curried prawns at Gibraltar. As a
former Parliamentary Under Secretary, he was qualified to offer
guidance in the tortuous maze of Maltese politics. Russell and
Munster, together with the A.D.C.s, John Gordon Duff and
Ford Geddes, provided the companionship of friends which was
indispensable to Gort in times of lonely responsibility.

Malta's painful resistance, and the refusal of the people to be
intimidated, were watched and applauded in Britain. In April
Mr. Leopold Amery, Secretary of State for India, had suggested
that the island be given the Victoria Cross. The King, much in
favour of such an imaginative gesture, nevertheless preferred the
George Cross, and on 15th April he announced its award. Gort
brought the medal with him, but so grave was the situation that it
was September before he could find a breathing space in which to
confer this unique distinction on the island, publicly and with due
ceremony, to bear witness, as the King proclaimed, "to a heroism
and devotion that will long be famous in history". Later, Gort
unsuccessfully proposed that, as an additional honour, Malta be
given the unique privilege of flying the Union Flag by day and
night.

By May, 1942, it was evident that unless a convoy was forced
through, gallantry would be of no avail. All efforts had to be

directed to survival and none could be spared for naval and air strikes against enemy shipping, so that from April to August the Axis forces in Africa received their supplies almost unhampered. In hopeful anticipation, Gort planned assiduously for a new convoy's arrival, mindful that in March the only three ships which struggled through had been sunk by bombs in the harbour and much of their cargo lost. In spite of opposition from the admiral, he had smoke canisters prepared to obscure the quays; he took steps to speed up unloading processes; and he made troops available to reinforce the unreliable stevedores.

As Russell put it, everybody on the island was bravely smiling but all too few were thinking. Food and petrol were the primary requisites. There were already Victory Kitchens, supplying some ten thousand people with stews of goat, horseflesh and vegetables, but officers and administrators were eating too well: five-course dinners were still available in clubs and restaurants. Gort changed all that. He made friends with the archbishop, Caruana, who helpfully pronounced that hoarding was a mortal sin. He instituted a strict allocation of supplies, requiring all figures to be checked and rechecked weekly. Sir Jack Drummond of the Ministry of Food was flown out, at Russell's suggestion, to advise on handling the food emergency. Amongst other measures Drummond recommended the slaughter of livestock. In the process several race-horses found their way into the Victory Kitchens, an incident which called for Munster's political tact since they belonged to the stepmother of Miss Mabel Strickland, the powerful and patriotic editor of *The Times* of Malta, in all other circumstances a stalwart supporter of Gort, of commonsense and of resistance to the last. There was another unfortunate incident when the guard at his palace of St. Anton were found to have caught the goldfish in the ornamental pond and sold them to the public at 1/9d. each. Concentrated vitamin tablets were sent by air and submarine for inclusion in the victory stews, both because scabies was becoming rampant and because the Colonial Office feared that the absence of vitamin E would deleteriously affect the islanders' reproductive powers. Gort observed that close proximity in the caves and shelters should be a sufficient antidote. In due course the Victory Kitchens were serving two hundred thousand people each day.

He placed himself and his staff on the basic civilian ration scale. Cut to its lowest in July and August, this was half the small weekly ration provided in Britain. Water was short, so that fleas and lice proliferated without the assistance of vitamin E; and children with emaciated bodies howled with the gnawing pain of hunger. The Governor not only ensured that he and his staff consumed the same calories as the poorest citizen, but also rationed them to one half-bucket of warm water a week for washing purposes. A little cold water was provided for shaving.

It was the same with petrol. Senior officers, used to driving in large cars, were shamed into economy when the Governor decided to ride a bicycle, which he would carry over rubble or other obstacles to his progress. He tended to head for danger in spite of Russell's efforts to restrain him. As they pedalled side by side towards the centre of an air raid, they conversed:

Gort: "Are you afraid, Guy?
Russell: Yes, Sir, terrified.
Gort: I thought the Royal Navy were never afraid.
Russell: If I was on my bridge, my Coxswain would be near me with a brandy flask. And you have been sent here to save the Island."

Some of the senior officers thought bicycling undignified: the Governor should motor round the island in a limousine with his standard flying. However, the Maltese preferred one who shared their hardships.

Seventeen merchantmen set sail for Malta, from east and west, in June. Only two arrived, bringing but 15,000 tons of cargo. Aviation spirit was so scarce that Gort decided it must be reserved for the fighters defending the island and denied to the bombers attacking enemy convoys, though small additional quantities were brought in by submarine. On 20th June Rommel captured Tobruk and it seemed that the enemy might now reach the Suez Canal. The aerodromes in Cyrenaica, providing some cover for convoys sailing from Alexandria, were lost to the British, and the Germans concluded that Malta would fall without the necessity of a costly invasion. Gort did not, of course, know this and as the news grew worse the probability of assault by sea and air seemed to grow. He was sure the garrison would fight to the last, but they were short of ammunition and would be overwhelmed by numbers. If starvation forced surrender, he intended to leave in a small fishing boat with a few volunteers and live as a guerilla in the Sicilian mountains. Perhaps some of the Sicilians, expert in banditry and faithful to their anti-Roman traditions, might have joined him in the enterprise.

Churchill had no intention of deserting Malta. A further

convoy was planned in the knowledge that its failure would mean starvation and surrender. By the beginning of August the estimated availability of supplies was measured not in weeks, but in days. On 4th August Gort told Hardinge: "Everything depends on the arrival of a convoy, and especially on the arrival of an oiler." A visit from Lord Cranborne, the only Cabinet Minister who went to Malta in these desperate months, was opportune. "It has been a great help having Cranborne out here," Gort's letter to Hardinge continued, "as he has managed to comb out difficulties the civil side was inclined to make. In places like Malta mountains are made out of molehills because so many people become temperamental under bombing."

Six days later fourteen large merchantmen, eleven British and three American, passed Gibraltar with a strong naval escort. The enemy mobilised twenty-one submarines and 600 aircraft to stop them and the ensuing battle gripped the attention of the whole combatant world. British naval losses were, as for all the Malta convoys, severe. Indeed, more lives were lost at sea in bringing supplies to Malta than from bombing raids on the island itself. But five ships, including the tanker *Ohio*, an American ship with a British crew, reached Valetta, mostly in sinking condition. With speed and successful improvisation 47,000 tons of cargo and oil were unloaded or salvaged. On meagre rations the island could now survive till mid-December.

Churchill, who had flown to Egypt along the North African coast at considerable risk, demanded a first-hand account of conditions in Malta. Thus on 20th August Gort and Munster went to Cairo. Their thin and haggard appearance brought vividly home to the assembled politicians, generals and diplomats what Malta had been through: they were in the early stages of starvation. Churchill was in Cairo with Brooke to reorganise the command in North Africa. He did not revive his earlier proposal to give Gort an army; for Malta ranked high on the list of active commands. Gort was, however, included in the military conversations and the Prime Minister went out of his way to tell Munster what store he set by Gort's advice. Also in Cairo was the commander-in-chief, East Africa, Lieutenant-General Sir William Platt, who had reason to be grateful for the foresight Gort had shown four years previously by instructing him to procure heavy transport from South Africa and organise Abyssinian guerillas against the Italian forces occupying their country. Platt said that without these two measures, taken in good time, he believed the remarkable success of the British campaign in Abyssinia could not have been achieved.

Back in Malta the struggle continued. It lasted, scarcely abated, till December and for ten days in October the air-raids were almost equal in strength to those of the previous spring. But, though still short of food, Malta was full of Spitfires which, with the help of efficient radar, engaged the enemy bombers over the sea before they could reach the island so that during nine days of the October raids 2,400 aircraft dropped little more than 400 tons of bombs on shore. Meanwhile the strikes from Malta against enemy convoys began again, and there was renewed dislocation of Axis supplies. Rommel said: "Malta has the lives of many thousands of German and Italian soldiers on its conscience"; but Malta's conscience was untroubled.

At the end of October the Battle of Alamein began. Gort wrote to Hardinge on 14th November: "I am overcome with joy at the great success which Alex and Monty have achieved and I am interested to note that Rommel's army broke into a thousand pieces under 'drum fire' as they used to call it in the last war." As the battle progressed, the Cyrenaican airfields were freed and new convoys could sail from Alexandria. On 20th November four ships reached Malta. On 5th December five more and a tanker arrived. In addition to oil, they brought 56,000 tons of cargo. The siege of Malta was over, the fleet returned to Valetta and early in December Gort suggested that command of the three services should revert to their respective commanders-in-chief.

His military responsibilities were at an end and he could concentrate on civil needs. He told Hardinge: "I am busying myself initiating plans for the future of Malta. It is essential to do so and a veil is best drawn over our administration in the past. I am sure you will have heard about our more pressing reforms from Cranborne. Unless we can get the start now Malta will drop out of the news and the money will not be forthcoming. It may be a mercenary outlook but I am sure it is the practical one. Amongst other things, I want scholarships at universities, technical colleges and polytechnics; towns at Home and elsewhere may be willing, if approached in the right way, to endow a scholarship. There won't be very many required but it is essential to get Maltese boys and girls out of the Island for a time if progress is to be made. I do not think many people at Home realise that a large proportion of the Maltese people have never seen a proper wood, a river or a railway train or even a tram-car . . .".

Nothing could stop him from dashing to the scene of action. One November evening, while he and his staff were eating their scanty supper, the mess sergeant reported a large fire in the direction of Hamrun. A petrol dump had been hit. Gort at once set off with Russell to see what steps were being taken to control the blaze. Once there, he forgot he was the Governor and assumed the role of fireman. Russell describes what followed: "Inactivity was always anathema to Gort who proceeded to rush in and start trying to haul out tins of petrol from a block already alight. One immediately burst and he was badly burned. I took him to be dressed at Hamrun Civil Hospital and then back to St. Anton. Had he been a Spitfire pilot or soldier he would have been hospitalised for some weeks, but he refused to give in, or have any proper attention or pain-killer, and insisted on being dressed in his proper uniform and carrying on without a single day off. I know how much he suffered because our rooms adjoined."

The burns took weeks to heal. Munster had returned to London in October and Russell left to command first H.M.S. *Nelson* and later H.M.S. *Duke of York*, in which he won fame by sinking the German battle-cruiser, *Scharnhorst*. After they had left, a new affliction, less painful but much more serious than the burns, struck Gort. At the end of the First World War he had developed cancer of the lip, but in spite of the insertion of mercury needles, hanging from his lips like matchsticks, he had evaded the notice of the army medical authorities and secrecy had been kept. The mercury had temporarily arrested the disease but it returned, twenty years later, and on 31st December, 1942, he was obliged to go to London for treatment.

Churchill had returned from Cairo the previous September with the proposal to make Wavell a field-marshal. P. J. Grigg, now Secretary of State for War, objected. He said he did not consider Wavell deserved it, and it would be unfair to Gort. The King and the Prime Minister decided that Gort, too, should be promoted. In fact, although Grigg did not know it, "the All Highest", as Gort called the Prime Minister, had already mentioned the idea to Gort in Cairo. When Munster wrote that Churchill had reverted to the matter in London, Gort was immediately and unnecessarily worried. He replied on 11th November that his promotion would arouse the indignation of Dill, Ironside and Brooke. Since Dill and Ironside were already field-marshals, this could only mean he believed they would think the commander of a defeated army unworthy of the honour.

"As you know," he told Munster, "all I want to do is to end my days after the Peace comes in peace and quiet. The things that so many people value mean nothing to me." He added that his own personal selection for field-marshals would be Wavell, Brooke and Alexander, in that order. Hardinge wrote to reassure him: it was the King's wish. He answered on 13th December: "What you said in your letter has set my mind at rest. I was frightened of the reactions in certain ambitious circles and I felt that harmony is all important in the Army in these days. Now that I know where the idea emanated, I feel it is all the greater honour. Indeed no greater honour could come my way." On New Year's Day, 1943, his appointment as a field-marshal was announced. Churchill, whom nobody had bothered to inform of Gort's return to London, telegraphed to Malta on 3rd January: "Heartiest congratulations on peak promotion. Delighted to hear it. Pray you are now on top and frowns of Fortune all passed." His congratulatory telegrams were seldom commonplace.

"Gort," Lawford recorded on 6th January, "had nothing but good words for the Maltese." They, for their part, rejoiced to see him return, on 15th March, 1943, to a relatively well-supplied island. He feared an epidemic and devoted much thought to preventive measures and to civil administration, but he found time to visit Algiers where Giraud was "exceptionally friendly and obviously delighted to see me". He had talks with General Eisenhower, who, many years later, wrote this letter to Dr. Richard Vereker:

"As a staff member of the American War Department I was normally present at the early meetings of the combined Chiefs of Staff in Washington. During the period when we were trying to set up a combined staff headquarters for a unified command in the Southwest Pacific, Lord Gort's name was suggested by the British Chiefs of Staff, all of whom talked about him in the most favourable terms. Many months later I was astonished and somewhat mystified when I heard bitter criticism of him voiced by other British officers.

My own contacts were of a personal nature but each of them was, for me, an interesting experience. He struck me as a thinker, completely free of thirst for personal aggrandizement or notoriety and well acquainted with the factors which were to have a great bearing upon the conduct of the war. He seemed a thoughtful, down-to-earth soldier who was thoroughly versed in his profession and whose sole idea was to perform his duty efficiently and selflessly in the war.

While my contacts with him were not of an official nature, my impression was that in his broad knowledge and understanding of war's demands, he had to take second place to none."

In May, 1943, the North African campaign ended in total defeat for the Germans and Italians. For the next step, the capture of Sicily, Malta was of obvious importance. The King came on 20th June by sea, and was ecstatically received by the people. He presented to Gort the field-marshal's baton. Then the allied commanders began to arrive, to prepare for the Sicilian expedition. Gort moved from St. Anton to more restricted quarters at Verdala, because he thought the commanders should be given the best accommodation in which to live and plan together. He was hurt and disappointed that they disregarded his gesture and that each preferred to set up a separate mess and headquarters. However, the success of the Sicilian landing drove such small cares into oblivion and in July the fall of Mussolini signalled the certainty of allied victory. Italy sued for peace. Her fleet, savaged by the Germans on its way, reached Valetta on 11th September, and on the 29th Marshal Badoglio signed the formal document of unconditional surrender on board H.M.S. *Nelson* in the presence of Eisenhower, Alexander and Gort.

There were a few glimmers of recognition for Gort at home. In May he was given the distinguished if mainly honorific appointment of Colonel Commandant of the Honourable Artillery Company and in June when his appointment as A.D.C. to the King expired, His Majesty decided to extend it. But in Malta his life was that of a spectator of world events responsible for the administration of a small, safe and now well-fed island. Churchill arrived in November, on his way to the Tehran Conference. Gort's courteous decision to put his own bedroom at the Prime Minister's disposal was ungratefully received because it was on the noisy side of the palace and Churchill had scarcely a wink of sleep. The Governor's domestic arrangements fell below Churchillian standards, but social errors and omissions were forgiven to holders of the Victoria Cross.

Roosevelt visited Malta on his way home from the Tehran and Cairo conferences. He presented to Gort an illuminated scroll recording America's admiration of Malta's resistance; but the effect of this agreeable gesture was marred by a subsequent drive during which armed security men, their guns at the ready, stood on the running board of the Presidential car and hemmed it in before and behind. The Maltese commented that six months previously the King had walked through their streets, and driven the length and breadth of their island, with Gort beside him and with no armed bodyguard. Another American visitor was General Patton, who asked himself to stay. Whether or not Gort was, as Alexander suggested, potentially the British Rommel, Patton was certainly Rommel's nearest American equivalent in dash, courage and initiative. He had recently been in trouble, with the American press in particular, for slapping the face of a soldier whom he thought a malingerer. Dining at St. Anton, he told Gort that if he had not so acted, he would have had few forces left at the front. Ford Geddes recalls that he then went on to ask: "Do you know why I have come to Malta?" "No," replied Gort. "I have come," Patton said, "because I wanted to see the bravest man in the British Army."

Meanwhile Churchill, also on his way home from the conferences, was smitten with pneumonia. On his sick-bed at Carthage he conceived the idea of a landing at Anzio to bestride the Italian peninsula and cut off the German forces opposing Alexander's armies which had landed at Salerno in September and were making but slow progress northwards. The attack at Anzio took place on 21st January. It was unsuccessful in its immediate objective and there were murmurs that Churchill had failed to learn the lesson of Gallipoli, while others blamed the general in command for pausing too long before he struck inland. Gort, reverting to a principle he had impressed on Liddell Hart twenty years before, maintained that the error lay in making the attack before the enemy's main reserves in south-east Europe were engaged.

In the ensuing fighting Gort's son-in-law, Major Sidney, performed a feat of valour which earned him the Victoria Cross. The Greek gods, plotting on Mount Olympus some capricious stroke on behalf of a temporarily favoured mortal, could not have conceived anything more opportune. Jacqueline's husband, by good fortune a Grenadier, had won the foremost distinction that can be bestowed on a soldier. Disappointed, misunderstood and in some quarters maligned, Gort had been looking inwards with increasing dejection. Now, for a brief interlude his wounds, real or imaginary, were of no account. On 3rd March, 1944, at Alexander's invitation, he flew to Naples in a Mosquito aircraft, meticulously noting the exact number of minutes of flight, and

With General Giraud and Harold Macmillan in Algiers, April 1943

With Alexander in Italy, March 1944, when his son-in-law
Captain Sidney received the Victoria Cross

was driven to Montacuto. There he watched General Alexander pin the ribbon (cut off one of Gort's own uniforms) on Sidney's tunic and the two V.C.s stood on either side of Alexander while the battalion marched past.

Earlier in the same month the people of Malta recognised their Governor's courage and leadership by giving him a Sword of Honour. They and their leaders would have endorsed the verdict of Air Vice-Marshal Hugh Lloyd, commanding the R.A.F. in Malta when Gort arrived. He said that nearly everyone except Gort claimed to have saved Malta; in his view Gort had a greater right to that distinction than anyone else.

The agreeable interlude was prolonged. In April he visited Tunis. At the airport he was received by the French army with a Guard of Honour of three companies and the colours. An escort of Spahis on white horses accompanied him into the town where the streets and balconies were thronged by cheering crowds. He began to feel better about the French. This impression grew stronger in Algiers, where there was a "guard of honour of gigantic proportions". De Gaulle gave a luncheon party during which he proclaimed that, looking back over the years, he could now see that the decision to retire on Dunkirk had been correct. Then there was a tea-party with Georges and Giraud. "Georges sat in a short black jacket and striped trousers looking a dignified figure, but he also said he was now the lowest form of animal life." Gort did not think so; nor did Churchill, who had aroused De Gaulle's impotent fury by inviting Georges to stay with him in Marrakech the previous January. Gort dined with Duff Cooper and stayed with Harold Macmillan. He found all the French most frank and open, and was delighted when Georges and Giraud accepted his invitation to pay a return visit to Malta. Fortunately they left no record of what they thought about the Governor's cuisine; but the bitterness had withered and Gort could once again feel towards the French generals something of the affection, if not perhaps the respect, in which he had held them before May, 1940.

In June, 1944, he followed with elation the progress of the allied armies in Italy and in Normandy. "I am delighted," he told Munster, "that Alex and Oliver Leese have had such successes and Monty is, as usual, carrying his good fortune as a soldier along with him. It is all good, as the Army has not had its deserts in the past, due to its being a Cinderella." "Here in Malta," he wrote to an old Harrow friend, Captain Arthur

M.V.—R

Fitzgerald, "life is dull as the war has left us far behind, so there is nothing to occupy attention except rehabilitation and local politics."

In July, he was offered the challenging appointment of High Commissioner in Palestine. Malta might now be a haven of quiet and comparative plenty: Palestine most certainly was not. An attempt had been made to assassinate the High Commissioner, Sir Harold MacMichael, and terrorism, dormant while the Germans were in the ascendant, was the policy of Zionist extremists. Gort accepted the offer with alacrity and in August he left with Ford Geddes for London.

Passing through Rome he was received in private audience by Pope Pius XII and shortly after his return home Eisenhower sent his own aircraft to bring Gort to his newly established headquarters at Versailles. It was a graceful tribute to the British commander who had been driven from France by a man, as generous in spirit as any military leader in all history, who now had more than a million British troops under his command. Back in London for a final briefing about Palestine, Gort went to the War Office. There he saw, amongst others, Sir John Kennedy, who knew him too well to be taken aback when he remarked: "It will be fun to be shot at again." As in St. Luke's summer, the gales were forgotten and for this brief spell the sunshine had returned, warm and comforting before the leaves began to turn and fall.

CHAPTER 20

PALESTINE

THE struggle between Jew and Arab for the right to possess the Holy Land was aggravated by contradictory pledges given by the British Government in the First World War. The Balfour Declaration of 1917 promised the Jews a home alongside the Arabs and the fulfilment of unquenchable yearnings for Zion; the letters exchanged eighteen months previously by Sir Henry Macmahon, British High Commissioner in Egypt, and the King of the Hedjaz had assured the Arabs, whose home Palestine had been for nearly two thousand years, that when they were liberated from the rule of the Turkish Sultan all Arabia, including Palestine, should be theirs to inhabit and to govern. The situation was exacerbated by an attempt in 1937 to imitate the Judgement of Solomon and carve the disputed child in two. The Peel Commission recommended the partition of Palestine. Like Solomon the British Government presently made it clear they had no intention of implementing the threat, but there was no happy ending because neither of the claimant mothers renounced the child.

The problem became still graver when Hitler decided to consummate his loathing of the Jews by wholesale massacre. Those who escaped saw in Palestine their last refuge and hope of a new life. From all over eastern Europe they began arriving in so-called Coffin Ships, often financed by American alms, only to find that the British Mandate authorities (for Britain had since 1922 ruled Palestine under mandate from the League of Nations) refused them entry. A White Paper issued in May, 1939, proposed to limit immigration to 75,000 over five years. This policy was deeply resented throughout the Jewish world, but it contributed to keeping the Arabs quiet when Rommel won his way to the threshold of Egypt.

Some of the Jews already in Palestine, in particular an organisation called Irgun and a still fiercer group called the Stern Gang, resorted to tactics of terrorism which Hitler himself might have envied and which, at any rate in the early stages, were abhorrent to the Jewish Agency and to its wise, dedicated leader, Dr. Weizmann. The Arabs, turbulent before the war, were now quiet but, thanks to Irgun and the Stern Gang, Jerusalem in 1944 was as troublesome and dangerous as Dublin in 1916, though fortunately much farther away and a less positive asset to the Germans. Jewish hatred was directed to the High Commissioner, Sir Harold MacMichael, who was held responsible for deporting illegal immigrants to the long suffering island of Mauritius. Meanwhile Zionist pressures had been brought to bear on President Roosevelt and the American State Department had developed an irrepressible desire to intervene in the Middle East, an area of which its members had little knowledge and no experience.

This was the background against which Gort set out for Palestine in October, 1944, pausing in Cairo for discussions with the new Minister Resident, Lord Moyne, whose difficult responsibility it was to hold the political balance in a Middle East recently relieved from the pacifying danger of invasion. On arrival at Lydda Airport Gort was welcomed by the Chief Secretary, John Shaw, his right-hand man in the task of administering the mandate and one to whom he quickly gave his confidence. As they drove into the Holy City through silent, sullen crowds, the contrast with cheering Tunis and ebullient, welcoming Malta was all too apparent. Gort said gaily to Shaw: "I suppose that at any moment we may be shot at?" Shaw replied: "Yes, Sir, we may. The trouble is that they will aim at you and hit me." It was the beginning of a short but close friendship.

The choice of Gort was an inspired one. It recalled the happy years when another field-marshal, Lord Plumer, had also been sent from Malta to govern Palestine. Ben Gurion found Gort "warm and humane". Arabs and Jews alike respected his reputation, his personality and the fearless way in which, to the consternation of the police, he went for walks through the streets of Jerusalem unarmed and sometimes unattended. Nor did he confine his personal explorations to Jerusalem. He told Captain Arthur Fitzgerald: "I am spending a lot of time chasing round the country looking at everything that goes on and being seen by those who are disposed to see one, whether of friendly or unfriendly disposition." They had tried to kill MacMichael; nobody made an attempt at the more readily available target of Gort. "They daren't shoot me; they will get something much worse," he remarked to one of his visitors, General Spears. On going to the theatre, Spears noticed that the whole house, stalls and gallery, Jews and Arabs, rose to their feet and cheered as the High Commissioner entered his box.

In "Cross Roads to Israel", one of the best accounts of this troubled time and country, Christopher Sykes wrote of Gort: "Considering the state of Palestine in 1944 and 1945, he may be said to have added to his many titles to fame that of being a respected High Commissioner in the most difficult of all posts at the most difficult of times. He had to carry out unpopular policies, but he was able to retain sufficient personal popularity to maintain a tolerable relationship between the ruler and the ruled. He restored the contacts that had been broken through the tensions of the last years. He had the gift of sympathy and to his initiative was ascribed the decision to allow those Jews who had been deported to Mauritius to settle in Palestine. There can be no doubt that the virtual suspension of terrorist activity . . . was greatly helped by the fact of Lord Gort being the man at the head of affairs."

On 6th November, shortly after Gort's arrival, the Stern Gang, with no motive except devotion to terrorism, murdered Lord Moyne in Cairo. The recoil of the Jewish majority from so dastardly a crime gave Gort a chance to pacify. In the same month, a visit by Dr. Weizmann, returning to Palestine for the first time since 1939, was a stroke for sanity, and little as Gort liked or understood politics, his honest determination to promote peace between the warring factions had its reward. The lions lay down with the lambs and the den of the cockatrice was rendered temporarily harmless by the gathering weight of moderate opinion. The High Commissioner helped to lower the temperature by being accessible to all men. "To listen patiently, to record what one is told, to avoid being drawn into controversial argument and to administer fairly and without discrimination," was, he wrote to Fitzgerald in March, all he could offer.

He was admired by the overworked civil administrators, little though he relished the minutes and memoranda which they conceived it their duty to offer him. Indeed he wrote home: "I have been used to hard work for years and years, but so far this place holds the record." In another letter he criticised the excessive centralisation of Government and added that "the civil secretariat live dogs' lives, burdened down by endless files". He considered the Crown Colony type of Government totally unfitted for the administration of a multi-lingual Mandated Territory.

So as not to seem overpowering to the soldiers, he dressed as often as possible in civilian clothes; and he took pains to improve the conditions of the Other Ranks and the British police. Each time his car drove out of Government House, the guard was turned out to present arms. Gort would stop the car, get out on to the drive and if in uniform salute, or if in mufti take off his hat. He said to Shaw that if a guard took the trouble to turn out for him, the least he could do was to return the compliment properly. In later years Shaw himself became a Colonial Governor and caused surprise by following the same ritual. He told inquirers that what was good enough for Lord Gort was good enough for him.

According to Shaw: "To dine at Government House was not a special treat as far as the victuals were concerned." Had he known Gort at almost any previous stage of his career, he would doubtless have made the same comment. However, Gort was now in ailing health, iller than he or anybody else knew, and perhaps if Lady Marjorie or Jacqueline could have been with him some of the sharper and more unnecessary austerities would have been avoided. The winter of 1944/45 was unusual for Palestine. Gort told Fitzgerald: "We have had an extraordinary winter here and it still freezes most nights. The rainfall has been more than double the usual amount and it has been painful to see the little enough soil on the hills being washed off." Government House, built of stone by Aston Webb in pseudo-Arab style, was scarcely heated, because Gort believed in saving fuel in wartime. The high vaulted rooms, archways and draughty corridors were as cold as a mortuary. If at meetings or interviews visitors were seen to shiver, Gort's sole concession was to push towards them a small electric heater which would scarcely have warmed a cubicle.

Major William Sidney had been returned to Parliament as the Member for Chelsea in the autumn of 1944. He and Jacqueline already had two daughters and in April, 1945, a son and heir was born. On 8th May, the day of victory in Europe, Gort wrote a letter to Philip Sidney:

"Although you came into this world under three weeks ago you arrived in time for this great occasion and I believe in years to come you may be interested to have in your possession a letter written on this ever to be remembered day in British history.

Twice in my lifetime have I marched out to war against Germany and twice has Germany been defeated. The British Empire and Germany were the only two peoples to endure the whole journey and for Britain to be the victor in both phases of the struggle constitutes a wonderful achievement. These two wars will always be remembered in our history as epics of British determination and endurance.

Some day you also may be a Grenadier and, if so, I know you will never fail to be impressed by the fine sense of comradeship and loyalty which binds all ranks together imbued with one thought and one thought only – the honour of the Regiment. Never must its name be tarnished.

It is my earnest wish that the world, in which Elizabeth, Catherine and yourself will live, will prove a truer, a friendlier and a happier world than the world we are now leaving behind us.

Your affectionate grandfather, Gort."

At the victory celebrations in Jerusalem the Senior Army Chaplain spoke of the days, five years before, when after a masterly retreat in the face of disaster, there had come the crowning miracle of a safe evacuation. This, he said, had been a symbol of divine purpose and who, from then on, could doubt the eventual outcome? "It made my thoughts wander rather, I am afraid, in the service," Gort wrote home. A few days later he was gratified to read an article in the *Daily Mirror* entitled: "The Three Forgotten Architects of Victory", and begging its readers to remember in the hour of victory the debt they owed to Gort, Dowding and Wavell. This timely thought was, however, exclusive to the *Daily Mirror*.

Gort now began to feel seriously ill and with illness came dejection. He wanted to finish the task he had undertaken, but he wrote to Lady Marjorie to ask whether she thought it would be reasonable for him to retire in the following year when he reached the age of 60. "One feels they will continue to use me as long as they can in these dirty jobs without ever giving me a word of encouragement of any sort. . . . The years ahead are for the younger generation to make or mar." Early in June he flew home for a medical check and X-ray. He was assured that all was well and he was back in Jerusalem on 14th June. It was not encouraging to find awaiting him a letter from Pownall who said: "It is quite true that Alan Brooke (tears in his eyes) did not care for G.H.Q. and any member of that G.H.Q. is likely to be looked on askance by A.B. now that he has the say-so. The various things that have happened to you in the past 5 years are quite a sufficient pointer. The blame for this attitude lies with him, not with you." True or not, this letter fed Gort's deep-seated belief that the military chiefs looked upon him as a disgraced and defeated soldier. He wrote to Lady Marjorie: "I have tried my best over a number of years to build up again with worn-out tools, but I am afraid one must face facts: it is not to be, because there are those who have power and who are quite determined it shall not be."

The Labour victory in the July General Election was welcomed in Jewish circles because, with that insouciant disregard for future convenience so often found in pre-election statements, Mr. Attlee had rashly pronounced in favour of a wholly Jewish Palestine. "Let the Arabs be encouraged to move out as the Jews move in," he had proclaimed at the Labour Party conference in December, 1944. The Jews therefore expected the sluices of immigration to be opened. They had not reckoned with the new Foreign Secretary, Mr. Ernest Bevin, who was impervious to pressure from Jerusalem, Washington or his own back-benches.

In the ominous pause which followed Gort began to feel seriously ill. Flying to London once again, he went straight to the Middlesex Hospital, but the doctors failed to diagnose the cancer which had gripped his liver. It was, they assured him, "merely a mild *B. Coli.* infection as a result of a chill on the tummy". While he was away Jewish patience became exhausted: the refugees were clamouring in their thousands for entry into Palestine and the moderate wing of the Zionists threw in their lot with Irgun and the Stern Gang. If the British Government were going to retain the mandate and keep the Arabs pacified by limiting immigration, they would have to use force; and they would have the United States against them.

Although Gort realised that increased terrorism was imminent, he did not despair. On 1st September he wrote from London to Ford Geddes: "I think that as we know the barometer is falling, we must get everything stowed and battened down and the ship will stagger home. It is the last lame duck I will command and I intend to get her into port, after which I shall step ashore for good." At the beginning of October he decided that, whatever his state of health, duty obliged him to return to his post. If he had been a little less humble, or had even spoken mildly to someone in authority, no doubt Transport Command would have been ordered to place an aircraft at his disposal. However, he left his travel arrangements in the hands of a Colonial Office clerk who despatched him via Cairo in an overcrowded, unheated and unpressurised Dakota which flew above the oxygen level for part of a long overnight journey.

Shaw, greeting him at the airport, was startled by his appearance, and Gort admitted that he had suffered greatly from chill and fatigue, even though he told Lady Marjorie in a letter written on 7th October: "I am picking up well now and my colour is coming back once more; so let us hope all will be well." It was far from well: in the course of the next few weeks Shaw and the G.O.C., Major-General John d'Arcy, realised to their dismay that he was becoming incapable of performing his duties. The emergency was approaching too. With an effort of will-power Gort forced himself to see and harangue the representatives of the normally well-behaved Jewish Agency who were, he said, putting out false stories and playing politics with an eye to the mid-term elections in the United States.

On the 14th he told Lady Marjorie: "I contrive to hold a balance between the two sides and am, I hope, wholly impartial. It is not always easy to do so when we live on top of a powder magazine." Again, on the 16th, he wrote of "the lull before the storm".

The storm broke on the night of 31st October when Jewish moderates and extremists, in unholy alliance, sank ships, wrecked railway lines and attacked the Haifa oil refinery, thus announcing the prelude to a struggle which has already scarred the Middle East for a generation and may do so for years still to come.

Gort had no opportunity to show whether his personal popularity with both sides, and the restraining influence he had successfully exercised for a year, might be used to avert excesses. Desperately though he tried to control his declining powers, Shaw and d'Arcy were obliged to consider whether, in the public interest, they should telegraph privately home suggesting that their chief be summoned to London for medical attention. It was against their personal inclinations and contrary to all the rules, but the political situation was graver day by day and a firm hand at Government House was essential. Their distasteful dilemma was resolved for them. Brooke and Montgomery arrived to stay at Government House with a number of other senior officers. After dinner that night the party went into the drawing-room for coffee and Gort sat down in his usual high arm-chair. While they talked there was a sudden crash and the High Commissioner fell unconscious to the floor.

Brooke's aircraft was sent to Cairo to fetch an eminent Harley Street consultant who was temporarily masquerading as a major-general in the R.A.M.C. He advised that Gort should return at once to England for urgent treatment in hospital. There was no choice, and there was little time for painful farewells. He found strength to break the news to his brother, Robert Vereker, who had lived much in Canada and of whom he had seen little for many years: "It is disappointing to end up forty years service this way and especially so as I was particularly anxious to see Palestine through her present troubles. I felt I could manage it successfully and it would have given me a happy end to my career which has been almost entirely spent in disappointing ventures with no honour or glory attached."

Amongst those who disagreed with Gort's assessment of his own achievements was Sir George Gater, Permanent Under Secretary at the Colonial Office. "I fully believe," he wrote, "that your personality alone has been a barrier to serious disorders in Palestine. Throughout your period of office you have maintained to an astonishing degree your personal popularity with both communities and you have secured their respect. Your departure now, on the eve of a new policy, is a national calamity." Before leaving, he composed a message to his staff: "The wheel of Fortune," it began, "has called me abruptly to lay down the task on which I embarked with such high hopes last year." And it ended: "To all of you I say good-bye with a heavy heart and a very real and deep sense of personal loss.

> Fare thee well! And if for ever,
> Still for ever, fare thee well!"
>
> (signed) Gort, F.M.

5.XI.45.   High Commissioner.

Arrangements were made for him to be carried to the aircraft on a stretcher, but he had no intention of taking leave on anything but his feet. He put on his field-marshal's uniform, drove to Lydda and walked from the car to the aeroplane. From the steps he waved farewell to Palestine and to public life. His successor was General Sir Alan Cunningham, the last holder of the ungrateful office of British High Commissioner. Gort bequeathed to him few hopes of a peaceful settlement, but he left behind many devoted admirers of himself. High on the list was his Chief Secretary, who pronounced this verdict: "He was the finest man I ever served. Like Gideon, he was a mighty man of valour."

CHAPTER 21

THE END

In the Nuffield Wing of Guy's Hospital an exploratory operation revealed the extent of the cancer and the hopelessness of a cure. He lived for four months, visited by a few faithful friends, courageous to the last and realising that he faced certain death. He wanted to live; for he was only 59 and he had been looking forward to retirement, to the company of Jacqueline and her family and to freedom to sail the seas again. "How well I understand the call of the sea," he had written to Fitzgerald at the end of his time in Malta, "and how it grows on me more and more."

His most intimate friend, Lady Marjorie Dalrymple-Hamilton, was dying of the same fell disease, so that they could not meet and could only speak words of mutual encouragement and affection on the telephone. It was a strangely fitting coincidence that they should be going together, after the long years of sympathy, understanding and companionship.

There was no Garter or Order of Merit for Gort. They had all gone to his successors on the Chiefs of Staff Committee and in the field of battle, a field to which he had vainly hoped he might be recalled. His leadership of the army in peace and war, the defiance of Malta under his command and his success in keeping the peace in Palestine for a brief but important interval, were recognised on 8th February, 1946, by a viscountcy of the United Kingdom. It was an asset of doubtful value to one who was already an Irish viscount, had no son and was too ill to take his seat in the House of Lords.

On 31st March, 1946, he died. He had no home, for East Cowes Castle had been sold before the war and the Irish estates had dwindled to a few acres. His body was therefore taken to Penshurst, the splendid home of the Sidneys where Jacqueline now lived, and buried after a private military funeral in the chapel of the twelfth-century church adjoining Penshurst Place. Sixteen years later his daughter, who so nearly resembled him and was so close to his heart, also died long before her time and was buried beside him.

There were tributes in both Houses of Parliament. In the Commons the Prime Minister, Mr. Attlee, spoke movingly and well; in the Lords, Alexander and Montgomery were abroad and Alanbrooke sent a message regretting that he was unable to attend. There was a memorial service in Westminster Abbey. Perhaps as the Last Post sounded, a few of those present may have reflected that if in May, 1940, Gort had taken the easy road of obedience to orders which he felt in his heart were wrong, there might have been no Stalingrad or Alamein and the breaking of the Axis might long have remained a daydream in the imaginations of a captive Europe and a helpless America.

Brief History of the Prendergast and Vereker Families

FEW Irish families experienced greater vicissitudes than the Prender-
gasts who arrived in "The Pale" with Richard Strongbow, Earl of
Pembroke, in the year 1169 and were powerful landlords in County
Tipperary. Having rashly backed King James II, they lost all their
lands. However, in 1696 Thomas Prendergast voluntarily confessed to
William III the details of a plot to assassinate His Majesty while out
hunting, a plot in which Thomas himself was implicated. Having thus
purged himself, and given away his confederates, he turned Protestant
(in the best tradition of his contemporary, the Vicar of Bray), married
Lord Cadogan's eligible sister, and recovered not only much of his
own family's forfeited property, but also the estates at Gort, in County
Galway, of some less adroit Roman Catholics called the O'Shaugh-
nessys. Thomas was made a baronet and fought boldly at Oudenarde
and Malplaquet where he was killed by a stray cannon ball fired after
the battle was over. On the death of his son, the last male Prendergast
of the elder line, the estates passed in 1760 to a nephew, John Smyth,
of Limerick, who was raised to the Irish peerage as Viscount Gort in
1810, even though he had been, as Member for Limerick, a strong
supporter of Henry Grattan and an opponent of the Union with
England and Scotland. He was a bachelor whose lands and, by Special
Remainder, his Viscountcy, devolved on his sister's son, Colonel
Charles Vereker, the hero of the strange battle of Coloony. Unfortunately, Smyth had been extravagant to an extent that none
suspected and instead of inheriting a fortune, painstakingly accumulat-
ed by marriages with at least half a dozen heiresses, Colonel Vereker
found himself encumbered with an enormous debt.

The Verekers had emigrated from Brabant in the reign of Charles I
and together with a number of their compatriots had settled in the
Fens where, with the specialised knowledge peculiar to their countrymen, they had drained and improved the land. When the Civil War
broke out, the men of East Anglia were solid for Cromwell, but the
Dutch settlers had royalist sympathies and John Vereker fled to
Ireland to join the King's Army. With the victory of the Common-
wealth he lost all he possessed, but meanly though many of the King's
most loyal supporters were treated at the Restoration there were
forty-nine officers, including John Vereker, who were provided with

arrears of pay by the sale of lands confiscated in Ireland from Cromwellian supporters. This untypical windfall enabled the Verekers to
purchase a "large thatched cabin and backside adjoining St. Nicholas'
Churchyard in the City of Cork". Subsequently, in spite of John's son
Henry backing the wrong horse at the battle of the Boyne, a convenient
heiress brought the family reasonable prosperity and enabled them to
acquire forfeited land in County Limerick from an English concern
called "The Company for Making Hollow Sword Blades" which had
diversified its activities into the lucrative trade of dealing in Irish
Jacobite real estate. The next Vereker married a still greater heiress,
but part of her fortune vanished in chancery law suits and her son,
Thomas, blew much of what remained. "After all", he is reported to
have said, "I get claret on tick and there is plenty of beef on the hill."
From the point of view of the family it was a great relief when Thomas
married Julia, John Smyth's sister and heiress presumptive to the
Prendergast estates.

Their son Charles was born in 1768 and joined the Navy at the age
of 13. In 1782 he sailed in H.M.S. *Alexandra*, a 74-gun ship of the
Line commanded by Lord Longford and took part in the relief of
Gibraltar by Admiral Howe. In spite of this early participation in so
successful an exploit, Charles decided to forsake the sea and at eighteen
he was gazetted to the First Royal Regiment of Foot stationed at Cork.
His military career was interrupted in 1789 by marriage to a widow
whom the *Limerick Chronicle* described as "a young lady possessed of
every amiable qualification to render the married state happy".
According to the same newspaper she was "possessed of an immense
fortune". Alas, she died young and she had children by her first
husband as well. Charles joined his uncle, John Smyth, as one of the
Members of Parliament for Limerick and in 1797 succeeded him as
Colonel of the local Militia, the Limerick City Regiment. It was with
this hitherto untried force that he won the Battle of Coloony.

Bibliography

PUBLISHED SOURCES

BARCLAY, BRIGADIER C. N., *Armistice 1918*, J. M. Dent & Sons 1968
BEAUFRE, GENERAL ANDRE, *1940: The Fall of France*, Cassell 1967
BEAUMAN, BRIGADIER-GENERAL A. B., *Then a Soldier*, P. R. Macmillan 1960
BENTWICH, NORMAN and HELEN, *Mandate Memories 1918–1948*, Hogarth Press 1965
BIRKENHEAD, THE EARL OF, *Halifax*, Hamish Hamilton 1965
BROWNRIGG, LIEUTENANT-GENERAL SIR DOUGLAS, K.C.B., D.S.O., *Unexpected*, Hutchinson 1950
BRYANT, SIR ARTHUR, *The Turn of the Tide*, Collins 1957
BUTLER, LIEUTENANT-COLONEL EWAN, and MAJOR J. SELBY BRADFORD, *Keep the Memory Green*, Hutchinson 1950
CAMERON, IAN, *Red Duster, White Ensign*, Muller 1959
CASEY, LORD, *Personal Experience, 1939–1946*, Constable 1962
CHANDOS, VISCOUNT, *Memoirs*, Bodley Head 1962
CHATFIELD, ADMIRAL OF THE FLEET LORD, *It Might Happen Again, Volume II*, Heinemann 1947
CHURCHILL, SIR WINSTON S., *The Gathering Storm*, Cassell 1948
  The Hinge of Fate, Cassell 1951
COLLIER, RICHARD, *The Sands of Dunkirk*, Collins 1961
CONNELL, JOHN, *Wavell*, Collins 1964
COOPER, SIR ALFRED DUFF, *Old Men Forget*, Hart-Davis 1953
DE GUINGAND, MAJOR-GENERAL SIR FRANCIS, *Operation Victory*, Hodder & Stoughton 1947
DIVINE, DAVID, *The Nine Days of Dunkirk*, Faber 1967
EDEN, ANTHONY (EARL OF AVON), *The Reckoning*, Houghton Mifflin 1965
EISENHOWER, DWIGHT D., *Crusade in Europe*, Heinemann 1948
ELLIS, MAJOR L. F., *The War in France and Flanders 1939–1940*, The History of the Second World War. H.M.S.O. 1953
GORT, GENERAL THE VISCOUNT
  First Despatch of the Commander-in-Chief, British Expeditionary Force. H.M.S.O. 1941
  Second Despatch of the Commander-in-Chief, British Expeditionary Force. H.M.S.O. 1941
HART, B. H. LIDDELL, *The Memoirs of Captain Liddell Hart*, Cassell 1965
HEADLAM, LIEUTENANT-COLONEL CUTHBERT, D.S.O., *History of the Guards Division in the Great War 1914–1918*, John Murray 1924
HOARE, SIR SAMUEL (VISCOUNT TEMPLEWOOD), *Ambassador on Special Mission*, Collins 1946
HORNE, ALISTAIR, *To Lose a Battle: France 1940*, Macmillan 1969
HOWARD, MICHAEL (editor), *The Theory and Practice of War*, Cassell 1965

HOWARD, MICHAEL, and JOHN SPARROW, *The Coldstream Guards 1920–1946*, Oxford University Press 1951

HUREWITZ, J. C., *The Struggle for Palestine*, (New York) 1950

IRONSIDE, FIELD-MARSHAL LORD, *Diaries 1937–1940*, Constable 1962

ISMAY, GENERAL LORD, *The Memoirs of General the Lord Ismay*, Heinemann 1960

KENNEDY, MAJOR-GENERAL SIR JOHN, *The Business of War*, Hutchinson 1957

LLOYD, AIR-MARSHAL SIR HUGH, *Briefed to Attack*, Hodder & Stoughton 1949

LOCKHART, R. H. BRUCE, *Comes the Reckoning*, Putnam 1947

LUVAAS, JAY, *The Education of an Army*, Cassell 1965

MACINTYRE, CAPTAIN DONALD, *The Fighting Admiral*, Evans 1961

MACKSEY, MAJOR K. J., *Armoured Crusader*, Hutchinson 1967

MACKSEY, MAJOR KENNETH, M.C., *The Shadow of Vimy Ridge*, Kimber 1965

MACLEOD, IAIN, *Neville Chamberlain*, Muller 1961

MACMILLAN, HAROLD, *The Blast of War*, Macmillan 1967

MARLOWE, JOHN, *The Seat of Pilate*, Cresset Press 1959

MARTEL, SIR GIFFARD Q., *An Outspoken Soldier*, Sifton Praed 1949

MAUROIS, ANDRE, *The Battle of France*, Bodley Head 1940
    Why France Fell, Bodley Head 1940

MINNEY, R. J., *The Private Papers of Hore Belisha*, Collins 1960

MONTGOMERY, FIELD-MARSHAL VISCOUNT, *The Memoirs of Field-Marshal the Viscount Montgomery of Alamein, K.G.*, Collins 1958

MORGAN, GENERAL SIR FREDERICK, *Peace and War*, Hodder & Stoughton 1961

NALDER, MAJOR-GENERAL R. F. H., *The Royal Corps of Signals*, Royal Signals Institution 1958

PEARLMAN, MOSHE, *Ben Gurion Looks Back*, Weidenfeld & Nicolson 1965

PEROWNE, STEWART, *The Siege Within the Walls*, Hodder & Stoughton 1970

PILE, GENERAL SIR FREDERICK, *Ack-Ack*, Harrap 1949

PITT, BARRIE, *1918: The Last Act*, Cassell 1962

PLAYFAIR, MAJOR-GENERAL I. S. O. and others, *The Mediterranean and Middle East, Volumes III and IV*, History of the Second World War, H.M.S.O. 1960

PONSONBY, LIEUTENANT-COLONEL THE RIGHT HON. SIR FREDERICK, *The Grenadier Guards in the Great War of 1914–1918*, Macmillan 1920

SHANKLAND, PETER, and ANTHONY HUNTER, *Malta Convoy*, Collins 1961

SLESSOR, MARSHAL OF THE ROYAL AIR FORCE, SIR JOHN, *Central Blue*, Cassell 1956

SMYTH, BRIGADIER SIR JOHN, BT., V.C., M.C., M.P., *Before the Dawn*, Cassell 1957

SPEARS, SIR EDWARD, *Assignment to Catastrophe*, Eyre & Spottiswoode 1966
    Prelude to Victory, Jonathan Cape 1939

SYKES, CHRISTOPHER, *Cross Roads to Israel*, Collins 1965

TEDDER, MARSHAL OF THE ROYAL AIR FORCE LORD, *With Prejudice*, Cassell 1966

War Office Committee of Enquiry into 'Shell Shock', Report of, H.M.S.O. 1922

WESTPHAL, SIEGFRIED, *Heer in Fesseln*, (Bonn) 1950

WOODWARD, SIR LLEWELLYN, *British Foreign Policy in the Second World War*, The History of the Second World War, H.M.S.O. 1962

UNPUBLISHED SOURCES

ARCHDALE, LIEUTENANT-COLONEL O. A., Diary, May 1940
Army Council, Minutes (1937–1939), (Ministry of Defence)
British Expeditionary Force, Military Headquarters Papers (1939), (Ministry of Defence WO 197 series)
COLVILLE, J. R., Diaries
Committee of Imperial Defence, Minutes of Meetings (1937–1939), Public Record Office: CAB/2 series
Committee of Imperial Defence, Chiefs of Staff Sub-Committee Memoranda (1937–1939), Public Record Office: CAB/53 series
Committee of Imperial Defence, Chiefs of Staff Sub-Committee Minutes of Meetings (1937–1939), Public Record Office: CAB/53 series
Director of Military Operations and Intelligence Papers (1939), Ministry of Defence: WO 106 series
GORT, FIELD-MARSHAL 6TH VISCOUNT, Manuscript diaries for parts of 1914 and 1915
GORT, 4TH VISCOUNT, History of the Prendergast and Vereker Families
Grenadier Guards, Regimental Records and Digest of Services
HAWKINS, ADMIRAL SIR GEOFFREY, Memorandum
IRONSIDE, FIELD-MARSHAL LORD, Unpublished diaries
LAWFORD, V. G., Diaries
MACLEOD, LIEUTENANT-COLONEL RORY, Proceedings of the Royal Artillery Historical Society 1968
POWNALL, LIEUTENANT-GENERAL SIR HENRY, Diaries
RUSSELL, ADMIRAL THE HON. SIR GUY, Memorandum
SHAW, SIR JOHN, Memorandum
War Cabinet. Conclusions (1939), Public Record Office: CAB/65/1
War Cabinet. Chiefs of Staff Committee, Memoranda (1939), Public Record Office: CAB/80/1
War Cabinet. Chiefs of Staff Committee, Minutes of Meetings (1939), CAB/79/1
War Diary of the Commander-in-Chief, British Expeditionary Force, 3rd September 1939 to 31st May 1940; with documents appended. (In the possession of Lord De L'Isle and Dudley)
War Diary of the Governor of Malta, 1942–1944
War Diary of 2nd Division (1914), Public Record Office: WO/95/1283
War Diary of 4th (Guards) Brigade (1915), Public Record Office: WO/95/1341
War Diary of 1st Battalion, Grenadier Guards (1918), Public Record Office: WO/95/1223
War Diary of 4th Battalion, Grenadier Guards (1917), Public Record Office: WO/95/1223

Index

202, 205, 212, 216-17; at Algiers, 257. Mentioned: 67, 125-26, 185

Gibraltar, 134, 238, 270; Gort's Governorship of, 240-46

Giraud, General H., 126, 153, 186, 195-96, 254, 257

Gloucester, H.R.H. Prince Henry, Duke of, 148

Godesberg, 101, 112-14

Goebbels, Dr. J., 101, 133, 164

Gonnelieu, 37-38

Gordon Duff, Lt.-Colonel John, 248

Gordon Finlayson, General Sir Robert, 136, 177

Gort, 1st Viscount, 238, 269-70

Gort, 2nd Viscount, 15, 16, 269-70

Gort, 3rd Viscount, 16

Gort, 3rd Viscountess (Mrs. Tudor), 16

Gort, 5th Viscount, 16

Gort, Eleanor, 5th Viscountess, 16, 17, 19, 57

Gort, Field-Marshal 6th Viscount. Birth and education, 17; joins Grenadiers, 18; character and appearance, 17, 50-51, 76-77; austere habits, 18, 156-57, 163, 242, 249-50, 253, 262; marriage and children, 20-21; outbreak of 1st World War, 22; retreat from Mons, 23-25; on Haig's staff, 28-30; commands 4th Bttn. Grenadier Guards, 32-39; commands 1st Bttn., 40-48; wins Victoria Cross, 46-48; pupil at Staff College, 50-51; instructor ibid, 52-54; divorce, 56; friendship with Dalrymple-Hamiltons, 56-57; correspondence with Liddell Hart, 51-53, 58-59, 63-64, 73; in Shanghai, 60-63; Director of Mil. Training in India, 65-68; obsession with detail, 66, 155-56, 244-45; commands Staff College, 68-69; meets Hore Belisha, 75; Military Secretary, 75-76; appointed C.I.G.S., 80-81; staff conversations with the French, 89, 93-94, 109-10, 126-27, 129-30; quarrels with Hore Belisha, 95-98, 135-38, 157-66; Sandys case, 98-100; Munich crisis, 111-15;

attitude to Munich, 115-17; struggle to equip British "Land Force", 88-93, 119-21, 127-28; discussions with Gamelin, 126-27, 129; attends 14th July parade in Paris, 129-30; appointed C.-in-C. British Expeditionary Force, 144; achievements as C.I.G.S., 145-46; establishes G.H.Q. at Arras, 149; accepts Dyle plan, 152-53; difficulties with Ironside, 172-73; and air support for the army, 173-75, 190, 197-98; leaves G.H.Q. for Command Post, 190; combines role of C.-in-C. and Army Commander, 190-91, 202; accepts General Billotte as "co-ordinator", 194; forms independent forces to defend Canal Line, 199, 207-8; refuses to retire to Scheldt, 200; considers alternative courses for B.E.F., 203; declines to March B.E.F. south to Amiens, 206-7; withdraws troops from Arras, 212; considers withdrawal to coast, 204, 213; abandons southwards sortie, 215-17; learns of Belgian surrender, 221; insists on continuing retreat to Dunkirk, 221-22; at La Panne, 222-24; recalled to England, 224-25; decisions which saved B.E.F., 225-26; Inspector of Training and Home Guard, 231; expedition to Rabat, 231; B.B.C. broadcast, 231-32; views on invasion prospect, 234; criticised in military circles, 235-37, 240, 254; death of Sandy Vereker, 237-38; Governor of Gibraltar, 238-39; constructs airfield, 240-41; relations with Spaniards, 243-44; compared with Rommel, 245; Governor of Malta, 246; assumes command of armed forces, 247-49; in Cairo with Churchill, 251; appointed Field-Marshal, 253-54; Eisenhower's opinion of, 254-55; Roosevelt and Patton visit, 256; attends award of V.C. to Major Sidney, 256-57; visits North Africa, 257; High Commissioner in Palestine, 258; respected by Arabs

R. Seine